The Medieval Soldier in the Wars of the Roses

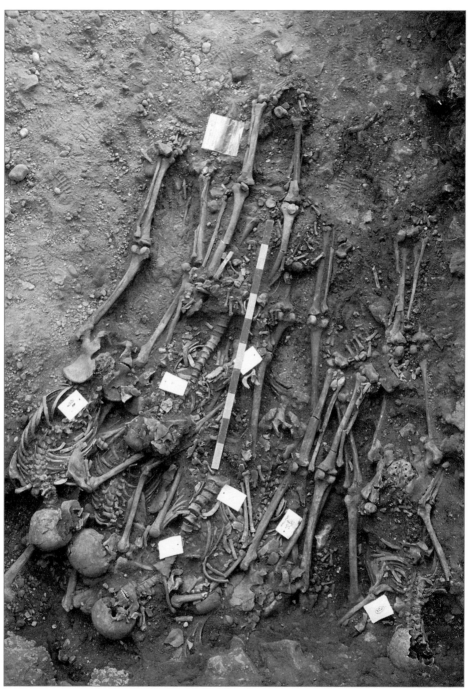

The grim reality of medieval combat during the Wars of the Roses, this is one of the many layers of bodies which were discovered in the mass grave at Towton, North Yorkshire. The find is unique since it is the first opportunity this century to investigate the casualties of a British battle dating to the medieval period. (Bradford University)

The
Medieval Soldier
in the
Wars of the Roses

A.W. BOARDMAN

SUTTON PUBLISHING

First published in 1998 by
Sutton Publishing Limited · Phoenix Mill
Thrupp · Stroud · Gloucestershire · GL5 2BU

British Library Cataloguing in Publication Data
A catalogue record for this book is available from the British Library

ISBN 0-7509-1465-3

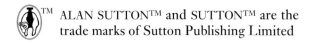
™ ALAN SUTTON™ and SUTTON™ are the
trade marks of Sutton Publishing Limited

Typeset in 11/12 pt Ehrhardt.
Typesetting and origination by
Sutton Publishing Limited.
Printed in Great Britain by
Butler & Tanner, Frome, Somerset.

Contents

For Sheree

Now are our brows bound with victorious wreaths;
Our bruised arms hung up for monuments;
Our stern alarums chang'd to merry meetings,
Our dreadful marches to delightful measures.
Gim-visag'd war hath smooth'd his wrinkled front . . .

King Richard III, Act 1, Scene 1,
William Shakespeare

Preface

While I was researching and writing the book *The Battle of Towton*, I became intensely interested in the individuals who had either intentionally or inadvertently become combatants in that day's bloody culmination of one of the most significant battles of the Wars of the Roses. Indeed, how the medieval soldier had coped, both mentally and physically, with this terrible and brutal battle began to fascinate me as a parallel interest. The more I learned about the battle, which took place during a blizzard on Palm Sunday in 1461, the more determined I became to explore what motivated medieval man to take part in such close-quarter slaughter on the battlefield. Thus I began to research the fifteenth-century soldier from a contemporary viewpoint, touching briefly on some of these primary sources in *The Battle of Towton* in an effort to bring to life the experience of medieval combat. The rest of this research was beyond the scope of that book.

The scarcity of reliable contemporary military evidence for the battles of Wars of the Roses provides few clues to the medieval battlefield experience. Indeed, because no fully corroborated account concerning these battles exists, one might conclude that so difficult a subject is best left well alone. Nevertheless, most historians have taken the opposite approach, and many books have been written in an effort to explain why and how medieval men fought. Similarly, the sites of other medieval battles, such as Agincourt, are repeatedly visited by historians in an attempt to form a balanced and realistic opinion about the soldier's battlefield experience.

My interest in the medieval soldier was initially fuelled by a number of contemporary fifteenth-century documents, in addition to the chronicles, which provide poignant glimpses of the individuals who had fought in the Wars of the Roses. These fleeting references to the medieval soldier were mainly contained in letters written after battles had taken place, in documents recording an individual's military service, and in musters where each soldier is named and his weapons described for recruitment purposes. Such documents allude briefly to the soldier's way of life during his short military service, but it is clear that more evidence is needed to fill the void between these factual documents and the romantic and chivalric ideology portrayed in some of the chronicles.

As regards the battle of Towton in particular, the medieval soldier's experience of warfare is shown to be singularly peculiar. This experience can be grouped into two main categories, physical and mental. The apparent long duration of the fighting in atrocious weather conditions would inevitably have led to mental attrition under stress. What effect did this have on the individual soldier? The effects of the awesome one-sided longbow attack that started the battle, the 'no quarter' hand-to-hand fighting, and the large-scale bloody rout and slaughter after the Lancastrian army broke ranks are three of the crucial factors that need to be analysed in this context. There are, of course, many other related questions.

The results of my research suggest a very different impression of the men who fought at such famous Wars of the Roses battles as St Albans, Towton, Barnet, Tewkesbury, Bosworth and many others. This is chiefly due to a military rather than political viewpoint. Contemporary chroniclers describing these battles only rarely mention the common soldiers, except collectively as part of an over-estimated total of an army's initial strength, or perhaps as numbers of casualties after the battle. But the soldiers cannot simply be regarded as a single entity. Each soldier had different reasons for taking up arms in the private struggles of the aristocracy, today known as the Wars of the Roses. But what were these reasons and did all soldiers wish to participate in the wars? The political and military ebb and flow of the wars provides some suggestions for this more 'personalised' research, but the lack of detail given by some of the chronicles about the battles themselves unfortunately hinders this kind of investigation.

Some contemporary chronicles were written by monastics and members of the clergy who were, quite naturally, more interested and concerned with matters having a direct bearing on their own lives, such as the fabric and antiquities of their church, rather than in the details of distant medieval warfare. However, they occasionally offer comments on the 'debatable' and 'appaling' loss of life caused by the fighting, and there is also one report in a monastic history that can be considered as an 'eyewitness' account of two particular battles.[1] Other chroniclers, mainly laymen, often with personal battlefield experience, were intensely interested in warfare, but wrote in the very best chivalric tradition of the period, applying a veneer of heroic romance to the bloodbaths they described. Indeed, their patrons demanded this style of writing. Such a style of narrative betrays all too clearly the overriding influence of propaganda, which is hardly surprising given the political nature of the Wars of the Roses. It is for this reason that foreign writers must be consulted, although their chronicles and letters are also influenced by some bias or favouritism, but to a lesser extent. Tudor writers particularly were writing to please their patrons, and thus show extreme bias; they are traditionally held responsible for most of the detailed information about the personalities and events during this period that we rely on today.[2]

I have tried to evaluate and analyse all the available evidence from the sources in this book. The written documentary evidence is factual, the conclusions drawn are my own. By examining sources such as musters, city records, state documents, and indentures, it is possible to present a much clearer picture of how the medieval soldier was recruited, what problems he faced on the march, how he was supplied and billeted, and how he actually fought, and lived or died on the battlefield. How he was led by his superiors, what he wore on the march and for protection in battle, and what weapons he used in combat are all important factors when considering his role and effectiveness in a Wars of the Roses army. What emerges from all the evidence is a new interpretation of the medieval experience of soldiering, stripped of its romantic imagery and propaganda. It is argued here that this veneer of glorious chivalry partly 'justified' war in the fifteenth century.

What it was *really* like to take part in a medieval battle cannot be extracted from the chronicles and letters of the period with any certainty, but with a little logic and imagination, I have tried to bring to life the horror and epic nature of a medieval battle. Details may be in part conjectural, but wherever possible I have tried to support the theory with a documented parallel case in the fifteenth century (or in an era not too far removed from the events described). Modern research into arms and armour of the medieval period also helps us to prove or disprove various theories regarding the soldier's battlefield experience.[3] How a man was equipped for battle obviously tells us much about the way he fought, while musters tell us how he was recruited. The English climate, especially the unseasonable and abrupt weather changes which occurred during particular campaigns, also plays a part in assessing how medieval armies moved about the country, and how they were supplied and billeted; it also helps to explain the physical constraints on medieval armies when they finally came face to face on the battlefield.

While I was researching and writing this book, a unique medieval war grave was discovered by workmen in the village of Towton in North Yorkshire. The grave contained the bodies of some of the soldiers who had fought at the terrible battle of Towton on 29 March 1461. Their bones provided many important clues not only to the soldiers' tragic deaths but also to their lives. This not only altered my perception of the medieval soldier but also changed the way this book was written. All the evidence is being carefully extracted with the help of forensic and archaeological science, and the preliminary results have already painted a much more detailed picture of the soldiers than was previously thought possible. Analysis of the bones and the conclusions that can be drawn from them, vividly brings to life the horror of medieval combat in a way that no documentary facts can, and therefore the Towton grave is as near as a modern historian can get to a medieval battle. I was very privileged to be consulted when the remains of the Towton dead were unearthed in July 1996, 535 years after their burial. Some of the results of the dedicated work carried out by the enthusiastic specialists at the Bradford University Department of Archaeological Sciences are contained within this book. Some of the conclusions drawn from the Towton grave are my own, others belong to specialists, to whom I am very grateful for sharing their knowledge with me. In my opinion, the Towton grave provides the best evidence yet as to the medieval soldier's experience of army life and the brutality and horror of fifteenth-century warfare.

The medieval soldier's attitude to warfare and violence is also discussed in this book, and the way in which war changed some men's lives forever is also described. The medieval soldier's view of combat was complex and depended much upon his social status, but his feelings are alluded to in contemporary writing in various forms. It is tempting for modern historians to assume that, since medieval man lived in a more violent age, he was in some way untouched by combat and violence. This is simply not true. Various attainder documents state the seriousness of local and national rebellion, and contemporary letters discuss the various injuries that men suffered in battle, and also the danger of wounds becoming infected after the event. Loss of goods, horses and equipment, bereavement, and deprivation caused by warfare are all clearly apparent through the window of personal letters. This evidence proves conclusively just how important it was to be on the winning side in such a conflict. How then did the threat of attainder and possible execution for treason, and previous knowledge of combat and the type of injuries suffered, affect the medieval soldier? How did some men escape attainder after a particular battle and later return to fight on the opposite side? Did the common soldier continue fighting indefinitely, or could he decide to opt out of taking part in the carnage on the battlefield again?

It is clear that the subject of the Wars of the Roses soldier cannot be taken in isolation, since he was a part of a continuously evolving process, some elements of which had been in existence already for centuries, and would persist well into the Tudor period. Bastard feudalism, for example, a system of recruitment and service which lay firmly at the root of social and military medieval administration during the Wars of the Roses, had been present, in virtually the same form, for an incredibly long period of time before this conflict. Indeed it would persist, in a different guise, long after the Houses of York and Lancaster had laid down their arms.[4] Most of the weapons used in the Wars of the Roses, and the formations and basic tactics adopted by the armies, had been in use for centuries as tried and tested methods of warfare. Therefore background evidence for some aspects of medieval warfare is available from other, perhaps better documented, periods. However, some aspects of the Wars of the Roses were quite unique to the conflict and these elements are examined in this book.

In a work such as this, it is important that the subject is set into the correct context and therefore the first chapter of this book explains briefly the history of the Wars of the Roses, with special reference to the military campaigns in which the common soldier took part. These military aspects are discussed in more depth later in the book with regard to the soldier's experience of warfare. The causes of the conflict are also touched on in chapter one, although the interested reader should turn to the books listed in the bibliography for a fuller account. The chronology of famous battles is central to the theme of the medieval soldier and therefore all the important engagements are briefly described here in relation to the major campaigns. Again more detail can be found in subsequent chapters, while books dealing with specific battles can be found in the bibliography.

The main section of this book focuses on the experience of the men who fought the Wars of the Roses, taking a number of individual contemporary case histories as examples and following them through a simple chronological sequence of events, culminating on the battlefield. From commander to commoner, from archer to man at arms, the role of the medieval soldier in the Wars of the Roses from recruitment to combat is explored, and the myths surrounding his role are exposed, discussed and re-assessed.

The preface of my book *The Battle of Towton* explained my 'indescribable fascination' with that particular battle, and my respect for the site where the

Houses of York and Lancaster struggled in the snow for the prize of the Crown of England. I now know, after completing the research for this book, that my fascination with this battle stems from a purely humane source – an appreciation and respect for the men who fought at Towton over five hundred years ago.

Acknowledgements

To thank everyone who has in some way helped me with this book would be impossible, as so many people have helped in so many different ways, but acknowledgement must be made to the following individuals for their special interest and support, and, in some cases, for sharing their dedicated research. I should also mention the Towton soldiers themselves who keep surprising us with even more evidence of their lives – and deaths – through the medium of twentieth-century archaeological science.

I would like to thank everyone at the Royal Armouries, Leeds, chiefly, the Master of the Armouries, Guy Wilson; John Waller for his special interest in the project and for organising the jacket photography; Thom Richardson for his translation of the Bridport Muster Roll; Graeme Rimmer; Philip Abbot for kindly researching and providing the bulk of the pictures included in the book; and the 'Towton archer', Frank Hammond. I would also like to thank everyone at Bradford University Department of Archaeological Sciences, especially Anthea Boyleston, Tim Sutherland, Malin Holst, Jenny Coughlan, Shannon Novak and Steve Dockrill, whose sensitive interest in Towton battlefield will now, I hope, be as great as my own. I would also like to thank many of my friends for their moral support over the past few years, especially Hedley Marsden, Phil Haigh, Dave Cooke, Kevin Bullimore, Stephen Bailey and Simon Richardson. I would also like to thank Robert Hardy CBE for his help and interest over the years; Michael Rayner of the Battlefields Trust; Chris Nickerson for the jacket photography; Paul Lewis Isemonger for the re-enactment photography; Paul Mason for supplying the medical reports featured in chapter 6; Chris Milnes of Trident Design for outputting the maps and diagrams; Veronica Fiorato and Anthea Burgess of North and West Yorkshire Archaeological Services for sharing their information on the Towton grave; the Borthwick Institute, York; Leeds City Library; the staff at Dorset County Record Office for providing information on the Bridport Muster Roll; and Geoff Wheeler for once again helping with some of the illustrations and pictures, and for kindly checking the manuscript. I would also like to thank Jonathan Falconer and all at Sutton Publishing for their indispensable help in producing this book.

Last but not least, I would like to thank my family and friends for their support through what has been a difficult period of my life. Most of all, I must thank the one person who has made this book possible: it could not have been researched or written if not for the constant support and patience of Sheree, to whom I dedicate this work.

CHAPTER 1

'Grim-visag'd war'

THE CAUSES OF THE WARS OF THE ROSES

At a basic level, the conflict can be blamed largely on the weakness and instability of King Henry VI, the son of the victor of Agincourt, whose inability to control the aristocracy enabled them to engage in private battles which inevitably escalated into civil war.

But responsibility must also be laid firmly at the door of the English nobility, who used bastard feudalism to create private armies throughout the fifteenth century. However, it would be a mistake to lay the blame for the conflict on any one individual, or on the effects of any socio-military system. During Henry VI's reign several nobles vied for supremacy, and the balance of power at court was a perpetual cycle of favour and demise. Similarly, bastard feudalism and the English nobles' 'overmighty' greed and political ambition had always been a reality, and a major threat to the Crown, well before the Wars of the Roses began. It was only when Henry VI shook off his minority at the age of sixteen that these elements combined, becoming a greater threat to the stability of the kingdom because of the king's weak leadership. King Henry's attempts to keep his nobles and their retainers in their place, as a strong ruling monarch had to do, only resulted in mismanagement.

Certain contemporary writers expressed great regard for King Henry's pious nature, portraying him as a saintly character, an opinion perpetuated by Lancastrian and Tudor propagandists. But, as the highest power in the land, he has to bear the greatest amount of responsibility for the outbreak of the Wars of the Roses; it is now generally accepted that the blame must be set squarely upon King Henry's shoulders. It is fair to say that his troubles were largely rooted in his weak nature, which was a total contrast to that of his warlike and strong-minded father Henry V.[1]

The origins of the Wars of the Roses can be traced back as far as the year 1453. In this year the Hundred Years War had finally ended with a humiliating English defeat at the battle of Castillon in France, and southern ports were full of thousands of disgruntled soldiers returning home to seek continued employment, protection and advancement in the only trade they knew. There were many more potential soldiers, under a similar obligation to serve when commanded to do so, who happened to be in England when the war with France finally petered out. The end of the wars also had a lasting effect upon public opinion, since failure abroad was bound to breed a sense of discontent. However, the gradual loss of

The Battle of Barnet, 1471. The Earl of Warwick tries to escape from the battlefield on horse-back (right) while his men, wearing ragged staff badges, fight desperately with Yorkist soldiers in the foreground. (Bibliothèque Municipale)

English territories abroad was not a direct cause of the Wars of the Roses, although it had a dramatic effect on King Henry's mental and physical ability to rule. The loss of French territories, won chiefly by the brilliant military ability of Henry V, was a major political disaster for his son, Henry VI, who was unable to cope with the repercussions of defeat. The incompetent Henry VI was soon caught up in the political backdraught which followed. The slow shift of power from the king to the nobility now increased dramatically, made easier by the misuse of bastard feudalism, unchecked by the king, until the aristocracy were able to intimidate whoever opposed their aims by mustering private 'armies'. In this unstable political climate, the king was at the mercy of his nobles if he could not control them – which is precisely what Henry VI failed to do.[2]

It is quite possible that the shock of the English army's defeat at Castillon triggered King Henry VI's first mental breakdown in August 1453.[3] Coupled with other personal inadequacies, this hereditary mental illness contributed to Henry's intermittent instability throughout his troubled reign, and enabled ambitious nobles to manipulate him to further their own ends.

The two prominent peers who vied for King Henry's favour in the 1440s and 1450s were Edmund Beaufort, Duke of Somerset, and Richard Plantagenet, Duke of York. Henry's French queen, Margaret of Anjou, not only dominated and manipulated her husband for her own ambitious political ends, but also fuelled the mutual mistrust between Somerset and York for many years to come. However, there is firm evidence that before Henry's collapse in 1453 he was 'consciously' in charge of his throne and, more importantly, he was personally making decisions as King of England, however wrong those decisions might have been.[4] His sudden 'inertia' in August 1453 can therefore be considered to have been the catalyst whereby England was plunged into insecurity, and thus into the Wars of the Roses themselves.

Richard of York was the most important English peer at this time. A very wealthy man with many ancient hereditary estates and titles attached to his name, Richard was descended from Lionel, Duke of Clarence, and Edmund, Duke of York, Edward III's second and fourth sons. He was also heir apparent to the then childless Henry VI, and was all too aware that his succession to the throne would be threatened if the inadequate king happened to fall into the wrong hands. He was particularly wary of Edmund Beaufort, Duke of Somerset, who was also descended from Edward III through a legitimatised, but debarred, line of succession stemming from the union of John of Gaunt, King Edward's third son, and Gaunt's third wife Katherine Swynford. Their mutual dislike flared into active hostility in the latter days of the Hundred Years War when English military incompetence abroad was at its zenith.

The Duke of York had seen military service in France as the king's lieutenant, but as the war turned in favour of the French, and the need to finance the army became an increasing drain on the English government, York was forced to use his own resources and was soon owed a vast amount of money. This debt was never paid back to him in full. In contrast, when the Duke of Somerset was given command of the army in France he received constant financial support to pursue the war with France. York was furious at this show of personal favouritism, and he complained bitterly to King Henry and his councillors. More importantly, it led to his feud with the Duke of Somerset, especially when Somerset became firmly established at court and replaced York as lieutenant of France in 1448.[5]

Somerset's appointment was a crushing blow to York's pride, but the situation was made even worse when York was dispatched to Ireland as King Henry's lieutenant for a term of ten years. Doubtless, King Henry had been persuaded by his pro-Somerset 'councillors' to remove York from the political scene and place

Somerset in the ascendancy at court. However, Somerset's military efforts to turn apparent stalemate in France into victory culminated in the complete loss of Normandy, and soon former English territories were being sold off by treaty and overrun by French troops, until at last only the port of Calais remained in English hands. The Duke of York naturally held Somerset personally responsible for the debacle, although in fairness, other prominent councillors had contributed to the defeat. Indeed, the ambitious Duke of Suffolk had already been blamed by the Commons, and had been banished and then clandestinely executed. In stark contrast, Somerset was not held responsible for the defeat and was recalled to England in 1450, following the tail of his retreating and disgruntled army into Kentish ports.

Popular opinion had turned against King Henry and his chief minister and a sense of resentment greeted the returning English soldiers. Led by Jack Cade, the common people of Kent had risen in arms, demanding reform through a petition. Some of the returning English soldiers took part in the rebellion that followed, and many fought in the skirmishes with the king's garrison troops who were ordered to protect London. Cade himself, a shadowy character with several aliases, had been a soldier in the French wars, and thus his rebellion appealed to the disenchanted commoners of all quarters of society. But the rebels were soon beaten as the disgruntled veterans of the French wars in the king's ranks gladly took any opportunity to attack whoever opposed them.[6]

Cade was later captured and executed, but the questions the common people had raised in their popular manifesto were to have far-reaching results, because rumours spread that the Duke of York had been involved in the Cade rising. The antipathy between York and Somerset escalated. These accusations, whether true or not, brought York back from his enforced exile in Ireland to try to clear his name. Unsure of his reception, he entered the kingdom with a large force of armed men for protection and immediately marched on London to petition King Henry for certain reforms, including the removal of certain named individuals from the Royal Council. Henry acquiesced to his demands, but did nothing because Somerset was back in favour; York's rash armed incursion now backfired, some nobles viewing his actions as an attempted usurpation. Thus failed York's first peaceable attempt at reform and he returned to Ludlow, his castle on the Welsh border, a bitter man. It would not be the only rash move that he would make.

During the next two years the Duke of York several times tried to enforce Somerset's dismissal, but he was to be defeated by blatant political manoeuvring. At Dartford in 1452, after meeting the royal army in the field, he was tricked and arrested; later he was forced to promise on oath never again to disturb the peace. The politically astute Somerset strengthened his position as the king's favourite and enjoyed humiliating York in front of his fellow peers. Ominously, a few months later, an English expeditionary force under the command of John Talbot, Earl of Shrewsbury, set sail for France in a last desperate attempt to win the war abroad. This military operation ended in complete catastrophe before the defences of Castillon in 1453.

If the English defeat at Castillon sparked off King Henry's 'insanity', which took the form of mental inertia and acute melancholia, it was a blessing for the

Henry VI creates John Talbot first Earl of Shrewsbury in 1442. Talbot's defeat at Castillon in 1453 shattered all English hopes in France, which may in turn have contributed to Henry's mental breakdown in the same year. (British Library)

Duke of York, since it brought him back into the political arena. When the Royal Council could no longer conceal the king's illness they had no other option but to appoint York as England's Protector because of his status as heir apparent. Quite naturally York's first move was to engineer the imprisonment of his enemy, the Duke of Somerset. This was the start of the open hostility betweeen the two men, which would eventually lead to the first battle of St Albans in 1455 and, more importantly, would divide the country as the aristocracy took sides according to their loyalties and ambitions. The great marcher lords, Neville and Percy, would play vital roles in the Wars of the Roses from this point on, chiefly because of their political problems in the north of England,[7] where feuding over ancient land rights and titles of office had been going on for years and had already brought the families of Neville and Percy to blows on more than one occasion, supported by their own private 'armies'. These 'private' quarrels were echoed all over England as belligerent nobles scrapped for power, but the large numbers of soldiers involved in the northern disputes made it important for the government to act quickly to prevent the skirmishing developing into private war.

The Duke of York's prompt intervention as Protector in one such northern dispute in 1453 shows his aptitude for strong action, in contrast to Henry VI.

However, York favoured the Nevilles and as a result, because Richard Neville, Earl of Warwick, had also argued with the Duke of Somerset over land rights in Wales, his family began to ally themselves with the Duke of York; the Percy Earls of Northumberland had little choice but to take the other side and found themselves supporting the royal party as Lancastrians from then on.

King Henry was incapable of ruling for the next eighteen months, but in October 1453 Queen Margaret gave birth to a son, Edward of Lancaster and fortuitously the king temporarily regained his sanity and blessed his son. Somerset was immediately released from prison and the tables were once more turned against the Duke of York. However, by this time Henry's fiery queen, Margaret of Anjou, was in firm control of the king's council and she secretly favoured Somerset, with all his faults, as her own personal instrument of political ambition. These events effectively brought to an end the Duke of York's Protectorship and heralded in a new era of suspicion as York began to realise that the queen was also intent on his political downfall. York's intense paranoia led him to believe that his life was at risk, and he immediately made plans for further military action to ensure his own safety.

FIRST BATTLES, 1455–60

It is hard to be precise about the first battle of the Wars of the Roses. According to some historians the 'civil wars' began in 1459 with the campaign that included the battle of Blore Heath; this places the first battle of St Albans – which took place in 1455 – alongside the Duke of York's other political attempts to remove his enemy Somerset from office before this date.[8] Other historians believe that the first battle of the Wars of the Roses took place at Shrewsbury as early as 1403.[9] It all depends on the degree of political importance attributed to each battle, and on the perceived length of the conflict overall. This problem is derived from the fact that the Wars of the Roses was not a continuous war, but rather a series of separate military conflicts over a long period of time, each fought for different reasons. Even the opponents changed over time. Nevertheless, it is apparent that the first battle of St Albans was a very important springboard to the wars, especially given the high status of some of the men killed there. It also provoked further hostility between noble families which was to have dramatic consequences as the Wars of the Roses progressed.

In May 1455 the Duke of York, threatened by the assembling of Lancastrian lords at Leicester, gathered his retainers and supporters and once more marched on London in an attempt to remove the Duke of Somerset from office. At St Albans, York's men met the king's small army, consisting of no more than 2,000 men, who immediately threw up makeshift barricades around the town's market-place as the Duke of York and his Neville allies, the Earl of Salisbury and his son the Earl of Warwick, arrayed their 'battles' in the fields outside the town. Negotiations between King Henry and the Duke of York began but soon broke down because of the king's unwillingness to deliver Somerset into the hands of the Yorkists. Not long after, a surprise attack was launched by the Yorkists on the barricades around the town, which were hastily manned by Lord Clifford and his retainers.[10] Despite the element of surprise, the Yorkist attack failed and the battle developed into a stand-off situation. But while the two sides were still locked in combat across the barricades, a single contingent of Yorkist troops found an unprotected gap between two of the town's ancient inns and the Earl of Warwick's '600 marchmen' suddenly burst into St Albans market-place, taking the Lancastrians completely by surprise. Some of the king's troops were routed immediately by the sudden appearance of Warwick's soldiers in the street, and when the Yorkist archers poured a hail of arrows into their confused and hemmed-in ranks, mass panic ensued. Finally, the Yorkist army took the barricades, and the king, who had been slightly wounded in the neck by an arrow, was promptly escorted to a nearby house for safety as the battle moved towards the last pockets of resistance, the Lancastrian nobles.

The Yorkist forces began to search out and execute prominent Lancastrians, a course of action which would reverberate throughout the Wars of the Roses. First Lord Clifford, then the Earl of Northumberland, a declared enemy of the Nevilles, were overwhelmed by 'northern' Yorkists and were butchered with their followers. The Duke of Buckingham was severely wounded, and the Duke of Somerset was found and savagely cut down as he tried to make a last stand with his faithful retainers outside the Castle Inn. Somerset's fate was a matter of political necessity considering his feud with the Duke of York and happened all too easily in the confusion of battle.

The first battle of St Albans was over in a very short time and casualties were relatively light, but despite Somerset's violent removal from office nothing had really changed for the Yorkists. However, from then on Queen Margaret's dominant influence was seen to be constantly at work to destroy them. As for the young Lancastrian nobles who had lost their fathers at St Albans, their determination to seek revenge became a convenient clarion call to arms, and more important, provided a ready source of troops for the queen to use under the king's standard. The lack of further retribution by the Yorkists immediately after the battle meant that there were plenty of Lancastrian nobles ready to take up arms, but a convenient time to begin the struggle was long in coming.

The Nevilles fared particularly well from the spoils of war after the first battle of St Albans. The Earl of Warwick was appointed Captain of Calais, and together with his father the Earl of Salisbury he was given the important wardenship of the West March to guard against Scottish invasion. However, the government, and indeed the country, was far from secure. The king had moved his court to the midlands in the face of continuing hostility in London. Further disturbances in the west country by feuding nobles, riots in London, and English piracy on the high seas at the expense of foreign fleets all contributed to a tense situation in what was now a virtually leaderless country. To make matters worse, King Henry had once more succumbed to illness which ultimately led to the Duke of York's further appointment as Lord Protector in an attempt to keep some semblance of law and order in the country.

In 1457 Sandwich was plundered by a French fleet under the command of the famous continental mercenary Pierre de Brézé, who was allegedly in the pay of Queen Margaret. Contemporary ballads related 'that the Duke of York had

[done] great wrong'[11] to the kingdom, and as the tension increased, nobles were constantly accompanied by large retinues of troops to council meetings. Conscious attempts at reconciliation were made by York and his followers in the years after the first battle of St Albans and compensation was ordered to be paid to the bereaved families of the Lancastrian casualties. The climax of these plans was celebrated in a charade of pomp and chivalry at St Pauls in London in March 1458, in which both parties willingly, if not wholeheartedly, participated. However, the following year both sides were preparing yet again for war.

Suspicions reached a new height in 1458 when Warwick was involved in a minor scuffle with some Lancastrian retainers and only just escaped with his life. Queen Margaret, naturally, blamed the earl for the incident and added insult to injury by accusing him of acts of piracy on the high seas in an effort to finance his unpaid Calais garrison. Commissions were sent out in May 1459 to loyal Lancastrians to meet at Leicester, but prominent Yorkists were deliberately excluded. During the subsequent council meeting in Coventry the Yorkists were indicted for their failure to attend the king in what can only be termed as a trap sprung by the queen. The civil war had begun.

The Duke of York's response to this new Lancastrian threat was to concentrate his forces at Ludlow, but the troops of his Neville allies were widely scattered in the north of England and at Calais. The Earl of Warwick crossed the English Channel with troops from the Calais garrison while the Earl of Salisbury's northern army marched south-west from Middleham Castle. Warwick, with some of the Calais garrison, managed to reach the muster point at Ludlow, narrowly avoiding some of the new Duke of Somerset's contingents, but the Earl of Salisbury's way was blocked at Blore Heath in Staffordshire by Lord Audley's Lancastrian force.

In the battle which followed, on 23 September 1459, the Earl of Salisbury occupied an elevated defensive position, which withstood several assaults from both cavalry and infantry contingents. While leading one of these desperate uphill charges against the Yorkist longbows, Lord Audley was killed, and soon after, through lack of leadership, the Lancastrians soon quit the field. Problems of troop concentration and communication difficulties before the battle meant that Audley's Lancastrian army had to fight Salisbury's men in an isolated battle. In fact, Lord Stanley's troops and Queen Margaret's main Lancastrian army had both been dangerously close to the battle zone when the fighting took place, but they had failed to link up with each other for concerted action at the crucial moment. The lack of Lancastrian troop concentration also gave the Earl of Salisbury the opportunity to slip through these forces under the cover of darkness, and his army was able to unite with the Duke of York's forces at Ludlow as planned.[12]

After the battle of Blore Heath the Yorkists again sent letters to King Henry in which they declared their innocence and expressed concern about the 'evil counsellors' who, they believed, were still intent on controlling the king for their own private reasons. The Yorkists stated categorically that even now their prime concern was for King Henry and that they had been forced into gathering their forces in self-defence. Their hopes for a favourable Lancastrian reply were doomed. Old grievances festered and could not now be healed. The Yorkists prepared their defences in anticipation of the Lancastrians' next move. The fields beyond Ludford Bridge were already planted with defensive wooden stakes and barricades, and guns were brought into position on carts. The Yorkists defiantly awaited the appearance of the royal banner in anticipation of yet more bloodletting on English soil.[13]

By now the sons of the leading nobles slain at St Albans had acquired their father's titles and were firmly entrenched in the Lancastrian ranks, eagerly awaiting the renewal of hostilities with the Yorkists. The new Duke of Somerset, Henry Beaufort, had himself been involved in the fighting at St Albans and had probably witnessed his own father's death there. The Earldom of Northumberland had also been perpetuated, and the new earl, Henry Percy, had acquired the traditional wardenship of the East March, thereby threatening the Neville influence in the west. The Duke of York and his Neville allies were therefore not only protecting their own lands and titles at Ludford; this continuing threat of personal blood feud between the nobles meant that almost everyone had some sort of stake in the outcome of future battles. In this respect the Yorkists were in great danger. As 'rebels' against their anointed king, whatever their intentions might have been towards his safety, they had committed treason and consequently they had nothing to gain from a limited victory. For them, it was all or nothing.

Loyalty was to play an important part in the events which followed on 12–13 October 1459. A message from the Duke of Somerset reached the vaward of the Duke of York's entrenched army at Ludford stating that the king would issue pardons to all those who would abandon the Yorkist cause. This took root in the Calais garrison, and especially in the conscience of one of the most famous soldiers of the day, Andrew Trollope. On hearing Somerset's offer, Trollope canvassed his men to search their souls and urged them not to commit treason against their rightful king and paymaster. As night approached the Yorkist leaders could only watch in horror as a portion of Warwick's 'trusted' garrison deserted to the Lancastrians, and the rest of the Yorkist line turned tail and fled in panic across Ludford Bridge. The Yorkist commanders had no choice but to flee, taking separate routes into Wales en route to the coast, from where they hoped to find refuge and safety abroad.[14]

The victorious Lancastrian soldiers swarmed over Ludford Bridge, broke into Ludlow and pillaged the town. Later, at Coventry, a parliament indicted the Yorkists for their treasonable actions at Ludford which resulted in the confiscation of their lands and titles to the crown and, even worse, the 'corruption' of their blood descendants so that they could neither inherit nor transmit any property in the future.[15] It is not surprising that henceforth Andrew Trollope was regarded as a traitor by the Yorkists. More importantly, the Lancastrian subterfuge at Ludford had dramatically shown that this form of 'treachery' in the face of the enemy was a commodity which could be bought and sold without warning; and treachery, and the fear of being betrayed, would be important issues in many of the battles of the Wars of the Roses.

The bloodless Lancastrian victory made possible by the 'rout of Ludford' effectively split the Duke of York's forces in two. York and his young son Edmund, Earl of Rutland, escaped to Ireland where the duke had been well liked during his enforced 'exile' as the king's lieutenant there in 1448. The Nevilles, with York's eldest son Edward, Earl of March, made for Calais where Warwick was, in theory at least, still captain of the garrison. Calais was to provide the Yorkists with a vital base of operations from which to plan and launch an invasion of England. It was equally important for the Lancastrian government to control Calais because both militarily and economically its strategic significance could not possibly be ignored. The English wool trade and the proximity of potential continental allies were two constant reminders to the Lancastrian government of just how volatile and insecure the situation now was. In fear of this, the Duke of Somerset was immediately dispatched to capture Calais but he found that Warwick's uncle, Lord Fauconberg, had already secured the position for the Yorkist earls. This forced the Lancastrians to embark upon a series of incompetent military actions in order to try to capture their objective. The Duke of Exeter was sent with 'a great navy'[16] to intercept the Earl of Warwick in the English Channel, but Exeter's ships were forced to disperse when no money was provided to pay for troops and provisions. At Sandwich, Warwick's ships, under the command of Lord Dinham, captured Lord Rivers' entire fleet before they had even set sail for Calais. Meanwhile Somerset's beleaguered army, badly in need of finance and supplies, valiantly tried to drive the Yorkists out of their position. Finally, however, the Lancastrians had to admit defeat. Warwick met with Richard of York in Dublin, a friendly bridgehead was secured by Lord Fauconberg at Sandwich, and in late June 1460 the Yorkists set sail for England with a small force. Their arrival was preceded by a well-timed canvassing of popular opinion in the shires, especially in Kent, where discontent and dissatisfaction with the king's chief ministers still prevailed. Against this turbulent background in south-east England, the Yorkists raised a new army and marched on London in an attempt to recapture the king.[17]

The three earls reached London virtually unopposed. In fact such was their popularity that some Lancastrian troops sent by the king to intercept their invasion at Canterbury turned their coats and joined the Yorkist ranks. However, the Tower of London had been well fortified by the Lancastrians, and under the command of Lord Scales its defenders defiantly secured the position, holding it against the Earl of Salisbury. With the Tower effectively bottled up, Warwick, Fauconberg and Edward, Earl of March, together with the major part of the Yorkist army marched out of the capital intending to capture King Henry who was then at Coventry. Before the Yorkists left London they reiterated that their plan was still only to deliver the king from his 'enemies'; in support of this their army was accompanied by a party of churchmen, including the Archbishop of Canterbury, whose role was to make sure that the Yorkists kept their sacred oaths. In the event even the efforts at mediation by these lofty prelates 'to avoid the effusion of Christian blood'[18] broke down and all-out slaughter once again decided the issue.

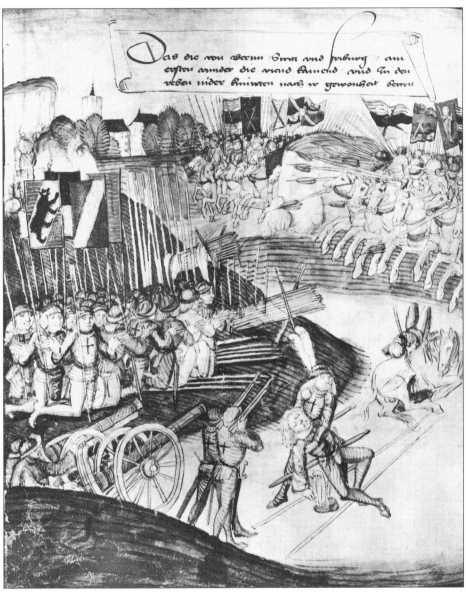

The taking of a fortified camp, as depicted in the Schilling Chronicle, 1484. (Royal Armouries)

King Henry and his loyal adherents had arrived at Northampton from Coventry some days before the Yorkists and, on receiving further news of Yorkist movements, the king's army had entrenched itself within a defensive redoubt of ditches and palisades, fortified with artillery, between the River Nene and Delapré Abbey. The Duke of Buckingham had been given overall command of the Lancastrian army, as he had been at St Albans five years earlier, with the Earl of Shrewsbury, Lord Grey of Ruthin and Lords Beaumont and Egremont in support. The Lancastrians must have been very confident of victory but in a very short time all these nobles, except Lord Grey, had either been slain on the battlefield or drowned in the River Nene trying to escape their attackers.

The battle of Northampton (10 July 1460) was a complete catastrophe for the Lancastrian cause. To begin with, their guns, which should have made any Yorkist attack on the Lancastrian defenses very costly indeed, had been waterlogged by heavy rain and their charges would not light or fire. Worse was to follow: the main disaster occurred when the Yorkist vaward, struggling up the slippery royalist redoubt, were actually helped into the camp by turncoat Lancastrians. Lord Grey and his troops, acting on what was most certainly a pre-arranged plan with the Yorkists, had changed sides and consequently Grey's troops made no attempt to prevent the Yorkists from attacking their amazed and already fleeing Lancastrian comrades. The Duke of Buckingham and the Earl of Shrewsbury rallied their men in vain at the king's pavilion to try to protect their sovereign, but they were quickly butchered by Yorkist soldiers; other Lancastrian nobles met a similar fate as they tried to wade across the River Nene and King Henry was soon recaptured. He was led triumphantly back to London where he once again became a puppet in Yorkist hands.[19]

Lancastrian resistance both at home and abroad disappeared in a cloud of retribution and negotiated pardon, and both the Tower garrison, still under the command of Lord Scales, and the Duke of Somerset surrendered to Yorkist pressure. Somerset fled first to France before joining Queen Margaret in the north of England, but in the meantime the Duke of York grasped the opportunity to re-enter the kingdom and reap the rewards of Yorkist victory. However, no one was prepared for the extraordinary way in which he would do this, nor what dynastic problems would arise out of the subsequent mediation.

The Duke of York's claim and right to the throne of England, although abstract until a time when King Henry and his son were no more, was, according to the law, still recognised by parliament and the Royal Council, but this was hardly the moment for the duke to claim the throne by 'right of conquest'. However, this is exactly what he did, in front of his dismayed supporters. What followed was an unprecedented settlement; in answer to the duke's claims, the Nevilles were forced to negotiate a compromise which effectively disinherited the Prince of Wales and made York heir apparent if King Henry should die.[20]

This so-called Act of Accord was not without its safeguards, however, namely that the king should not be 'removed'. After all, did any true Yorkist supporter believe the king worthy of his crown, considering the difficulties caused by his inability to rule? Nevertheless it was clear that most Yorkists, including Warwick himself, still preferred to keep the anointed king on his throne, even as a figurehead monarch, and frowned upon the Duke of York's attempted usurpation. For the moment restoration to office would have contented most Yorkist nobles but inadvertently York's actions had set in motion events that would prolong the struggle, namely by making a relentless enemy of Queen

Margaret because of her son's disinheritance. Consequently the Act of Accord neither solved the developing dynastic problem nor prevented further hostilities. In fact, it may also have led to disunity in the Yorkist ranks. This same dynastic claim would within a year cause the Duke of York's death and, in turn, bring about his son's successful usurpation of Henry's crown in a welter of English blood.

THE NORTH–SOUTH WAR, 1460–61

There was very little continuous active campaigning during the Wars of the Roses between 1455 and 1487, but the 1460–61 mid-winter conflict must be considered to have been the longest, bloodiest and most closely followed episode of the period. Between December 1460 and March 1461 there were fought no fewer than four major pitched battles on English soil; in addition there were several sharp skirmishes, not to mention an unruly pillaging *chevauchée* which cut a swath of destruction along the main artery of the country. Add to this the effects of the unusually harsh weather conditions which prevailed at the time, and this period earns Shakepeare's description as the 'grim-visag'd war'.[21]

It was during this series of individual, but consecutive, short military campaigns that the medieval soldier was tested to the limit, both on the march and on the battlefield; here he faced the ultimate horror and confusion of close-quarter hand-to-hand combat when these winter operations culminated in the bloodiest battle ever fought on English soil. It was also a time when the north and south of England were divided by a wave of scaremongering and widespread propaganda that would persist for generations to come.

In December 1460 Queen Margaret secretly gathered a large army in the north of England with which she intended to restore her son's rightful inheritance, removed by the Act of Accord. She then left Hull, her base in the north, and travelled to Scotland to recruit additional troops to prepare for the expected march south to free King Henry from further Yorkist manipulation. Meanwhile, the Lancastrian leaders, based at Pontefract Castle, proceeded to pillage the Duke of York's lands in Yorkshire; this brought the Yorkists hotfoot out of London to quell what they thought was a purely local issue. Old grievances, and the desire for revenge, would soon be the order of the day as the Duke of York's meagre army of about 5,000 men struggled northwards with their baggage train and artillery through the rain and mud of the December roads.[22]

The Duke of York's army advanced without support from London, although commissions had been issued to 'trusted' Yorkists, including Lord Neville, who subsequently took his recruits over to the enemy instead of fulfilling his contract.[23] Warwick was left in charge of the capital, while York's eldest son Edward, Earl of March, had been sent on a recruiting drive in the Welsh Marches with the intention of linking up with his father some time later. However, a skirmish involving York's advance guard at Worksop proved that the Lancastrians were active in, if not wholly in control of, the north, which forced the Yorkists on to the defensive; they quickly sought refuge in York's castle at Sandal near Wakefield. It is said that at this point a chivalrous truce was negotiated between the two sides to allow the Christmas festivities to proceed, but it was to be a raw season for the Yorkist garrison when supplies and food ran out at Sandal and foraging began in earnest at the end of December 1460.

The battle of Wakefield (30 December 1460) began when Lancastrian troops attacked some of these Yorkist 'scourers' who were searching for victuals in the neighbouring countryside; it soon escalated into a major engagement when part of the Lancastrian force arrived outside Sandal Castle. His supply line to Wakefield now cut, the Duke of York had no option but to seek battle with what seemed like a much smaller Lancastrian army than he had anticipated. His advisers counselled caution, but the duke was determined; tragically, within half an hour, the Duke of York himself and many of his followers were killed, trapped in the maelstrom of a pincer movement made by diligent Lancastrian commanders. In the rout, York's second son Edmund, Earl of Rutland, was stabbed to death by Lord Clifford, avenging his own father's death at St Albans in 1455. Similarly, the Earl of Salisbury was captured, denied ransom, and then executed at Pontefract Castle along with other Yorkist soldiers soon after the battle was over.[24]

Yorkist heads were spiked on the gates of York to signal the Yorkists' final humiliation and defeat in the north, and soon the Queen arrived from Scotland with more troops which she had bought with the surrender of Berwick upon Tweed and an unscrupulous marriage pact with the Scottish king. With York dead, the way was now clear for the Lancastrians to push south to free King Henry from Warwick's clutches. The advance began with the sacking of Beverley by Lord Neville's troops; such behaviour continued unabated and uncontrolled as the queen's army moved slowly towards London, its ranks swelled by others looking for an opportunity to loot and pillage but who had no intention of fighting for their king. The swath of destruction was obviously painted 'blacker than black' by contemporary southern chroniclers,[25] and the Earl of Warwick had every reason to exaggerate the horrors of the Lancastrian advance to encourage the recruitment of troops for the expected encounter with the Lancastrian army. Doubtless, every shire levy's muster was coloured with this patriotic call to protect both families and property from the unruly northerners whom southerners now held in the utmost dread. After all, towns like Grantham, Stamford, Peterborough and others had already felt the effects of the renegade element in Queen Margaret's army, and reports of indiscriminate pillaging were rife in London; this not only caused widespread panic, but also infused the coming issue with northern prejudice.

However, the queen's unruly northern army was not the only problem that faced the Yorkist faction. After hearing news of the deaths of his father and younger brother at the battle of Wakefield, Edward, Earl of March, the new Duke of York, received reports of a further Lancastrian army advancing into England from Wales. This 'motley creu' of foreign mercenaries and Welshmen was commanded by the Earls of Wiltshire and Pembroke who were intent on linking up with Queen Margaret's troops. Edward, then recruiting in the Marcher lands of his ancestors, the Mortimers, was ideally placed to deal with the western threat, and with the support of what was to become over the next two months a vastly experienced army of loyal Yorkist retainers and battle-hardened soldiers, he

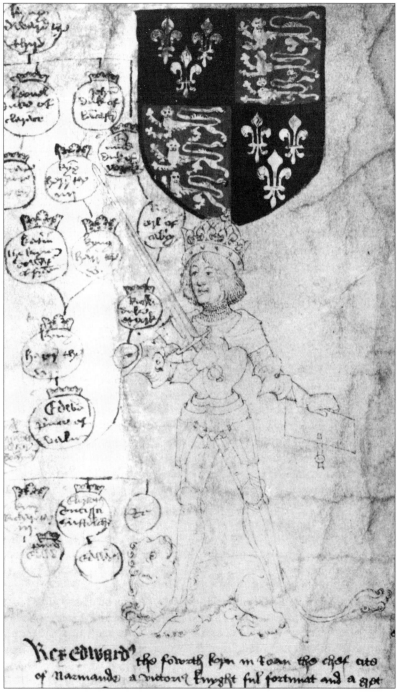

A young Edward IV from the 'Rous Roll'. Edward was still only eighteen years of age when he fought in the crucial campaigns of 1461 which finally won him the English throne. (British Library)

confronted the Lancastrian army at Mortimers Cross near Hereford. Although he was only eighteen years old at this time, Edward was already commanding great respect from his supporters, both militarily and, more recently, politically, as the new head of the House of York. He had been directly involved in the Ludford fiasco and the Calais campaign and had fought at the battle of Northampton. He may also have been present at, although not directly involved in, the battle of St Albans five years earlier; therefore he already had some experience of warfare by the early 1460s.[26] However, he also had several experienced 'captains' present in all these campaigns to give advice; although in battle, authority was situated beneath the commander's standard, the thinking behind the army's tactics was largely derived from the experienced and valued captains who led the 'battles'.

On 3 February 1461 at Mortimers Cross Edward's Yorkist army thoroughly beat the Lancastrians, chiefly because of the quality of his troops compared to the mixture of nationalities opposing them. In addition some of Edward's adherents were, in effect, protecting their own lands in the Welsh Marches, and thus had a further incentive. Before the battle, a natural phenomen known as a parhelion – three suns – was seen in the sky; to prevent the more superstitious of his men interpreting this as a bad omen, Edward told his army that it meant God was with them and that the three suns represented the Trinity; after the battle Edward's heraldic achievements included the 'sun in splendour', which he used as a livery badge from then on. Many Lancastrians were killed or executed in the rout after Mortimers Cross; Owen Tudor was beheaded in Hereford market-place with other Lancastrian prisoners, but the Earls of Wiltshire and Pembroke, undoubtedly Edward's two main targets, managed to escape the battlefield and lived to fight another day.[27] After the battle the victorious Yorkists immediately marched towards London and en route received news of Queen Margaret's pillaging army. Initial reports were followed by others which indicated that Warwick's army had been beaten in battle and driven out of St Albans, and that, even worse, King Henry had once more been taken back into Lancastrian hands.

The second battle of St Albans (17 February 1461) was an engagement that developed in an unusual manner and was therefore very different from the other set-piece actions of the Wars of the Roses. The main reason for the running battle that ensued in the streets and through the outskirts of the town was the poor intelligence supplied to the Earl of Warwick by his scouts; after marching out of London to confront the queen's pillaging army, he was forced to deploy his forces too thinly in an effort to cover all the routes into the town. This lack of intelligence forced Warwick to split his army into numerous small forces and consequently, when battle was joined, the Yorkist army was unable to maintain a continuous and cohesive battle line against the repeated Lancastrian attacks from different directions.

As the queen's army advanced into the centre of the town, the Yorkists fared well at first, one contingent of archers succeeding temporarily in turning back the Lancastrians. However, the Lancastrian commanders quickly found another route into St Peter's Street and the Yorkist archers were soon outflanked and overrun. The Lancastrians then advanced on to Barnards Heath and towards the Yorkist 'battle' positioned there. This section of Warwick's 'line' had been fortified with various ingenious defensive contraptions to make the Lancastrian approach and attack more difficult; it also contained a contingent of mercenary Burgundian handgunners. However, none of these defensive measures was of any use to Warwick because the 'battle' had been deployed in the wrong direction to confront the Lancastrian army. This misalignment could not be redressed in time to meet the assault of the queen's troops effectively, and consequently the fight developed into a running mêlée.

The Earl of Warwick, commanding the main Yorkist battle at Sandridge, soon became aware of the problem, but once again poor intelligence and his distance from the developing action made it difficult for him to march in support of his hard-pressed contingents. He decided to quit the field with what was left of his army and as night closed in the Yorkists took their chance to escape, skirting the thin Lancastrian picket lines to reach safety. Warwick left King Henry near St Albans in the care of some trusted Yorkist knights. The queen's army made short work of the last remaining pockets of Yorkist resistance on the field – and then promptly executed the king's keepers in a fit of savagery. Warwick rallied his men and marched westwards to link up with Edward, Duke of York, while the Lancastrian army, now seriously depleted because of the continuing pillaging problem, marched on London towards what seemed like certain victory.[28]

Outside the capital, however, the Lancastrian advance suddenly ground to a halt. The Londoners, terrified of the marauding northern army, a terror created mainly by Warwick's scaremongering propaganda, had closed the city gates. King Henry himself craved admittance, but nothing could remove the spectre of 'mykel dread'[29] that had seized the minds of the citizens. Even food supplies en route to the Lancastrian army were stopped. Emissaries sent by the queen to negotiate with the Londoners were attacked at Westminster out of fear, and as the Lancastrian leaders faced the prospect of dwindling supplies and a rapidly disintegrating army, they learned that Edward and Warwick had united their forces and were already marching towards the capital. The Lancastrians had no option but to retreat back to York and attempt to regroup their army in more 'friendly' territory.

The atmosphere in London was now perfect for the triumphant Yorkists to enter the city, and for Edward to claim the English throne. He was welcomed by the Londoners as their saviour and on 4 March 1461 the Yorkists acclaimed their new sovereign at Westminster, although his coronation was postponed until the Lancastrians had been dealt with.[30] Edward's priority now was to march north as quickly as possible, recruiting on the way, to try to prevent a large concentration of Lancastrian strength building up in Yorkshire. Aware of the Lancastrians' ability to muster large numbers of experienced troops in the north of England, the Yorkist commanders took different roads to an arranged rendezvous with the intention of recruiting as many men as possible en route. By the time Edward, Warwick and Lord Fauconberg joined up in Yorkshire, the Yorkist army numbered some 20,000 men. However, the Duke of Norfolk had failed to link up, and when Edward's army encamped near Pontefract Castle, Norfolk's contingents were still a day's march behind the main army. The newly recruited Lancastrian northern army was much larger by comparison, although it is difficult to give precise figures because of conflicting evidence.

A skirmish at Ferrybridge in the early hours of 28 March caused the Yorkist army to move forward to dispute the River Aire crossing; the bridge at Ferrybridge was defended by Lord Clifford's retainers who had been sent out from Towton, where the main Lancastrian army was encamped. The task of harassing the Yorkist advance had begun, and a battle ensued for the crossing, which the Yorkists gained by an effective flank march and attack by Lord Fauconberg's vaward who then proceeded to chase the retreating Lancastrians back up the Towton road. Lord Clifford and his men were wiped out by the Yorkist vaward's mounted contingent near Dintingdale, only two miles from their own main battle lines. In freezing conditions the Yorkist army crossed the River Aire and the next day the Yorkists could see the now massive Lancastrian army camped on a high plateau between Saxton and Towton and preparing for what would prove to be the deadliest and most horrifying of all medieval battles.

Amid snow and freezing temperatures the long-standing blood feuds of the Wars of the Roses reached a terrible climax on Palm Sunday, 29 March 1461. By the end of the bloody battle of Towton between 20,000 and 28,000 soldiers lay dead in great heaps on the battlefield or drowned in the two adjacent rivers which ran red with blood. Here the medieval soldier faced his greatest test yet. The battle began with a longbow attack of remarkable proportions which put the Lancastrians at a grave disadvantage and forced them to assault the Yorkist line prematurely. During the deadly hand-to-hand combat that followed, 'the dead carcasses hindered those that fought',[31] but gradually the larger Lancastrian army began to push the Yorkists back towards Saxton. All now depended on the arrival of the Duke of Norfolk's reinforcements as battle fatigue began to cast a shadow over the two opposing armies. Late in the afternoon, the appearance of Norfolk's fresh forces on the field caused the Lancastrian battle line to give way and a terrible rout ensued over treacherous terrain; the two rivers would severely impede the soldiers' escape from the battlefield. Lancastrian soldiers were cut down in their thousands, their bodies spread over an area some six miles long by three broad, and although some of King Edward's main enemies, namely the Dukes of Somerset and Exeter, the Earl of Wiltshire and Lord Roos, managed to escape with King Henry into the north, many Lancastrian nobles and gentry were killed during the day's slaughter and in the bloody aftermath.[32]

The casualty list after the battle of Towton included the Earls of Northumberland and Devon and numerous other Lancastrian leaders; as noted above, Lord Clifford had been killed the previous day at Dintingdale. The battle not only cut down to size the militarily 'active' nobility of England at that time, but also depleted the available Lancastrian manpower for some time to come. Indeed, it is unlikely that the Lancastrians could ever again put into the field such an effective and unified army without resorting to the use of mercenaries or continental allies, although it is certainly not true that the Lancastrian nobility ceased to exist after Towton.[33] However, it is true that the armies which took part in the battle of Towton would never be equalled in size during the Wars of the Roses, and never again would so many soldiers be slain on English soil.

The battlefield cross at Towton (North Yorkshire), marking the site where York and Lancaster struggled in the snow for the crown of England on Palm Sunday, 1461. (Author)

THE BORDER WAR, 1461–64

The operation in the north of England to root out further Lancastrian opposition after Towton was left in the capable hands of the Earl of Warwick and his brother, Lord Montagu. After his triumph at Towton, King Edward's numerous attempts to take command of his forces in the field in person would flounder, and on a number of occasions he would find himself uncharacteristically leading from the rear in the next phase of the Wars of the Roses. Consequently, over the next three years Edward IV never took an active part in the various pitched battles and sieges that took place in the north of England.

After the battle of Towton the Yorkists pushed back the remaining Lancastrians over the border into Scotland, while other men of dubious loyalty took refuge in the great castles of Northumberland. But it would be another three years of intermittent fighting and fluctuating fortunes before the north was even partially secured by the Yorkists. King Edward travelled south soon after the capture and execution of the Earl of Wiltshire at Newcastle, and was formally crowned at Westminster Abbey on 28 June 1461. His first act was to create a new Yorkist government which passed an act of attainder on 113 Lancastrians who had rebelled against him.[34] He also advanced his friends and relatives to high office, bestowing dukedoms on his two younger brothers Richard and George, while soldiers who had served with him in the Towton campaign were rewarded for their services with knighthoods or annuities for life.

King Henry and the royal family, on the other hand, soon took the opportunity offered by an alliance with Scotland to disrupt the north by renewing the sporadic border raiding which had traditionally threatened England in the past. In this way the Lancastrians, now with Scottish troops in their ranks, began a campaign in which fortune would favour first the Yorkists and then the Lancastrians, and which would be reminiscent of continental warfare, where strategy and tactics were mainly based on diplomatic manoeuvres, and where confrontation in open battle was avoided at all costs. The Wars of the Roses had been reduced to guerrilla warfare.

In April 1461 the key garrison town of Berwick upon Tweed was officially handed over to the Scots by Queen Margaret as payment for previous military aid; later Carlisle was to be similarly threatened with forfeiture to pay for Scottish troops. Unrest among Welsh Lancastrians led by the Earl of Pembroke and the Duke of Exeter caused the Yorkists some concern, but King Edward mobilised an army, under the command of Lords Herbert and Ferrers, to contain the problem. The Yorkists succeeded in capturing Pembroke Castle, and during the next few months they went on to subdue most of the Lancastrian strongholds in Wales. Only Harlech Castle held out, remaining for a few more years as a safe haven for the Lancastrians. The Yorkist campaign in Wales was a great success, although both Henry Tudor (then a refugee in Harlech) and Jasper Tudor were still at large to threaten the Yorkist cause.[35]

Edward's attention now turned to the north of England where the situation was not so easily remedied. The Earl of Warwick, newly appointed the warden of both the East and West Marches, was having great difficulty in keeping the key strongholds of Alnwick and Dunstanburgh under control. In September 1461 the Percy castle at Alnwick surrendered to the Yorkists and soon after the fortress at Dunstanburgh also capitulated, but both castles were soon back in Lancastrian hands, chiefly because of a Yorkist miscalculation. Rather foolishly, the Yorkists retained Sir Ralph Percy, a staunch Lancastrian, as the commander of Dunstanburgh Castle, and it wasn't long before the stronghold was back in

Lancastrian hands when Yorkist operations were directed elsewhere. Similarly, within a few months Alnwick's fickle Yorkist garrison also surrendered to Lancastrian opposition.[36]

It is worth noting that Edward's forgiving and chivalrous nature was in part responsible for the duration of the border war. His misplaced trust in his enemies shows that he would overlook the previous attitudes and opposition of even staunch Lancastrians in his efforts to garrison and control the northern castles. Inevitably, the cocktail of shifting alliances, misplaced faith and chivalrous offers of pardon were to cause great problems for Edward's generals in the field. Despite the excesses meted out to the king's own family during and after the battle of Wakefield in 1460, Edward decided that even die-hard Lancastrians were to have their attainders reversed; his trust, almost inevitably, would be betrayed, causing the border war to flare up once again. However, despite his crushing victory at Towton, between 1461 and 1464 Edward IV's throne was still very insecure, and would remain so as long as Henry VI and his son lived as a focus for Lancastrian supporters. Edward's policy was to try to win over the nobles who held sway in those areas of England hostile to the Yorkists, especially the Percies, and thus many Lancastrians who sought mercy and favour from Edward were granted in return the reversal of their attainders. Edward's misplaced trust not only led to various acts of treachery during the northern border war, but also caused serious problems when Edward married into a staunch Lancastrian family in 1464, a family that had been shown similar mercy and preferment after the battle of Towton. On the basis of promises, pacts of allegiance and dubious alliances, this new phase of the Wars of the Roses was played out in the most unscrupulous manner before the walls of the north's greatest strongholds, on the ever-shifting sands of continental diplomacy.

In 1462 Queen Margaret, true to her industrious nature, was pressing for further military support from abroad and had been in close political contact with the new King of France, Louis XI. However, her absence from Scotland provided a lucky political break for the Yorkists who were able to establish a brief Anglo-Scottish truce which enabled them to seize several key Lancastrian strongholds. Margaret's political bargaining with the French king was eventually to secure only the help of Pierre de Brézé (who had allegedly already helped her with military matters); in return she 'promised' to hand over to the French the English garrison town of Calais. However, de Brézé's small contingent of mercenary troops enabled Queen Margaret to extend Lancastrian influence in the north, and in 1462 Bamburgh, Alnwick, Dunstanburgh and Warkworth – four of the most formidable of the Northumbrian castles – all opened their gates to her troops either through treachery or weakness on the part of the defenders.[37] It was clear that King Edward could not allow such Lancastrian consolidation on the borders of his kingdom to continue, and therefore an army was rapidly mobilised to deal with the threat. Warwick was sent north with a commission to recruit troops, and Yorkist ships set sail for Newcastle with a cargo of heavy artillery in anticipation of siege warfare.

By all accounts the Yorkist army was impressive by the standards of the day, so much so that Queen Margaret decided to retreat into Scotland immediately, leaving all the newly won Lancastrian strongpoints at the mercy of Yorkist retaliation. King Edward himself had intended to command the army in the north in person, but an attack of measles prevented him from taking any further part in the forthcoming campaign. Nevertheless he gave explicit orders that castles were to be seized intact, without resorting to artillery bombardment; fortuitously, only Dunstanburgh and Bamburgh proved difficult for the Yorkist army to subdue. At both these castles the Lancastrian defenders grimly held on, even though some were reduced to eating their horses, but in the end lack of food and supplies forced them to capitulate, and the terms for their surrender were agreed on Christmas Eve 1462.[38]

True to form, Edward's over-generous nature meant that once again leading pro-Lancastrians were given the command of key garrison towns and strongholds. Even the Duke of Somerset, newly received and recruited into King Edward's favour, was helping Warwick to besiege Alnwick Castle, which was held by his former allies. However, the timely appearance of a Lancastrian-Scottish relieving force under the command of Pierre de Brézé and the Earl of Angus forced Warwick's larger besieging army to withdraw from their positions around Alnwick. Having been entrenched in their siegeworks for so long the Yorkist troops lacked the incentive to attack and this gave the Lancastrians the opportunity to escape unimpeded over the border to safety.[39]

The capture of Alnwick gave the Yorkists the upper hand once more, but astonishingly, despite the precarious Yorkist hold on the north, Warwick and Edward returned to the south of England. In March 1463 Sir Ralph Percy allowed French and Scottish troops back into Bamburgh and Dunstanburgh. The Lancastrians also tricked their way into Alnwick Castle. Once again the distant Yorkist commanders faced the problem of isolated garrison troops, lacking support and leadership, changing sides. However, the Yorkists had learnt important lessons, and the situation was remedied by the much-needed appointment of a more permanent northern commander. Warwick's brother, John Neville, Lord Montagu, was given the wardenship of the important East March, a post traditionally held by the Percy family. The appearance in the north of the Earl of Warwick himself with more troops aided his brother's new position considerably, and their successes in the field even led to an unruly burning and pillaging raid by the Yorkist army into Scotland.

The Scottish regency council now became intensely frustrated with Queen Margaret's costly military efforts in the north, and refused to tolerate her 'she-wolf' tactics, no matter what lucrative incentives she offered. The Scottish army retreated and the Lancastrian cause collapsed. Queen Margaret and Prince Edward found sanctuary at Bamburgh, where they learned that the Lancastrian cause had been undermined by King Edward's secret diplomacy. Edward had not only agreed a truce with Scotland, but had also secured a one-year cessation of hostilities with France: it was this that had forced the Scottish split with Lancaster. Queen Margaret immediately took ship to Flanders and King Henry was moved to Bamburgh, the most formidable of the northern strongholds.

The Duke of Somerset now made his move, openly declaring his Lancastrian allegiance for the last time in his eventful career. Forced into hiding by the pressures of a hostile Yorkist England, he eventually met with Henry VI and other staunch Lancastrians, including Sir Ralph Percy, at Bamburgh Castle. Taking up what was left of the Lancastrian king's authority in the north, Somerset went on to the offensive, capturing several important northern border strongholds. However, Somerset's desperate bid to resurrect his own personal ambitions was not to last. On 25 April 1464, while escorting Scottish emissaries back to meet King Edward at York, Lord Montagu was attacked by Somerset and Percy at Hedgeley Moor. The Lancastrians were defeated in open battle, leaving Sir Ralph Percy dead on the field. However, Somerset managed to escape

A drawing of the tomb of Pierre de Brézé and his wife, now destroyed. (Geoffrey Wheeler)

from the battlefield and set about rebuilding his army with which to renew further hostilities with the Yorkists.[40]

Meanwhile, King Edward had mobilised his artillery and was preparing for yet another major military campaign in the north at the expense of the hard-pressed English taxpayer. Somerset decided to strike quickly before Edward's army could move, but the extremely able Lord Montagu was soon hard on his heels, and on 10 May 1464 at Hexham he surprised Somerset's Lancastrian army in camp and pushed them into a nearby river after a brief fight. Henry Beaufort's career as a soldier had come to an end; captured in the rout from the battlefield, he was executed for treason at Newcastle.[41] King Henry's last line of Lancastrian defiance now lay behind the solid walls of Bamburgh Castle.

Between 1461 and 1464 many of the northern castles had changed hands at least three times, but only one sustained a real siege including artillery bombardment and spirited attack: Bamburgh was held for King Henry by Sir Ralph Grey who refused to succumb to the Yorkists, turning down political incentives and defying efforts to starve out the garrison. Edward's military policy in the north dictated that 'the jewel' of Bamburgh, being so close to the Scottish border, was too valuable a fortress to be destroyed by heavy artillery. In the end, though, Warwick was forced to use his bombards, warning the beleaguered defenders of Bamburgh that 'for every stone that fell from the walls of the castle a Lancastrian head would fall likewise thereafter'.[42] But the Lancastrian commanders had too much to lose and refused to submit; on 25 June 1464 the king's great guns, 'Newcastle', 'London' and 'Dijon' opened fire on the castle.

The great walls were soon breached and during the following assault the castle fell to the Yorkists. Grey was captured amid the smoke and rubble of the last Lancastrian stronghold in the north and was taken to Doncaster where he was executed. As a reward for his services in the north King Edward granted Lord Montagu the earldom of Northumberland.

The Lancastrian hold in Northumberland had been broken at last, and in July 1465 King Henry was found wandering in the north of England, and was captured. A pathetic remnant of a lost cause, he was taken to London on horseback, his feet tied to the stirrups. He was imprisoned in the Tower of London where he would continue to be a thorn in the Yorkist side for some time to come.[43]

YORK AGAINST YORK, 1465–71

Edward IV ruled a relatively peaceful England for the next four years and united the English people behind him by proclaiming renewed aggression against the French king. With the support of Burgundy and other foreign powers, Edward began to lay plans for an invasion of France, energetically taking up the mantle, and the cause, of Henry V, hoping perhaps that a war abroad would help to erase some of the bitterness of the civil wars of previous years. However, not all Edward's decisions as King of England were good at this time. In 1464 he had secretly married Elizabeth Woodville, formerly Grey, who had brought to court with her a large brood of greedy relatives all expecting to be provided for and entered on to an already full nobility list. Clearly Edward was beyond reproach and his chief advisors and councillors could do nothing about the infatuated king's choice of queen, even though the Woodvilles had been prominent Lancastrians. However, Edward's secret marriage was to have far-reaching consequences. Most people chose to accept it with as much grave as they could muster, but not the Earl of Warwick.

Edward's extraordinary marriage and his single-minded overseas policy caused a severe rift between the King and Warwick: the 'Kingmaker' believed that he was the greatest diplomat and puppetmaster of English politics, and that Edward was still his faithful protégé. Indeed, Warwick may even have coveted the crown for himself. Doubtless he was aggrieved by Edward's new-found independent behaviour, but whatever Warwick's motives, his plans to marry Edward to a French princess were dashed by the Woodville marriage and this left him in an acutely embarrassing position with the French king. Later, adding insult to injury, Edward refused to allow Warwick's daughters to marry into the royal family, as Warwick had no doubt hoped. Warwick could only watch as the door of royal patronage closed on him inch by inch, while others profited from Edward's open-handed generosity.[44] In short, Warwick's role as the 'kingmaker' was no more. Not to be thwarted, however, Warwick would soon enlist further support and find another protégé to manipulate, stoking the fires of the Wars of the Roses once again.

By 1467 Warwick had very easily cajoled Edward's 'false, fleeting'[45] brother George, Duke of Clarence, into his confidence, priming him for the attempted usurpation of Edward's throne. Clarence had no real reason to betray his brother – he had been well rewarded by Edward, and was also the Yorkist heir apparent – but he was greedy, foolish and easily led. It was because of these characteristics that he followed Warwick's plan to discredit Edward, first by causing a widespread popular rebellion in 1469 centred primarily in Yorkshire.

The two predominantly tax-related rebellions of Robin of Redesdale and Robin of Holderness were brought partially under control by John Neville, Earl of Northumberland, who was still acting as the king's lieutenant in the north. The demands of Robin of Holderness included the restoration of the Percy family to office,[46] so the new Earl of Northumberland had a vested interest in curbing this particular disturbance. However, it was Robin of Redesdale, identified as Sir William Conyers, who caused the greatest concern to King Edward. Conyers was related to the Nevilles by marriage and, having fortuitously evaded capture by the Earl of Northumberland, he began to recruit a large army in support of his popular manifesto to seek a remedy for 'the great hurt and empoverishing of this land',[47] a manifesto that Warwick and Clarence openly distributed for propaganda purposes in July 1469.

Earlier that month, the Duke of Clarence had been hastily married to Isabel Neville, Warwick's daughter, in Calais. Rumours reached King Edward that Warwick and Clarence were plotting against him, but the king took no action, although it became clear that numerous problems at home and abroad were linked to Warwick's activities. The king reacted to Redesdale's rebellion by ordering the Earl of Pembroke (William Herbert) and the Earl of Devon (Humphrey Stafford) to come to his aid at Nottingham, but problems of troop concentration and an argument over billeting facilities prevented the Yorkist contingents from linking up for concerted action against the rebels.[48] In the meantime Warwick had landed in Kent – the traditional breeding ground of popular revolt – and was marching on London at the head of a small army.

Because of the quarrel over billeting conditions the two main Yorkist forces had now split up, leaving Pembroke's force deficient of archers. Meanwhile Redesdale's army had bypassed King Edward's small force at Nottingham, thus cutting him off from London, and clashed with Pembroke's contingents at Edgecote on 26 July 1469. Lacking archers, Pembroke's Welshmen were utterly defeated by the reinforcement of Redesdale's army by Warwick's troops later in the day; they suffered heavy casualties. As might be expected, the Earl of Pembroke and his brother were beheaded at Northampton the next day.[49]

Edward IV was now vulnerable to capture. His own small force had deserted him when they learned of the Yorkist defeat at Edgecote and Edward was forced to throw himself on Warwick's mercy. He was taken prisoner at Olney and was later confined in the Neville stronghold of Middleham Castle. There he awaited his fate and contemplated the opportunity to get even with the Kingmaker when the time came. However, the very propaganda which had made Warwick's *coup d'etat* possible in 1469 was soon discredited, a matter of weeks after the king's capture. The commons' grievances which had been so powerful in causing unrest and dissatisfaction with King Edward's excessive taxation for military and private purposes, was now replaced by a general return to lawlessness and disorder in the kingdom which Warwick's limited powers of authority were unable to control. Lacking the necessary support from his fellow peers during his takeover bid, Warwick was unable to establish any solution to the crisis and was forced to release Edward from captivity.

Edward's policy of mercy towards his declared enemies returned, but this time was moderated by a number of moves to isolate Warwick politically.[50] However, the personal differences between Edward and Warwick had not yet been settled, and while each man outwardly tolerated the other, behind the façade both waited for a further opportunity to strike. Continuing unrest in the country would prevent the final reckoning for some time yet, but this enabled Warwick to strengthen his forces, ostensibly to put down outbreaks of unrest. The resulting campaign would end disastrously, but would later pave the way for Warwick to oust Edward not only from power, but also out of his own kingdom.

The Lincolnshire rebellion of 1470 centred around the fortunes of Lord Welles and his son Sir Robert, who, not unlike most fifteenth-century gentry, had become embroiled in a personal feud with one of the king's men.[51] As the quarrel escalated Welles found himself seeking support from Warwick and Clarence. Perhaps at Warwick's instigation, Sir Robert Welles caused further trouble when he issued a proclamation in Lincolnshire to the effect that King Edward was about to punish the shire for its part in previous rebellions. Alarmed by this threat, recruits flocked to his standard, ready to defend their county. The crisis proved so serious that Edward believed that he would need the support of Warwick and Clarence to put down the unrest; the Earl of Warwick and his all too willing protégé, given the king's commission to recruit troops, now made their move.

Lord Welles was interrogated by the king and confessed to his part in the rebellion. Then a letter was dispatched to his son Robert warning him that if he did not submit immediately his father would be executed forthwith. Abandoning his part in Warwick's plan of action – to catch Edward in a pincer movement – Sir Robert Welles dutifully veered off to rescue his father. His contingents unexpectedly met the king's army, with banners displayed, at Empingham, five miles from Stamford, where King Edward promptly executed Sir Robert's father for treason, in full view of both armies. The battle of Empingham, on 12 March 1470, was a brief affair, on account of the king's superior forces. Edward's field guns opened fire on the rebel position, forcing them to advance or be annihilated where they stood. The majority of Welles's men took to their heels, and in the ensuing rout they discarded their weapons and livery jackets, giving the battle the name 'Losecoat Field'. Their tell-tale jackets in Clarence's livery proved beyond any doubt who had instigated the rising and after the battle various documents were also found which further implicated Warwick and Clarence. Later, Sir Robert Welles was brought before the king to confess, but remarkably, rather than issuing demands for their arrest, King Edward offered both Clarence and Warwick a chance to give themselves up. However, Edward had further problems in the north, where some rebels were still active, and he immediately marched north to put down the rising. On the way he had Sir Robert Welles beheaded. After negotiating with the rebels, Edward agreed to reinstate Henry Percy to the

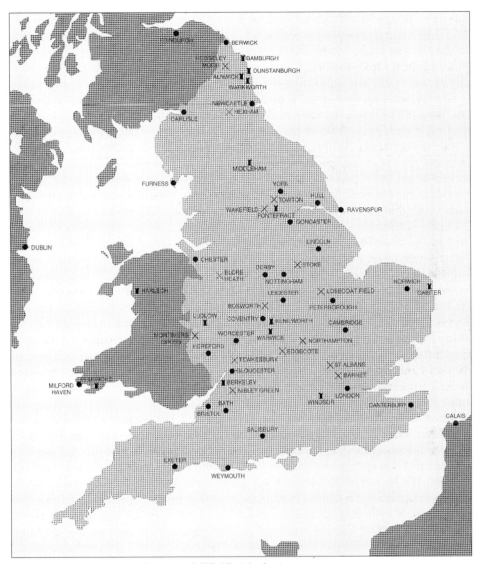

The battles of the Wars of the Roses, 1455–87. (Author)

Earldom of Northumberland which solved the immediate crisis in the north.[52] John Neville was made Marquis Montagu to compensate for his loss of office in Northumberland while his brother Warwick, who had not surrendered, had a £1,000 price put on his head.

Warwick and Clarence, their support in the country dwindling, were soon forced to flee abroad. Their way was almost blocked at the English coast, then at Calais their fleet was refused entry to the town by Lord Wenlock, acting on Edward's orders. Warwick sailed on, and characteristically set about buccaneering his way through the English Channel. However, Lord Howard's fleet attacked Warwick's ships and after a fierce sea battle the Kingmaker was forced into Honfleur. On French soil, Warwick's political fortunes once again began to flourish at the court of Louis XI where he proceeded to cement the most unusual alliance yet of the Wars of the Roses.

French and Burgundian politics had a dramatic effect on English affairs during the Wars of the Roses, notably on the events leading to Henry VI's 'Readeption'. In 1470 Louis XI's plans to pursue further military action against Burgundy rested on the reconciliation of the Earl of Warwick with his arch-enemy Margaret of Anjou, already a refugee at Louis XI's court. The plan was centred on Warwick spearheading an invasion of England to topple Edward from his throne. Henry VI was then to be reinstated as King of England, with Warwick, naturally, acting as chief councillor, and then war was to be declared against Burgundy on two fronts. This ambitious plan was cemented by the marriage of Warwick's daughter Anne Neville to Edward of Lancaster, the Prince of Wales. This marriage, of course, left the grasping Clarence out in the cold as far as his own personal ambitions of kingship were concerned, but for the moment he went along with Warwick's plan.

Supported by the French king, Warwick sailed for England. He was forced to land in the west country because of bad weather, but he soon gathered enough support to enable him to march north to confront King Edward, who was then at York. Edward's forces were insignificant at this time, but his position became desperate when news came in that John Neville, Marquis Montagu, had turned his coat in favour of his brother Warwick, and was marching against the king with men gathered under the king's own Commission of Array. Edward had no time to react and was forced, with only a few loyal adherents, to take ship to Burgundy. Warwick and Clarence entered London in triumph, released Henry VI from the Tower and placed him on the throne for the last time.

Edward's sea journey to Holland was a hazardous one, but once there, under the dubious protection of his brother-in-law Charles the Bold, he began making plans for a return to England. Five months later, subsidised largely by Burgundian money and fuelled by Charles's animosity for his French enemy, he mustered a small force of continental mercenaries. In March 1471 Edward, together with his brother Richard of Gloucester, Lord Rivers and Lord Hastings, set sail from Flushing to embark upon a desperate gamble to win back the crown of England.

In sharp contrast to his apparent lack of military foresight and slow reactions during the previous ten years of intermittent crisis, the way in which Edward IV recovered his throne in 1471 is an object lesson in medieval military excellence. Edward's forced landing at Ravenspur, at the mouth of the Humber Estuary, marked the start of a dangerous, and largely unsupported, march westwards to York, then southwards, skirting Montagu's forces, towards London. This unhindered march was chiefly made possible by the non-committal stance of the Earl of Northumberland, Henry Percy, who, not for the last time in his career, preferred to stand back, supporting neither side. However, the very fact that he remained inactive enabled Edward to reach Derbyshire, where royal commissions were issued and the retainers and adherents of Lord Hastings made possible further progress to Nottingham.[53]

The Earl of Warwick, then bottled up in Coventry, refused Edward's challenge to meet him in open battle. This is not surprising considering that Warwick was waiting for reinforcements to arrive, especially the contingents of the Duke of Clarence. But the fickle Clarence had other plans. Dissatisfied with his role in Warwick's plan, Clarence changed sides. He was welcomed back into the fold by Edward, who badly needed the additional troops, but from then on, the king would keep his brother on a short leash both in battle and, later, at court. After a brief and 'touching' reconciliation the Yorkist brothers marched on London, with Warwick in pursuit, and entered the capital with little difficulty.

On 13 April 1471, only two days after reaching London, Edward's army marched north once more, dragging the unfortunate King Henry with them. In the afternoon Edward's 'aforeriders' made contact with Warwick's scouts at Barnet and drove them out of the town. Warwick's army was spotted, in the fading light, half a mile beyond the town, but by the time the main body of the Yorkist army had arrived there it was pitch black and Edward's battle lines, forming up in the dark, became slightly adrift of Warwick's 'hedge side' position. During the night, Warwick's artillery began to bombard Edward's position, but overshot because the king's troops had inadvertently manoeuvred closer than expected. These two factors – the overlapping of the battle lines and the proximity of the two armies – were to prove significant the next morning when a thick, damp April mist enveloped the battlefield.

Very early the next day the armies clashed on a low ridge in thick fog. The overlapping lines meant that the left flank of each army was overwhelmed by superior numbers, and during the desperate hand-to-hand struggle that followed, Edward's left was soon routed by the Earl of Oxford's contingents. The fighting in the centre, on what turned out to be the pivotal axis of the battle, was intense, and once again treachery was to have a hand in the final outcome of the battle. As Oxford's troops returned to the fray after routing Edward's wing, their heraldic badge, a star, was mistaken by Warwick's men for Edward's sun in splendour. Warwick's men opened fire and word quickly spread that Oxford's men had turned their coats. Warwick's line disintegrated in panic amid cries of treason. The ensuing rout claimed the lives of both Montagu and the Kingmaker himself, who was cut down while trying to reach his horse behind the lines.[54]

Luck certainly played an important role in the battle of Barnet, as it did in most of the battles of the Wars of the Roses. But King Edward's next campaign, culminating in the battle of Tewkesbury, was a brilliant example of medieval military strategy and tactics, which would prove decisive in sealing the fate of the House of Lancaster forever.

While Warwick's battered body was being stripped naked and taken from the field of Barnet, Margaret of Anjou's fleet landed at Weymouth. News soon reached her of the earl's defeat and she decided to advance inland in order to link up with Jasper Tudor, then rallying Welsh support. Strengthened by troops supplied by the new Duke of Somerset, Edmund Beaufort, and the Earl of Devon, the Lancastrian army pressed on in an effort to cross the River Severn into Wales. King Edward, then at Windsor, spurred his refreshed army into action and, realising that good intelligence and timing were going to be the key factors in catching the Lancastrians before they could concentrate their forces, he immediately dispatched scourers to seek out the enemy.

The chase which followed highlights the importance of accurate intelligence in medieval warfare, when it was not uncommon for scouts to deliver information either too late, or incorrectly, to enable the army commanders to implement competent strategy. In the march to intercept the Lancastrian army, King Edward was given the slip several times when Margaret's army made a quick change in direction, and Edward drew up the Yorkist army for battle several times, only to find that the Lancastrians had taken evasive action. Yet Edward's intelligence was more competent than usual on this occasion, and this enabled the Yorkists to prevent the Lancastrians, after a forced night march, from crossing over the first bridge over the River Severn at Gloucester. Edward's promise of relief caused the loyal town to close the gates on Margaret's army and the Lancastrians had to press on to Tewkesbury, with Edward shadowing their every move on a parallel course.

Both armies were already exhausted by their intense activity in very hot weather conditions. Margaret's army had had little rest during the long march from Gloucester, while the Yorkists, always having 'good espialls upon them' from the Cotswolds escarpment, also suffered from a lack of victuals.[55] These problems forced the Lancastrian army to halt short of its next objective and they pitched camp a little to the south of Tewkesbury where they hoped to cross over the River Severn the next day. The presence of the Yorkist army, now encamped only three miles away, prevented any hope of a crossing being attempted, and so both armies spent the night preparing for the inevitable clash of arms which would follow the next day.

Early the following morning (Saturday 4 May 1471), Edward arrayed his army opposite the Lancastrian position, which was bounded by a field called 'The Gastons', having already concealed a force of mounted 'spears' in a wood to his left. The terrain played a crucial part in the battle; reluctant to advance against the very strong Lancastrian position, Edward opened the battle with a missile bombardment. The 'right-a-sharp shower'[56] of arrows and cannon balls which fell on the Duke of Somerset's battle line forced his men to advance through the enclosures, dykes and lanes which had previously protected his front. However, chiefly because of a low hill which hampered their manoeuvre, his troops emerged not on the flank of Edward's army, as Somerset expected, but at the junction of two Yorkist 'battles'.

The disarray that resulted from this mistaken alignment meant that Somerset's troops were now caught in a trap without any support and, attacked on two fronts, they were soon pushed back by superior numbers. The Yorkist cavalry hidden in the wood now turned a difficult situation into a disaster for the Lancastrians, suddenly charging down on their exposed flank. Somerset's battle line collapsed and his men fled back towards Tewkesbury and the River Severn. In the rout the Prince of Wales and the Earl of Devon were both slain, while in the ferocious aftermath of the battle other Lancastrians who had sought holy sanctuary were irreverently dragged out of Tewkesbury Abbey and put to the sword.[57]

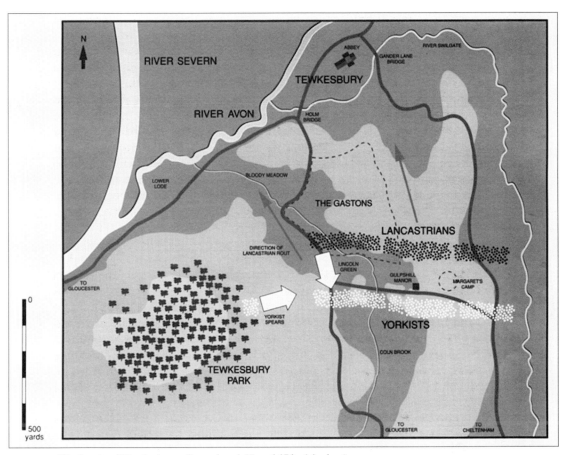

The battle of Tewkesbury, Saturday 4 May 1471. (Author)

The Lancastrian cause was now in ruins. The Duke of Somerset was executed after the battle along with other prominent Lancastrians in Tewkesbury market-place, and Queen Margaret herself was soon captured. Reports of her son's death reduced her to a broken woman, and she was imprisoned by Edward. In 1476 she was ransomed by the French king and died some years later in France, a shadow of her former self. But Edward had to face one last rebellion. Lord Fauconberg's bastard son Thomas Neville, another of Warwick's kinsmen, planned to rescue Henry VI from captivity in the Tower while Edward was otherwise occupied, and to this end he had raised the commons in Kent, yet again, to march on London. With the dubious authority of his dead uncle's commission, part of the Calais garrison was mustered and, supported by a small fleet, Fauconberg arrived in London on 12 May 1471 and moored his ships a safe distance from the Tower of London. On his instructions the commons tried to cross the Thames bridges and when they were prevented from doing so, he ordered the guns on his ships to bombard the Tower from across the river. Further action followed when a land assault was made on the gates of the city and against the Tower walls, but Lord Rivers managed to disperse the rebels temporarily in the name of King Edward. Time was running out for Fauconberg: soon news arrived that Edward's victorious army was marching towards the capital and the rebellion soon evaporated under this threat. Fauconberg was captured, and was at first pardoned, but was later executed for his treasonable action when he became too much of a threat to be allowed to live.[58]

It was now painfully clear that as long as the saintly figure of Henry VI still lived he posed a threat to the security of Edward's throne and there could be no rest for the Yorkist dynasty. His death would mean the complete eradication of any Lancastrian hopes. Thus the Lancastrian 'saint king' achieved his martyrdom, being put to death in the Tower on the very same night that Edward arrived in London.[59]

THE FALL OF YORK AND THE RISE OF TUDOR, 1475–87

Edward IV had at last seen his final battle, and had finally achieved a dynastic ambition which had been realised ten years previously on the battlefield of Towton. His two young sons, Edward and Richard, made doubly sure of the Yorkist dynasty as heirs to his throne, and in 1475 he felt able to turn his attention abroad, fulfilling his promise to seek renewed conflict with Louis XI in an effort to secure the dual crown of England and France. His invasion force was the best-equipped English army ever assembled for continental warfare and consisted of retinues supplied by most of the English nobility. However, the resulting campaign, undertaken with the backing of Burgundy, was little more than a show of strength, and Edward was paid off for his expensive adventure by King Louis without a drop of blood being shed.[60]

King Edward became decidedly inactive after this episode, preferring to leave military matters in the capable hands of his brother Richard of Gloucester, who had already replaced Warwick as the king's lieutenant in the north of England. The Duke of Clarence, unable to resist dabbling in the murky waters of political intrigue and treason, was executed on Edward's orders in February 1478, but it was not until 1483 that another major threat appeared to spark off renewed internal conflict. The sudden death of Edward in the spring of that year left his eldest son to cope with an inevitable power struggle that was more divided, violent and ruthless than any that had gone before. The ensuing fight for political supremacy resulted in Richard III's usurpation of Edward V's throne.

The masterly timing and subtle moves made by Richard, Duke of Gloucester, to secure the throne for himself are well documented, but his motives can only be guessed at because contemporary chroniclers failed to put Richard's character into context with his age, preferring to please their Tudor masters by portraying the last Yorkist king as a monster in order justify the 'new' and uncertain Tudor regime. Primarily, Richard acted against threats to his brother's firmly established Yorkist policies, and even though some of his violent actions may seem drastic to us today, they were none the less necessary in his eyes to ensure the future political stability of the Yorkist dynasty during the young king's minority.

When his father died, Prince Edward was living in his own household at Ludlow Castle, under the supervision of Anthony Woodville, Earl Rivers. The Woodville family immediately planned to have Edward crowned under their protection. But Richard of Gloucester, then Lord Protector, considered the Woodvilles' prominent position at court to be a threat, and with the support of the Duke of Buckingham, Richard reacted quickly to take control of the new king. He intercepted Lord Rivers and the new king's small royal retinue at Stony Stratford and arrested the king's keepers for allegedly plotting to seize the government and suppress the old Yorkist nobility. He later had them executed, but Elizabeth Woodville, anticipating Gloucester's next move, took sanctuary at Westminster with her younger son.

Lord Hastings, Edward IV's most trusted advisor and retainer, reassured the city and the Royal Council that all would be well, but soon he too was to fall under Richard's suspicion even though his hatred for the Woodville faction was well known. Richard's 'ambition' made Hastings suspicious of the Protector's intentions. Not only was Richard's action contrary to Hastings's promised loyalty to the Prince, but Hastings would also be in breach of his contract of royal indenture to protect the Prince from his enemies if he did nothing to prevent such dynastic aggression. Hastings bravely chose to remain loyal to his new king, and spoke out against Richard's actions; he paid the price for his loyalty, being summarily executed for blocking the Protector's path to the throne. Richard then removed Edward V's younger brother from sanctuary, and his plan to secure the crown for himself rested on the fate of the 'Princes in the Tower'.[61]

Using the ploy of a previous pre-contract of marriage between Edward IV and Nell Butler, daughter of the Earl of Shewsbury, as proof, Richard argued, and had it proclaimed by others, that Edward IV's children were illegitimate. This accusation (and a further revelation that Edward IV himself was also a bastard) placed the crown within Richard's grasp at last. The doubts cast by this dynastic uncertainty led to Richard being offered the crown – which he refused several times by all accounts – at Baynards Castle. But he was formally crowned King Richard III on 6 July 1483, an action which in effect signed the two princes' death warrants. Their last reported sighting was in July of that year.[62]

Richard's crown had been attained with the help of his northern retainers and with the dubious backing of the Duke of Buckingham who, not unlike other nobles in the Wars of the Roses, had hoped to secure his own advancement by supporting Richard's cause. However, dissatisfied with his rewards, Buckingham turned against Richard, and planned to rebel by procuring another contender for the throne, in this case Henry Tudor, Earl of Richmond. Buckingham's plan involved creating an unstable atmosphere in England, thereby bringing about renewed rebellion in the southern shires so that Henry Tudor could invade and attempt to take the throne by force and legitimate right.

Henry Tudor had been under the Duke of Brittany's protection since 1471. His claim to the throne depended on his descent from Margaret Beaufort, daughter of John Beaufort, Duke of Somerset. This Beaufort line of succession had now come full circle from John of Gaunt, Edward III's third son, and it presented a very real threat to Richard's throne even though Henry's claim was, at best, tenuous. The Buckingham rebellion highlighted his claim considerably, but Richard's foreknowledge of the rebels' intentions, and Buckingham's own bad luck, gave the king the opportunity to raise a large force with which to counter the rebellion. The Yorkist army soon caught up with the renegade duke and he was executed in Salisbury market-place on 2 November 1483. This forced Henry Tudor to turn back to Brittany as soon as the news broke.[63]

It is worthy of mention here that even at this stage support for King Richard from Lord Stanley (Margaret Beaufort's husband) and the Earl of Northumberland was dubious, and would prove decisive in August 1485 when the outcome of Richard's final battle depended on their actions. Only John Howard, Duke of Norfolk, remained entirely loyal to Richard, and he was entrusted with the defence of London while Richard attended to Buckingham's rebellion elsewhere. However, most nobles, including those who chose to join Henry Tudor abroad for safety at this time, realised that their lives depended on the survival or fall of the Yorkist dynasty. Matters worsened for Richard in April 1484 when his only son and heir died; this tragedy was followed not long afterwards by the sudden death of his wife, Anne Neville.

With the death of his only legitimate son, Richard's hold on the crown began to slip. In the eyes of some of his supporters, his judgement also seemed impaired by the sad loss of his family, but nevertheless in August 1485, he was forced into military action yet again, in order to meet the long-expected invasion of Henry Tudor, whose ships and small army had landed at Milford Haven in Pembrokeshire. Henry's contacts at home and abroad had procured him the military services of the Earl of Oxford and the French troops of Philibert de Chandée and he had written to his mother and his stepfather Lord Stanley, as well as to Sir Gilbert Talbot and other English gentry, asking for support against Richard. Henry headed inland, evading potential opponents, and crossed the River Severn into England while Lord Stanley, always the careful player, moved with his contingents towards London. Henry's ultimate objective was to gain support from his stepfather, but Stanley dithered, bearing in mind that his own son George, Lord Strange, was in Richard's custody. Lord Stanley made camp at Atherstone while his brother Sir William Stanley independently went to talk with Henry. Thus Henry was still without the troops he had expected, and was dangerously out on a limb in the middle of England without any large-scale support. It was an unenviable position, to say the least, in view of his limited military ability.

King Richard mustered his Yorkist army at Leicester, with contingents chiefly supplied by the Duke of Norfolk and the Earl of Northumberland. The royal army advanced and made camp in and around Ambien Hill near Sutton Cheney in Leicestershire. Henry Tudor's small force, still without the promised support of the Stanley brothers, made camp at Whitemoors while the Stanley brothers took up position between the two opposing armies, probably both to the north (or south) of what would the next day become the battlefield of Bosworth. Sir William had little to lose by committing himself to military action for Henry the following day as he had already been declared a traitor by

Richard, but his brother Lord Stanley was still playing a waiting game. Lord Stanley had been, on more than one occasion, very cool to King Richard's cause, as he had been to other parties during the Wars of the Roses, and to ensure his loyalty Richard had threatened that Stanley's son would be executed if he did not place his contingents favourably the next day. Richard's plan to isolate the pretender's small force might well have worked, but as the sun rose on that hot August day in 1485 Henry advanced early, taking the royal army by surprise. His line of march took him towards the Stanley brothers and around the marshes which lay at the foot of Ambien Hill while, stunned at the pretender's audacity, the king's army hastily arrayed their battles in line astern on the crest of the ridge, with their archers to the fore under the command of the Duke of Norfolk. Henry's intention was to attempt to force the Stanleys to join him, but this immediately failed and battle was joined when Henry's vaward under the Earl of Oxford came under attack from a hail of Yorkist arrows and artillery now in place on Ambien Hill. The Duke of Norfolk then launched his attack, and the two opposing vawards clashed on the plain below the hill, leaving Henry and his small main battle isolated somewhere near the indecisive Stanley forces.

A fifteenth-century sallet with an unusual lower protective plate attached to the visor. This relic from St Michael's Church, Caerhays (Cornwall) is said to have belonged to one of the Trevanions who fought for Henry Tudor at Bosworth in 1485. (Geoffrey Wheeler)

Oxford's experience enabled him to withstand Norfolk's onslaught by contracting his battle line and as the battle raged Norfolk himself was soon cut down; this caused immediate disarray and confusion among the Yorkist troops, to the extent that Richard decided to intervene personally with his household men. 'Inflamed with ire' that the Earl of Northumberland had not, and would not, come to his aid when commanded to do so, Richard decided to lead a mounted charge against Henry Tudor's isolated force, midway between Oxford's vaward and the Stanley forces. In the process, the execution of George Stanley was forgotten and Sir William Stanley now saw an opportune moment to strike while Richard was stubbornly cutting his way through towards Henry's standard. In a flanking movement his troops quickly enveloped the king's household men and rapidly brought the battle to an end. In the confusion Richard was unhorsed and killed in the fierce mêlée which followed.[64]

This was the most politically important battle of the Wars of the Roses. The battle of Bosworth crushed once and for all the Yorkist dynastic claims in England, and once again treachery had proved the decisive factor. Some of Richard's main adherents had failed him at the eleventh hour, preferring not to commit their forces to the uncertainty of combat, while Henry Tudor's crowning on the battlefield itself immediately after the conflict speaks volumes about his own uncertain support. His victory, snatched from the jaws of defeat by dubious allies, and a traitorous subject who preferred not to engage, must have left him feeling somewhat insecure, his claim to the throne still largely unsupported. Consequently, the death of Richard, Duke of York's last surviving son did not solve the dynastic question and the Yorkist cause lingered on for several more years, threatening Henry VII's reign and perpetuating the Wars of the Roses for at least another decade of political and military uncertainty.

Although the fall of Richard III had sounded the death knell of real Yorkist claims in England, the existence of the son of Richard's brother, the late Duke of Clarence, stirred further action in the Wars of the Roses. Henry VII's quick imprisonment of the young Earl of Warwick in the Tower of London after Bosworth had, in effect, the reverse effect as it promoted the fifteen-year-old boy as a credible contender for the throne. Henry's second move was to imprison the Earl of Northumberland for his inaction at Bosworth. Dissident nobles, some of whom had escaped from the battlefield, were quick to exploit Henry's tenuous dynastic claim, and in April 1486 Viscount Lovell and Humphrey Stafford came out of hiding to raise men in the north and in Worcestershire in support of the imprisoned Earl of Warwick. Henry VII was unprepared for the rising, but quickly dispatched troops to deal with Lovell, who was deserted by his Yorkshire tenants after they accepted the king's terms of surrender. Stafford's rebellion similarly held no weight, and both rebels once more fled into hiding, Lovell to Flanders and Stafford into sanctuary from which he was forcibly ejected and later executed for treason.[65]

However, the most serious threat yet was to come from a scheme conceived by a priest called Richard Symonds. He had trained a young man named Lambert Simnel whom he intended to pass off as the unfortunate Earl of Warwick. The real earl was taken from the Tower immediately as proof of identity, but questions still remained as to which was the real son of Clarence. The bizarre sequence of events culminated in a serious problem for Henry VII, when three influential people – Gerald Fitzgerald, the Earl of Lincoln and Viscount Lovell – found a common, if self-centred, interest in Simnel and had him crowned King Edward VI in Dublin on 24 May 1487. With contingents supplied from Ireland and Germany (the latter supplied by Margaret of Burgundy), the three rebels sailed to England and landed at Furness in Westmorland to stake their own claims to power under the cover of loyalty to another puppet king.

Sympathies were still running high in the north for the old Ricardian regime and Simnel's rebel army was soon augmented by former Yorkist retainers, hoping to avenge the Tudor usurpation after Bosworth. By 15 June 1487 this army, commanded by the Earl of Lincoln, was marching on Newark and the king advanced to meet the rebels with a large force. Once again, as at Bosworth, the Earl of Oxford led the Tudor vaward and yet again he bore the brunt of the forthcoming battle while Henry remained at the rear for safety.

On 16 June 1487 the Earl of Lincoln, aware that his force was heavily outnumbered, drew up his mostly foreign and allied troops near East Stoke and proposed to ambush or assault the royal army. It transpired, however, that the Tudor army was unsure of the rebel position, and after marching blindly for some miles, the Earl of Oxford's vaward 'found' the Earl of Lincoln's force, positioned on a hill now known as Burnham Furlong. The rebel army immediately attacked downhill, and the outcome of the battle lay in the balance for some time, while the king's main force raced to the field in support. Matched against Oxford's superior troops, the Irish 'naked' contingents under Fitzgerald sustained heavy casualties, as did the German mercenaries under the command of Martin Schwartz, but finally, the king's fresh forces arrived and soon broke the rebels who subsequently fled the field.[66] Lincoln, Fitzgerald, Schwartz and later Lovell were all killed, or had disappeared without trace, but the last battle of the Wars of the Roses had been fought, although it would be some time yet before Yorkist sympathies were quelled. Ever alert for treachery, Henry took up the reins of power. Nobody was safe, and even Henry's rescuer at Bosworth, Sir William Stanley, was some years later found guilty of treason and executed for his suspected complicity in the Perkin Warbeck rising of 1497.

In this brief re-appraisal of the Wars of the Roses we can see that its political aspects were decided by the highest in the land, but the battles themselves were decided by the soldiers, who became caught up in a bloody void between loyalty and fate on the battlefield. As we have seen, loyalty to a local overlord spelled an uncertain future for most, while others moved open-eyed within the confines of danger at the expense of repeated family loss. Other soldiers' loyal military service walked hand-in-hand with repeated acts of treachery and war crimes towards both friends and enemies. The medieval soldier in this respect is therefore a very complex individual to analyse, and the examination of how the battles of Wars of the Roses were fought needs to be placed into context with the experiences of the soldier himself, from his recruitment at home to his appearance amid the steel-tipped ranks of his fellow countrymen on the English landscape.

CHAPTER 2
'... of feats of arms and chivalry'

MILITARY THINKING DURING THE WARS OF THE ROSES

The modern term 'soldier' is hardly applicable to the medieval fighting man, even though the word is used in many contemporary documents of the Wars of the Roses, and it is important to understand its meaning in the fifteenth century. In modern terms a soldier is a professional, or at the very least a conscript, who accepts strict discipline and is trained and drilled in tactical formations and weaponry in a permanent army. This professionalism, discipline, and training was not the norm in the Wars of the Roses, because England did not have a standing army.

In a very broad sense, certain parallels can be made between the army structures of almost any period. Military management and structure has changed gradually over the centuries, each era bringing its own developments, but generally it is difficult to draw comparisons between army recruitment, structure, training, logistics, strategy, tactics and actual fighting methods in the medieval period and those of the present day. In particular the demands of the Wars of the Roses dictated the introduction of new ways to recruit troops and wage war. These ways were influenced of course by myriad contributing factors such as the effects of neo-feudal methods of recruitment, the introduction of new weapons, the locality of operations, civil warfare and blood feuding, all based on deeply ingrained concepts and ideals, such as religion and chivalry.

All these important factors shaped the Wars of the Roses to some extent. Religion also played an important role, many soldiers believing that God would intervene to influence the outcome of battles. Medieval kings took religious intervention in battle very seriously indeed. Edward's quick thinking at the battle of Mortimers Cross in February 1461 transformed the ominous vision of the three suns 'in the firmament shining full clear'[1] into a religious symbol, and hence gained a distinct psychological advantage by persuading his men that God was on their side. Later in the Wars of the Roses, King Edward IV's right to the throne itself was justified 'by victory given unto us by our Lord Almighty God in divers battles against our great adversary Harry [Henry VI]',[2] rather than attributing

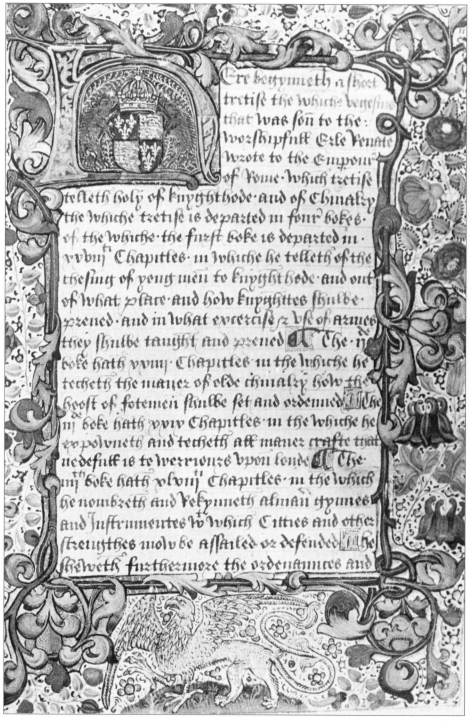

A page from Richard III's personal copy of Vegetius, De Rei Militaris. *(British Library)*

such victories to hard-fought hand-to-hand combat. Similarly, common soldiers followed their commander's example by hearing mass before going into battle. The Church instilled the fear of purgatory and death into medieval man as part of his everyday existence, and therefore soldiers were anxious to seek absolution from sin before a battle commenced. The prospect of an eternity in purgatory if they were killed was portrayed in the medieval period as a fate far worse than death. However, such religious devotion did not stop English soldiers killing their fellow countrymen, nor did it dissuade them from fighting on feast days or saints' days: the battle of Towton took place on Palm Sunday 1461 and the battle of Barnet took place on Easter Sunday 1471.[3]

The medieval soldier's willingness to take up arms depended partly on how he was recruited and partly on his incentive for fighting. The soldier's expectation of witnessing his 'rightful' king in person on the field of battle also had a marked effect on an army's unity of aim. Medieval monarchs enhanced their status and power by leading their subjects to war, which explains why Henry VI's martial deficiencies had such a marked effect, not only on his kingdom but also on his troops in the field. The rebel, or opposing side, had a different problem to contend with: they had to persuade their men to fight against their anointed king. Regularly during the early power struggles between the Houses of York and Lancaster (1452–1460) leading nobles hesitated before trading blows, and exchanged well-worded messages through mediators and heralds in an effort to explain their actions. Swearing sacred oaths that the king's person should not be harmed was also a common feature during this period. In some cases proclamations of innocence were used very cleverly, especially in the early 1450s, to justify Yorkist aggression towards the 'evil councillors' who were then entrenched in the Lancastrian government. However, this excuse became progressively less convincing as the wars went on, and was offered less often as the conflict became centred more on family feuding and dynastic issues than an issue between subject and king.

On more than one occasion in the Wars of the Roses, armies tried to avoid confrontation at all costs, and either fortified their position in the field, dispersed, or took cover behind city walls and castle ramparts for greater protection. Fifteenth-century church chroniclers repeatedly lamented the spilling of English blood as a waste of manpower. Such slaughter, they concluded, would have been better directed against the 'enemies of the Christian name'.[4] Prominent ecclesiastics like George Neville, Bishop of Exeter, for instance, commented on the immense casualty figures inflicted at the battle of Towton in 1461 for purely self-centred reasons, and most of his contemporaries doubled and tripled the reported battlefield death tolls for similar purposes, adding to the overall confusion of the conflict. However, the oft-quoted phrase, used by all the factions, 'hereto we have forborne and avoided all things that might serve to the effusion of Christian blood'[5] is a reminder that battles were not entered into lightly nor without some justification in the eyes of God. When it was pursued, however, it seems that mercy, humanity and chivalry were abandoned, to be replaced by single-minded all-out slaughter on the battlefield. Because medieval warfare was carried out in the most brutal and savage way imaginable, it had to be justified by religious intervention in some way. This justification could then be called upon instantly to encourage a reluctant army to fight. Obviously such religious ideology was not a medieval invention, and elements of it can still be found in modern warfare.

The fourth-century theories of Publius Flavius Vegetius Renatus concerning Roman military thinking were translated for a medieval audience and may well have had some influence on fighting methods in the Wars of the Roses. Most 'great captains' and commanders were literate and would doubtless have read the ancient writings. Vegetius presented his theories to his Emperor in the form of a step-by-step manual entitled *Epitoma Rei Militaris*, by which he hoped to restore the rapidly deteriorating Roman army, infiltrated and weakened by the presence of foreign auxiliary troops, to its former glory.[6] Vegetius's manual was translated and updated several times in the fifteenth century by writers such as Christine de Pisan, Viscount Beaumont and the anonymous author of *Knyghthode and Bataile* for similar reasons and thus was readily available to literate captains.[7] The medieval writers adapted the manual to highlight the fact that in late fifteenth-century England there was a noticeable – and increasing – disregard for medieval military tactics and chivalry. Viscount Beaumont, who literally echoed Vegetius's concepts but reworded his text in ballad form, presented Henry VI with a copy of his work, perhaps with the hope of inspiring the indifferent king with a more martial and aggressive attitude towards his enemies. Similarly, Margaret of Anjou was given a copy of Christine de Pisan's book, *Livre des fais d'armes et de chevalerie*, by John Talbot, Earl of Shrewsbury; in view of her close involvement in the main military campaigns of the Wars of the Roses, this was probably of great use to her and her chief commanders in the field.

Christine de Pisan's military manual was later printed by William Caxton in the vernacular for popular consumption under the title *The Book of the Fayttes of Armes and Chyvalrye*. But although most military commanders knew of the theories presented in such manuals, actual personal experience in medieval combat must have counted for much more on the battlefield. Acting as captains, such experienced veterans of 'olde and exercised sapience',[8] especially those who had commanded in France, were coveted by army leaders and sought out by those commanders who generally had little knowledge of battlefield tactics – but to the enemy they were marked men. At the other end of the social scale, the common fighting man was largely ignorant of such theories and manuals and, in all but the execution of his duty, understood very little of the 'art of war'. Such men simply fought for their lives under the good or bad leadership of their captains.

Another fifteenth-century military writer, William Worcester, took a more political stance, infusing his *Book of Noblesse* with nationalistic propaganda and at the same time pointing an accusing finger at the reason behind the English defeat in the Hundred Years War. He discussed the responsibilities of knights and commanders in warfare, but wrongly blamed the peace with France for causing the Wars of the Roses. Worcester's work gives us some idea of how things looked to the defeated captains and their troops after the loss of Normandy in 1450 and also highlights the responsibilities of knights and commanders in an age when the principles of chivalry and military training were irretrievably breaking down.

Worcester produced his work in the 1450s in an attempt to persuade King Henry VI to adopt a more warlike policy towards the French, but his book was later remodelled to attract Yorkist patronage between 1461 and 1472, then slightly revised again in 1475 in time for Edward IV's abortive invasion of France. Clearly military training was not being adhered to during these periods, especially by the English nobility, and this fact is all too apparent in Worcester's repeated attacks on the aristocracy:

> But now of late days, the greater the pity is, many one that [has] been descended of noble blood and born to arms, as knights sons, esquires, and of other gentle blood, [has] set himself to singular practice, strange faculties from that set, as to learn the practice of law or custom of land, or of civil matters, and so waste greatly their time in such needless business.[9]

Worcester states that noblemen should, instead, receive good military training and should not study law or engage in civil occupations, as some were beginning to do, and although this may be seen as little more than Worcester's personal opinion, the overall picture is certainly not one of a country of well-trained, military minded and battle-hardened veterans. In fact it is clear that the majority of noblemen who fought in the Wars of the Roses were entirely the opposite. However, there were notable exceptions, and these men were valued all the more highly, either because of their experience in France, or because of their natural military genius.

The 'chiefest captains'[10] of the Wars of the Roses were those who advised their superiors on the 'art of war'. Each captain's knowledge and personal experience of warfare would permeate through to those with less experience and thus sound strategy could be employed to good effect before actual fighting commenced. Those of an older generation would still use tried and trusted tactics, such as the power of the longbow, or the use of entrenchments, on the Wars of the Roses battlefield, in order to try to gain some sort of advantage over the enemy rather than adopting new methods. Sixty-year-old grizzled veteran captains, such as Lord Fauconberg, who had served in France with distinction, were still going strong some thirty years later at the battle of Towton. The Duke of York, the Duke of Buckingham and the Earl of Salisbury had all commanded and led armies during the latter part of the Hundred Years War and had each experienced different degrees of success and failure on campaign. Lord Hungerford had served with John Talbot at Castillon in 1453, while Lord Fitzwalter, Lord Welles and Sir Thomas Kyriell were all veteran campaigners. There were many more like them who had seen active service, as their forefathers had done before them, in France; crucially, they had served during the latter part of the French war when the English had begun to lose their military dominance.

New military talent was bound to emerge to add to (and in some cases to stifle) conventional military thinking during the Wars of the Roses. In time this brought about changes in strategy by the employment of new weapons and 'unchivalrous' tactics, in contrast to the traditional and deeply ingrained concepts of warfare. The extremely competent Lancastrian military advisor Sir Andrew Trollope, for

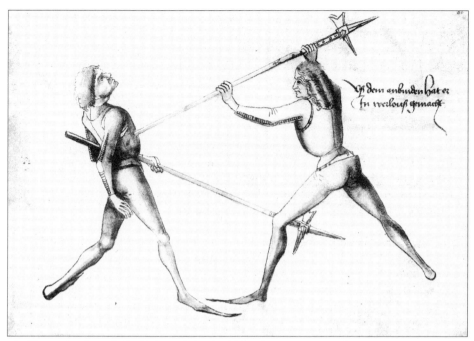

An illustration from Talhoffer's Fechtbuch, *1467, showing two men fighting with poll-axes. (Royal Armouries)*

instance, was regarded by the contemporary chronicler Jean de Waurin as 'un tres soubtil homme de guerre',[11] while of a man who was called simply 'Lovelace', Waurin reports that he 'had the reputation of being the most expert in warfare in England' during this period. The identity, and indeed the morality, of this second individual, who commanded the Yorkist artillery in 1460 and 1461, is still open to question because of certain issues of alleged treachery. However, Trollope in particular was a man ahead of his time in military matters. His talents, coupled with the authority of the Duke of Somerset, enabled him to engineer Lancastrian successes on the battlefield several times until his death at Towton in 1461.

However, it is my opinion that all these military men, old and new, failed to some degree in the Wars of the Roses, some of them losing their lives in the process. Their failure can be attributed not to their own incompetence but rather to the nature of medieval warfare itself, especially with regard to the general lack of organised and practised manoeuvres on the battlefield. Armies might be conducted admirably on the march, which might enable commanders to gain some advantage over the enemy before battle commenced. But once the armies clashed face to face, warfare was inevitably extremely confusing and disorientating. In the ensuing chaos the outcome was in the hands of the individual soldier fighting in his local contingent for the common aim; only the 'feats of arms' of front line captains could in any way influence this horrific, isolated, and extremely violent hand-to-hand fighting.

Edward IV was the most able strategist and front line commander of his era, possibly of the whole fifteenth century, but how much of his knowledge was derived from his veteran captains? During his early career Edward had inevitably learned something from his valued captains both on the march and in battle, and he was to continue to use their advice to the best possible advantage in all his future campaigns. Indeed, most medieval commanders followed this advisory route with much success and had been, and would continue to be, subservient to the great captains' knowledge of warfare for some time to come. Certainly Edward was a copybook medieval soldier of proven courage who defied death time and time again on the battlefields of the Wars of the Roses. Taking his place boldly in the front line he instilled confidence into his troops. It comes as no surprise that most contemporary chroniclers attributed his military successes to his willingness to face danger.[12] Certainly his presence in the front line increased his troops' morale, encouraging them to make a greater effort when all was not going well on the battlefield. Consequently, as most of his contemporaries were so impressed by Edward's valour, they tended to overlook or disregard the humble captain's role in such actions.

Military training in medieval England was sadly lacking in any national standards, although almost all commanders employed the most basic tactics, using the traditional triple 'battle' formation. This division in medieval armies derived from the need for control and manoeuvrability on the battlefield, where different contingents and retinues could be brought together to form manageable groups or divisions. The average soldier was taught his role in this triple battle formation, but the men were not drilled regularly on a large scale, hence the training was hopelessly deficient. It was essentially up to the veteran captains to keep order on the battlefield, relying on their previous experience and using a prick from a poll-axe to enforce discipline among their soldiers. However, violence was a common fact of everyday life in medieval England and people were used to carrying – and using – weapons; hence, without the captains, the amalgamation of large numbers of undisciplined troops would lead to an uncontrollable rabble.

All men between the ages of sixteen and sixty were expected to bear arms, complying with the accepted Anglo-Saxon methods of recruitment, and loyally support their rightful king in times of need. There was some degree of basic military training in fifteenth-century England for foreign war in France, but it was neither widespread nor permanent during the Wars of the Roses. Essentially, troops had time to 'shake down' in foreign wars because they were expected to be much longer campaigns. Most of the campaigns of the Wars of the Roses were sudden and generally short-lived and so there was no time for basic training, nor for familiarisation with other contingents. As regards comprehensive training, every man was forced by law to practise archery with a longbow and there is abundant evidence in contemporary chronicles that English archers, under experienced captains, could apply their traditional skills with the bow to great effect. However, in the Wars of the Roses, the commanders on both sides knew the power of the longbow, and hence adopted new weapons and devised new tactics to try to neutralise the longbow's dominance.

Most men took up arms as necessary, usually armed with bow or bill. The exceptions were those born into landed families who were expected to train in the use of arms from an early age. These knights and esquires, and all ranks above them, loosely referred to in this book as 'men at arms', were therefore the only individuals who were professionally trained as 'soldiers' in the accepted modern sense of the word. Such men, if they chose to follow the drum, lived in a kind of semi-conscious expectation of combat and were obligated to fight by their superiors through either their civil or military connections. They lived by a social system that was chiefly developed for general administrative purposes, but also had the capability to breed violence and victimisation. In extreme circumstances, this darker side helped fuel the civil war which broke out in 1459.[13]

Other more experienced soldiers had served in English garrisons. Inevitably these troops were more seasoned because of their exposure to isolated bouts of warfare while defending the vulnerable parts of the kingdom. The Scottish, Welsh and Calais Marches therefore provided pools of battle-hardened troops in the fifteenth century. It should be remembered, however, that garrisons were neither permanent nor stationary. The wardens and lieutenants of the Marches who were given the responsibility of securing these extremely volatile areas traditionally had to use their own territorial manpower (often their own personal retinues) to form garrisons. Indeed, in times of great need nobles were expected to muster large contingents of men to subdue the king's enemies on the borders of his kingdom. A contemporary document states that as many as 20,000 men were recruited by Richard, Duke of Gloucester, for his invasion of Scotland in 1482.[14]

Providing their employer could afford to pay and control these troops this system of recruitment by specific nobles acting as wardens worked well, but occasionally soldiers could prove difficult. For example, the English garrison at Calais during the Wars of the Roses had to be continually augmented and demanded more and more money; these experienced troops, subsequently serving in England, could have a dramatic effect on the outcome of some battles, especially when pay or loyalty came into question. The Calais garrison mutinied on several occasions because of lack of wages and even stole wool from the warehouses they were employed to protect, in order to obtain money. Therefore control of soldiers was very closely associated with pay. Wages were also important when foreign mercenaries were recruited to serve alongside English troops, and especially significant when political allies offered financial backing to the leading protagonists in the Wars of the Roses. These paid contingents were to play vital roles in the conflict when various individuals invaded England to seek the recovery of the kingdom.

The fact that by law every man was obliged to practise using the longbow, and that some men had served in garrisons, might be seen as contradictory to the suggested lack of training mentioned above. However, in the Wars of the Roses English archers were never used in the same large ratio to men at arms as they were in foreign wars such as in the Hundred Years War. Longbowmen generally amounted to approximately one half of the total army strength in any particular battle, compared to the ratio seen in battles abroad where there might be as many as eight archers to one man-at-arms. Troop types were disproportionate in the era, and indeed some armies in the Wars of the Roses lacked archers, because these forces were not specially recruited invasion troops, carefully chosen to take advantage of the known military deficiencies in foreign armies. Occasionally so-called 'armies' contained only the small personal bodyguards of nobles. Various town militias armed with bills, tenant farmers with jacks, sallets, swords and daggers, shire levies with farm implements, and mercenaries with dubious handguns and artillery could be called upon to augment the strength of an army; but none of these were permanently 'trained' troops, nor were they drilled in formations and kept in a state of constant military readiness. Men-at-arms and their retainers – the only real professional soldiers in any army – were always a very small percentage of the overall total, mainly because of the cost of their profession and their military equipment. Moreover, garrisons were generally small (or non-existent in peace time) in castles on the borders of the kingdom, chiefly because of the cost of keeping men continually on duty. The notable exception to this was Calais, where as many as a thousand men were in service to protect the vital port for both commercial and political reasons. But garrison duty in general was very much a case of occasional service and erratic payment; we can by no means say that these troops were either 'crack' or elite professional soldiers, although those who served on the Marches against invaders obviously had some combat experience and knew what to expect. Mercenary troops appear only briefly in the early wars between York and Lancaster, but later in the conflict they feature more often as rebel army strengths became more deficient in English soldiers.

A noble or knight's much sought after 'feats of arms' on the battlefield had to be supported by a vast amount of food and supplies for his armies on campaign. However, it is difficult to analyse the thinking behind logistics in this period because warfare in the Wars of the Roses was completely different from that conducted by English armies abroad. The medieval commander had to plan in advance to finance, feed, supply, and even clothe his army to the best of his ability. Harbingers, victuallers and the like were employed as experts in this field, while 'scourers' foraged on horseback for supplies when food was scarce and 'engineers' also had their tasks to perform and materials to gather as specialist troops in a marching or sieging army. Draught animals were needed to drag wagons and carts, artillery had to be supplied with shot and black powder, and billets had to be found for both nobles and soldiers. An army could live off the land to a certain extent, but the locality dictated how far this could go unchecked; in some isolated instances armies ran out of control to the point where troops looted a town indiscriminately or pillaged the countryside at will. Commanders were all too aware that a badly fed or unpaid army could disperse at any moment through lack of supplies, even before battle was joined. Similarly an advancing army might encounter a 'scorched earth policy' during mid-winter campaigning, the resulting lack of supplies leading to desertions and deaths in their ranks.

The single most important factor governing warfare in this period was the commander's problem of financing the medieval army in the field. This problem had been especially applicable to the armies involved in the Hundred Years War and indeed, lack of funding, as well as lack of competent generalship,

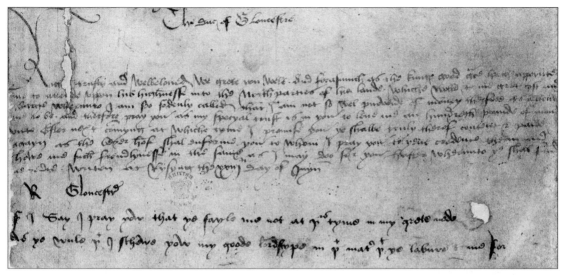

A letter written by Richard, Duke of Gloucester, from Castle Rising to Sir John Say requesting a loan of a hundred pounds in 1469. (British Library)

had contributed to the loss of the English territories in France in the latter years of the conflict. The convention for waging English war abroad was for the king to seek loans by imposing taxes levied at a percentage of personal turnover, and also by securing Church funding. Many of the leading nobles who fought in France also bore the cost of warfare, to their great displeasure. During the Wars of the Roses the same conventions were applied through parliamentary decision and by taxing the population accordingly. The nobility and gentry would pay their men to fight and the king would then repay them in coin or in kind for their military service and financial expenditure. However, this system could not be used to finance a rebellious army, and 'rebel' nobles had to muster forces through their own network of retainers and 'well willers' using their own personal funds; some even resorted to acts of piracy on the high seas to pay their men.

On a number of occasions during the Wars of the Roses English kings had to secure vast loans before putting their armies into the field; consequently there was immense pressure on parliament, and on the English people, to provide adequate funding for war. However, obligatory service, both through a noble's family ties and his tenants' affiliation to him, was the fundamental reason for a man-at-arm's fighting, even without pay. The benefits from this form of service were widely accepted at the time and the prospect of gaining land and titles from their 'lord', or benefiting in some way from the death of his enemies in battle, far outweighed the needs for short-term finance for everyone concerned. For the common soldier sufficient supplies and payment for service were deciding factors, and of course the chance to loot a battlefield, or in some cases the English countryside, also had its attractions.

This problem of financing the medieval army could, and did, lead rebel commanders into deception; they would make use of a royal Commission of Array to recruit men for their own private purposes. However, the mechanism of recruitment worked admirably when nobles enlisted their retainers' support. This service sometimes went unpaid, but was just as effectively repaid in 'good lordship' which was in effect far more important to an ambitious medieval knight serving his master as a man-at-arms. Such payment in kind was effectively recovered from an overlord if, for example, a retainer's lands were threatened by others of similar status, if he had a private family feud to solve, or if he had a criminal matter to resolve in the law courts. The retainer's 'master' could be expected to apply the required pressure, or enlist others of a higher status, to help his man win his corner. This medieval 'gangsterism' could, and did, involve bribery, corruption, and even on occasion, murder, to either fulfil a promise or return a favour. In return the retainer would support and fight for his overlord when called upon to do so.

It is very difficult to understand the mind of the medieval soldier without modern precedents colouring our theories and conclusions. We only have the words and descriptions of the chroniclers, the written lists and indentures of certain officials and nobles, and the ballads and poems of the Wars of the Roses, which speak so sparingly about the medieval soldier, and thus any comparisons we make today must be examined very carefully indeed. Medieval warfare and tactics must be analysed in conjunction with many other factors, and it is difficult for modern historians to take all these factors into account. In the medieval period, warfare was more simplistic in its 'art' and was ruled in part, in medieval eyes, by the intervention of God, and was influenced by the force of waning and distorted chivalric values. Sometimes apparently 'well documented' medieval battles appear irrational and miraculous today because we cannot fully appreciate the effects of medieval military thinking and tactics. Therefore caution must be applied when using modern attitudes and reasoning (such as A.H. Burne's famous theory of Inherent Military Probability)[15] to interpret the events of a particular battle, especially when contemporary evidence is lacking.

The only men trained in the constant expectation of warfare were the men-at-arms, as well as the esquires, knights and all ranks above them. When not actually on campaign, these men were training and preparing for action through the medieval 'sports' of hunting and jousting. Honour was paramount, and was achieved through exposure to danger on the battlefield fighting for the Church, the king, country or family. Ancestry, proudly illustrated in the symbolism of heraldry, was also of prime importance, and heralds were employed to protect and control its workings and principles. The code of honour practised by the upper classes was called chivalry, but in the Wars of the Roses it is possible that the knightly code changed in some way because of the very nature of the conflict?

THE EFFECTS OF CHIVALRY

In the late spring of 1467 two illustrious medieval knights participated in a joust which was to become the most famous confrontation of its kind in the fifteenth century. Queen Elizabeth's brother, Anthony, Lord Scales (later Earl Rivers) and

Anthony, the Bastard of Burgundy, the son of Philip the Good, were both champions of the lists in their own right, and they came together on Thursday 11 June at West Smithfield in London. For three days they fought out the epitome of chivalrous expectation in an age which demanded both honour and spectacle.

The lists at Smithfield had been specially smoothed and prepared for the tournament. Pavilions and grandstands had been custom-built to house the dignitaries, including King Edward IV, while spectators jostled for the best vantage points to witness the important event, amid all the panoply of banners, pennants and blaring trumpets that medieval London could offer. After the Lord Mayor and his procession had taken their places in the arena the two champions entered the lists with their entourages and did reverence to King Edward, before going off to arm themselves. Lord Scales armed himself in his pavilion while the

Edward IV greets Lord Scales before he prepares to fight in the lists at Smithfield in 1467 against the Bastard of Burgundy. (Royal Armouries)

Bastard of Burgundy preferred to arm in the open. When all was ready the trumpets sounded and the two knights, mounted on their faithful coursers, charged towards each other down the 90 yard long lists, lances couched. The Tudor chronicler Edward Hall has passed down to us his version of what happened next:

> And on the first day they ran together certain courses with sharp spears, and so departed with equal honour. The next day they entered the field, and the Bastard sitting on a bay courser, being somewhat dim of sight, and the Lord Scales having a grey courser on whose schaffron was a long and sharp spike of steel, when these two valiant persons came together at the tourney, the Lord Scales' horse, by chance or by custom, thrust his spike into the nostrils of the horse of the Bastard, so that, for very pain, he mounted so high, that he fell on one side with his master; and the Lord Scales rode round about him, with his sword shaking in his hand, till the king commanded the marshal to help up the Bastard . . . And when he was remounted, he made a countenance to assail his adversary; but the king, either favouring his brother's honour then gotten, or mistrusting the shame which might come to the Bastard, if he were again foiled, caused the heralds to cry a lostel, and every man depart. The morrow after, the two noblemen came into the field on foot, with two poleaxes, and there fought valiantly like two courageous champions; but at last, the point of the axe of the Lord Scales happened to enter the sight of the helm of the Bastard, and by pure force he might have plucked him to his knees, when the king suddenly cast down his warder, and then the marshals severed them. The Bastard, not content with this chance, very desirous to be avenged, trusting on his cunning at the poleaxe, required the king, of justice, that he might perform his enterprise: the Lord Scales not refused it. The king said he would ask counsel, and so he called to him the constable and marshal, with the officers of arms. After long consultation had, and laws of arms rehearsed, it was declared to the Bastard, for a sentence definitive, that if he would prosecute further this attempted challenge, he must, by the law of arms, be delivered to his adversary in the same case, and like condition, as he was when he was taken from him; that is to say, the point of the Lord Scales' axe to be fixed in the sight of his helm, as deep as it was when they were severed. The Bastard, hearing this judgement, doubted much the sequel, if he should so proceed again. Wherefore he was content to relinquish his challenge.[16]

This contest impresses on us Edward IV's chivalrous nature and his political attempts to avert unnecessary bloodshed between two well-known medieval champions. In other words we may see this particular contest as being a 'controlled' fight, in comparison with the unrestricted combat on the battlefield. Although sometimes dangerous and bloody, for the aristocracy such tournaments provided a training ground for actual warfare, and thus the joust was an important 'sport' in their eyes. Chivalry was an integral part of the overall structure governing medieval tournaments and its workings in this respect were therefore at least partly non-aggressive. The above example shows that the codes and rules of chivalry were used to permit controlled violence in an increasingly violent society. However, the total opposite applied when this training was transferred to the medieval battlefield. This was especially apparent during the Wars of the Roses when the codes and rules of chivalry were gradually deteriorating.

Limiting rules derived from the code of chivalry and governing all aspects of warfare had been in place well before the Wars of the Roses began, and it was common in battle for important people and other notable individuals to be captured and released for ransoms; anyone who could offer good compensation in return for mercy on the battlefield would be spared. This aspect of warfare is confirmed in contemporary chronicles where these 'limiting rules' concerned matters such as the treatment of prisoners, the granting of safe conducts through war zones, the recognising of immunities from combat, and the limiting of battles to a specific time and place. Thus the codes of chivalry can be seen as the forerunner of international law which meant that its rules and ideas could be transposed into the political realities of the time through the mediation of the various orders of chivalry. However, the reality was far removed from the theory because there was an inherent contradiction present in the workings of chivalry which, in effect, diluted its meaning. This meant that on the one hand chivalry justified war, but on the other hand its limiting aspects effectively contradicted all the chivalric works which firmly set forth the correct attitude of a model knight. In the words of one contemporary,

> The shedding of his own, or others' blood cannot dismay or frighten him; death seems a small penalty to endure in order to gain honour and great renown.[17]

The word chivalry conjures up for most people a world of 'knights in shining armour' participating in jousts and tournaments amid all the heraldic pomp and splendour the medieval world could offer. Following a code of honour to defend the Church, the weak and the oppressed, and at the same time offering their foes professional respect on the battlefield, the knight in this Arthurian guise was the essence of the medieval world. However, in my opinion, the word chivalry is an abstraction, and although we can explain what is meant by the word knight – the supposed possessor of chivalric qualities – the actual ideology and practice of chivalry is not so easily pinned down to a precise definition. In short, medieval chivalry is fraught with inconsistencies and contradictions.[18]

Sir John Hawkwood, the English mercenary knight of the White Company in the service of the *condottiero* in Italy, was well aware what chivalry meant to him in the 1300s. At the gates of Montecchio in Italy he was met by two friars who wished him peace; 'May the Lord take away your alms,' he replied. 'Do you not know I live by war and that peace would be my undoing?'[19] Hawkwood was convinced that for him chivalry meant the route whereby he might overcome his foes, destroy property, and glorify himself on the battlefield – ambitions he realised in abundance during his military career. In this instance, the word chivalry was used as a cover to enable him to commit brutal acts in war. In isolated instances it could also be seen as downright sham if we are to believe the exploits of Sir John Harleston, sitting with a group of English knights all drinking from silver chalices that they had just looted from a nearby church.[20]

The knight errant was an individual who could, when required, equip himself with weapons and armour; mounted on a suitable horse, he could fight as a heavy cavalryman in a medieval army. Dubbed a knight either by his king or his immediate superior for his services in battle, he was usually, though not always, of noble or aristocratic birth, since only wealthy families could accept the high financial expenditure required to be recognised for such a distinction in the first place. Such ceremonies of knighthood on the battlefield abound during the Wars of the Roses: Edward IV personally knighted John, 2nd Lord Cobham, 'in the field of gastum [Gaston] besides Tewkesbury'[21] after the battle there in 1471; the Earl of Northumberland knighted William Gascoigne at the battle of Wakefield in 1460; Andrew Trollope was knighted at the second battle of St Albans in 1461, and so forth.[22] However, chivalry – the code by which the knight lived and fought, and the cultural world he lived in, are less easily described.

Effigy of Sir Henry Pierrepoint at St Edmund's Church, Holme (Nottinghamshire). After the battle of Tewkesbury in 1471, he was one of the Yorkists knighted by Edward IV on the field (Geoffrey Wheeler)

Chivalry was a code that regarded war as the hereditary profession of knights, but in the fifteenth century major changes were at work in northern Europe which would affect the knight's role as a heavy cavalryman. The high casualty rates among French heavy cavalry detachments at great battles such as Agincourt, Crécy and Poitiers had proved dramatically that massed archers, properly placed, could completely destroy knightly prowess in the field. Later in the fifteenth century the knight's role was diminished still further by the development of field artillery, and in the sixteenth century he ceased to exist altogether in his traditional medieval guise. Given that the code of chivalry was already on the wane in the Wars of the Roses, it is important to question its role. How did it apply to the knights as the only permanently 'trained soldiers' in the armies? Did such knights still give quarter to their enemies, and if they did, were such prisoners ransomed off in the same way as before? Or did the bitter family feuding that developed and the effects of civil war prevent such acts of mercy?

Other questions also arise concerning chivalry, especially with regard to the effects of developments in tactics and weaponry; it was the power of the longbow that dictated the decision by English (and French) knights to fight their battles on foot. But did fighting dismounted alongside men of a lower class and status affect a knight's attitude to war? Did he think he was demeaning himself, and more importantly, degrading his code of honour because of this? Was the knight punished if chivalry was abandoned in favour of treachery or 'war crimes', and what did the knight hope to achieve on the battlefield? Indeed, how did he justify his actions afterwards, if no code of honour existed in war? These are just a few of the questions that need to be addressed in any assessment of the Wars of the Roses soldier because these knights were the commanders of men, and therefore they had a direct influence on how battles were fought in the front line. They were the officers of their own contingents of recruited men-at-arms and tenants, and were looked up to for guidance, example, and in many cases survival on the battlefield by the men they led.

Dr G. Bernard suggested that war 'was not an aberration . . . war was the supreme expression of the social purposes for which the military aristocracy existed'.[23] Warfare in the Wars of the Roses was an extremely personal matter, and the stakes were high, especially among the nobility and the gentry who were directly involved in the conflict and generally suffered most because of it. Battlefield protection had become a fine art by the end of the fifteenth century and the increased protection afforded by the best suits of armour in Europe convinced the knightly class that honour and advancement through feats of arms in battle was a risk worth taking. This statement is substantiated by the large investments made by the knights and men-at-arms in the very latest weapons, armour and horses (usually more than one) needed to wage war successfully. The results of this investment in armoured protection meant that the knight was in some ways divorced from the harsh realities of war by a kind of psychological barrier (his armour), at least until he began to suffer dehydration and exhaustion, the real problems for armoured knights.

Casualties were extremely high among the knightly classes during the Wars of the Roses, especially compared to any other English medieval campaigns, but why was this so when chivalry was in effect created as a buffer to this kind of aristocratic slaughter? It seems that in the Wars of the Roses there was a reluctance on both sides to capture knights and ransom them, as might have been expected in the Hundred Years War for example. Even kings and princes were killed without hesitation at battles such as Wakefield, Tewkesbury and Bosworth. Similarly, many prominent nobles were executed instead of being offered quarter and ransom as the laws of chivalry had previously dictated. Families repeatedly lost loved ones in feuds that were perpetuated for generations and were settled in battles that were sometimes specifically sought out by individuals for the express purpose of revenge. Therefore we may conclude that during the most intense periods of the Wars of the Roses, factional opposition rendered the codes of chivalry, and the merciful aspects of quarter, almost obsolete on the English battlefield.

In order to prove this theory further, and also in order to offer some further explanations as to why casualties were so high among the aristocracy in the Wars of the Roses, we must briefly look at the nature of the conflict as a civil war from 1459 onwards. But it is important to remember that even before this date the daggers had been already drawn between the factions, and had been liberally soaked in family blood at the battle of St Albans in 1455. Indeed the bloodthirsty execution of specifically targeted nobles at St Albans had created a tide of 'unchivalrous' behaviour that would persist for the duration of the Wars of the Roses, and culminated in the 'legal' execution of opponents both on and off the battlefield. This merciless behaviour became more and more commonplace as the wars progressed, even after weapons had been laid down in submission; this gives us further cause to question such unchivalrous action, given the fact that most of this killing occurred when battles had ended. Even among the relatively few casualties inflicted at St Albans in 1455, prominent nobles such as the Duke of Somerset, the Earl of Northumberland and Lord Clifford had been killed during or after the battle by ambitious Yorkist lords aiming at political supremacy and local dominance. The Yorkists' disregard for the codes of chivalry in favour of political necessity and family feuding at St Albans effectively set the trend for all future confrontations.

All the nobles slain at St Albans had sons who were intent on avenging their fathers' deaths, and restoring their family honour; through what we may describe as a distorted image of chivalry to fulfil their private aims, the sons of the St Albans dead succeeded in bringing down the head of the House of York – the perpetrator of their fathers' deaths – at the battle of Wakefield five years later. Here, young Lord Clifford took this revenge to its extremes, murdering one of the Duke of York's sons in the rout after the battle, and further retribution was levelled at the Earl of Salisbury, who had also been present at St Albans in 1455 and was therefore an accomplice to what happened there. Salisbury, denied ransom by the Lancastrians, was dragged out of Pontefract Castle by a mob and beheaded like a common criminal. Even before the battle the talk had been of the Lancastrians breaking a chivalrous truce in order to fulfil their unchivalrous ambitions. Therefore threats to the code of chivalry, both on and off the battlefield, were already present early on in the wars.

Even before the battle of Wakefield, the threatening aspects of attainder placed on the Yorkist lords after Blore Heath and Ludford Bridge in 1459 had brought about renewed conflict and new grievances, chiefly because of the dynastic issue. This new phase of the Wars of the Roses finally came to fruition after the battle of Northampton in 1460 when Richard, Duke of York, staked his claim to Henry VI's throne at Westminster. In view of this, Edward, Duke of York's victory at Mortimers Cross in February 1461 was immediately followed up by the execution of Lancastrian captives at Hereford, notably Owen Tudor, in revenge for the deaths of Edward's father and brother at Wakefield. At the second battle of St Albans, which took place during the same month, family feuding was once again an underlying issue, Lord Bonville being executed soon after the battle because of his strained relationship with the Courteneys of Devon. A few weeks later at the battle of Towton the blood feuding, exacerbated by the crucial dynastic issue, reached a terrible climax which resulted in the deaths of Lord Clifford, Lord Neville, the Earl of Northumberland, Lord Dacre, Lord Welles, and many others; the Earl of Devon was executed the next day, and another forty-two knights were executed or died after the battle.[24]

After Towton Yorkist aggression resulted in the systematic execution of further prominent individuals who had previously evaded capture in the wars. The Earl of Wiltshire was apprehended and beheaded, and Sir Ralph Percy was later killed at Hedgeley Moor. The Duke of Somerset, Lord Roos and other

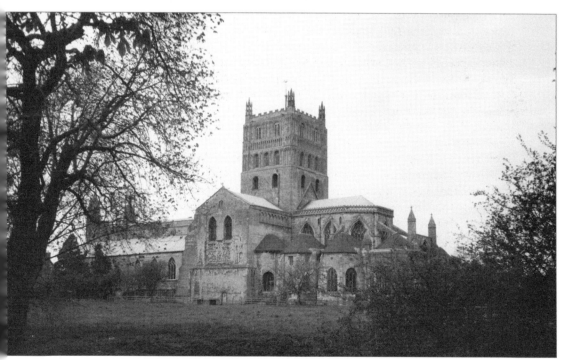

Tewkesbury Abbey from the south, where a number of Lancastrian soldiers sought sanctuary after the battle there in 1471. Edward IV, ignoring the abbey's safe haven, is said to have ordered them dragged out of the abbey and executed. (Author)

refugees from Towton were also executed after being captured at the battle of Hexham in 1464 – but this was only the beginning. In April 1471 at the battle of Barnet Marquis Montagu was killed in action and his elder brother, the Earl of Warwick, was cut down while attempting to escape from the field. Another Beaufort, the third Duke of Somerset, was executed after the battle of Tewkesbury and the Prince of Wales himself fell victim to a Yorkist blade during the rout from the battlefield. Shortly after Tewkesbury some Lancastrian fugitives were unchivalrously dragged out of the sanctuary of the nearby Abbey on Edward's orders and were put to death, proving that even fear of the Church and divine retribution were powerless against this type of blood lust and political execution. Even the private family feuding, which was a common feature of the period, led to individual knights and nobles being singled out and murdered, as occurred at Nibley Green in 1470. A year later, strained dynastic insecurity meant that King Henry VI himself was put to death in the Tower of London. Where was the code of chivalry in all this slaughter?

Alternatively, all these deaths may be regarded as the price for treasonable actions against the Kings of England during this period, and therefore not subject to the knightly code of honour at all. This is in part true, but does not explain the role of chivalry in the Wars of the Roses, and whether it actually existed in some distorted form. Perhaps the answer should be sought in the knights' perception of chivalry when they dismounted to fight on foot, and in the weapons ranged against them on the battlefield. These factors may have prevented the knights from fulfilling their knightly, and traditionally chivalrous, acts of mercy in battle, not to mention the fact that unmounted knights could not easily escape. The answer also lies in the knights' perception of civil war, the resulting breakdown of law and order in the country, and the influence of bastard feudalism.

Geoffery le Baker tells us that English men-at-arms, imitating the Scots, fought on foot for the first time at Halidon Hill in 1333.[25] There are two important aspects to this, one of which was later forced upon the knights by the longbow. First, by dismounting and tethering their horses in the rear to prevent easy flight the knights were seen to be better integrated with their troops, thereby increasing their soldiers' morale by demonstrating their own willingness to face a common danger; secondly, they presented a much smaller target to the enemy longbowmen. This second factor was emphasised by the aristocracy, and even kings, on the medieval battlefield, since commanders on both sides were all too aware of what devastation could be caused by massed archery against cavalry. This point is highlighted in various chronicles, but some cavalry still came to grief in this way during the period when it appears that typical medieval cavalry attacks took place as at Blore Heath in 1459.[26]

Philippe de Commines' comments on the typically English manner of dismounting to fight on foot brings us more up to date. He says that during a conversation with Edward IV, he stated 'modestly' that he had won nine important battles all of which were fought on foot, which if nothing else proves that it was common during the Wars of the Roses for all knights to fight dismounted in the same manner as their king, and in the midst of their own contingents, surrounded by the protection of their household men.[27] This decision to fight dismounted is the main reason why so many nobles and gentry came to grief in the mêlée, although a good deal of protection was afforded by field armour. However, many more, including the Earl of Warwick at the battle of Barnet, were caught while attempting to retrieve their mounts from behind the lines. In most cases, nobles were captured and sometimes executed for treason later, but on the field the knights were at greater risk because of their heavy equipment; they were often caught and slain as they tried to flee, especially by victorious common soldiers in search of plunder. The demise of chivalry in such routs is dramatically echoed in Edward IV's less than chivalrous cry after he had won the field to 'save the common soldiers, and put the nobles to the sword, by which means none, or very few of them, escaped'.[28]

By leaving their beloved mounts tethered in the rear of their battle line the knights themselves signalled the demise of chivalry as we would traditionally accept it today, even though it lived on in the minds of some who saw its true virtues, even when fighting on foot. It also was perpetuated by those who wrote about it in chivalrous works, and in attempting to resurrect chivalry in some form writers such as Viscount Beaumont and Christine de Pisan blatantly illustrated the fact that it was already on the decline in England during the second half of the fifteenth century. It had to be – or why would they write about a proposed revival? The advent of artillery on the battlefield completely destroyed both the knights' and the literary philosophers' ideas of chivalry, because the mounted knight was no longer the master of 'shock tactics' on the battlefield. Indeed, in the Wars of the Roses the footmen played the more dominant role. If we add to this the apparent absence of a knight's willingness to ransom his opponents because of the effects of family feuding and civil war, then it was even more astonishing that Edward IV should hold out a glimmer of mercy and forgiveness to his mortal enemy the Duke of Somerset in 1464, only to be betrayed by Somerset's unchivalrous trust as the wars progressed.

However, the fine line between the political and the chivalrous must be stressed here. Indeed, such individual motives must be analysed alongside many other contributing factors. For instance, treachery by individuals and whole contingents of soldiers was one of the worst possible aspects of the Wars of the Roses and gives us further reason to accept the demise of chivalry in warfare during this whole unstable period. How could chivalry possibly exist on the battlefield when acts of mercy, avoidance of combat, or capture of individuals for ransom could be seen as a treasonable act? Noble acts of fealty to a king, such as Andrew Trollope's action towards Henry VI at Ludford Bridge in 1459, left individuals marked for life by rebels and therefore candidates for execution if captured later on. The whole episode of Lord Grey's treachery at the battle of Northampton was probably linked to a political pact with the opposing side, or possibly a breach of indenture. In this insecure environment whole battle lines could be penetrated and the seeds of distrust were irretrievably sown for future conflict. Treachery could also be 'accidental', as at the Battle of Barnet in 1471, but experience and mistrust of it coloured the soldiers' fear of such acts to the point where one side could be intensely paranoid of the other's intentions on the battlefield. What price chivalry in such an unstable environment as this?

However, knights who found themselves on the opposing side and guilty of treason; men such as Somerset, Trollope and Grey, could still hold their chivalrous honour, however distorted, in great regard, and it was a considerable insult to have it stripped away from them before they faced the headman's axe. After the spirited and stubborn Lancastrian defence of Bamburgh Castle in 1464 Sir Ralph Grey found himself at the mercy of King Edward IV:

> The king hath ordained that thou [Grey] should have thy spurs stricken off by the hard heels with the hand of the master cook . . . The king hath ordained here that thou may see the King of Arms and heralds and thine own proper coat of arms, that which they should tear off thy body, and so thou should as well be degraded of thy worship noblesse and arms, as of the order of knighthood, and also here is another coat of thine arms reversed, the which thou should wear of thy body going unto death ward, for that belongeth after the law.[29]

After these ritualised actions Sir Ralph Grey was beheaded for his crimes, and his name was disgraced for eternity and his property was stripped away from him. The fact that Grey's honour was taken from him in such a manner before his execution clearly shows that a distorted form of chivalry did exist in the Wars of the Roses, but was regarded more as an ideal than a practical mode of behaviour. Chivalry was, nevertheless, in its darker aspect, an excuse to kill and commit cold-blooded murder and, in the Wars of the Roses at least, it offered a chance to execute political opponents at will; therefore it represents a completely different concept to that generally attributed to the image of the perfect knight of medieval legend.

Orders of medieval chivalry, such as the Order of the Bath, the Order of the Garter, and in Burgundy the Order of the Golden Fleece, dignified and solemnised the general cover-up of the kind of slaughter, pillage and destruction that could, and did, occur in warfare. Formalised with oaths, vows, vigils and exchanges of heraldic tokens between princes and kings, the hereditary right to kill was maintained in glory and honour as an example of how the knight should behave and thereby achieve great personal renown. This was the whole *raison d'être* of the knights, and because of it the knights were trained for war on a grand scale in the lists and at tournaments. The importance placed on this mock combat helps modern historians to understand the aims and ambitions of the well-trained and well-armoured knight and man-at-arms.

However, we may take the mockery of chivalry as a justification for violence one step further if we consider that this knightly behaviour was not only levelled against their enemies, but also in some instances against their allies. For example, French knights at the battle of Crécy in 1346 mercilessly rode down the survivors of their own ineffective crossbowmen soon after their Genoese allies had succumbed to an English arrowstorm. Chivalry here dictated that the flamboyant mounted aristocrats in the French army should prevail and so-called cowardice be avenged, even though the French knights were doomed to a similar fate, annihilated by the English cloth-yard arrow.[30] Similarly, in 1465 at the battle of

Charles the Bold is taken by the Swiss in 1476. Tapestries such as this not only depicted the confusion of fifteenth-century hand-to-hand combat, but also infused the whole idea of warfare with the myths of chivalry and heroism that condoned such violent action. (Royal Armouries)

Montl'héry, Philippe de Commines, who was an eyewitness, described an incident when mounted knights in the Count of Charolois' Burgundian army rode down their own archers to get at the enemy.[31]

Innocent men, women and children were butchered in sieges and during ruthless *chevauchée*s by English knights and their soldiers in the Hundred Years War, and in some parts of France vast tracts of land were laid waste on numerous occasions in the name of glory, honour and chivalry. Starvation and death resulted among the French peasantry at the expense of their aristocrats' quest for noble feats of arms. Therefore English shires during the Wars of the Roses were very lucky indeed to escape comparable devastation from the knights and their followers, and instead many English farmers may have consoled themselves in the fact that the aristocracy were content to kill only their counterparts in arms in an effort to carve out a name for themselves on the battlefield, and not to lay waste to their own country in the process.

Michael Hicks has pointed out that the dangers of the code of chivalry actually helped to produce this retrograde effect in warfare whereby plunder and looting had become a direct product of a knight's career. In this respect the knight could even become a mercenary in his own land if he wished, and thus an enemy to his own people. Hicks claims that by the mid-fifteenth century 'much that had been typical of chivalry . . . if not the core of the chivalrous mode of life itself began very gradually to lose its significance'.[32] This can clearly be seen in the numbers of casualties inflicted upon the aristocracy during the Wars of the Roses who were generally not shown, nor did they expect, any mercy on the battlefield. Such indiscriminate slaughter among the aristocracy, the result of blood feuds, civil war, and factionalism, was bound to help the gradual demise of chivalry in England much more quickly than anywhere else. Therefore it seems that the knight's disregard for his opposite number on the battlefield proves that no code of chivalry was followed or even existed in the Wars of the Roses. We may also say that 'true' chivalry was destroyed in England at the first battle of St Albans in 1455.

CHAPTER 3

'. . . and ordain them jackets of my livery'

RETAINERS

The main factor affecting our analysis of the medieval soldier in the Wars of the Roses is the way in which he was recruited. To place this in context, we must first look at the various methods of recruitment used by the king and the aristocracy during the fifteenth century. There were four main methods of recruiting, all of which overlap considerably: the process of retaining troops through contracts of indenture; the ability of the monarch to recruit men from the shires through Commissions of Array; the mustering of village, town and city militias and garrisons by both the above methods; and the ability of the king, and indeed his 'rebel' counterpart, to gather foreign troops and mercenaries.

The prospects of mutual benefit, advancement, protection and solidarity were sought after by most men in such an uncertain and unstable environment as that which prevailed in the Wars of the Roses. Of course, any social system that embraced all of these ideals would also produce a number of retrograde effects, especially when land-hungry neighbours vied for position or, in extreme cases, when a nobleman aimed at the crown. Sir John Fortescue, reflecting in Edward IV's reign on past unrest in England, fully understood the perils of 'overmighty' subjects and their retainers. Writing in 1471 he pointed out that this was increasingly dangerous to the crown: 'Whereof it hath come that often times, when a subject hath also great livelihood of his prince, he hath aspired to the estate of his prince, which by such a man may soon be got . . . for the people will go with him that best may sustain and reward them.'[1]

Social status dictated the level of involvement in local and national politics, and inevitably the higher echelons of society took a great interest in both, with the great and ancient families of England taking leading roles in government. Some of these 'overmighty' subjects created the factional problems inherent in the Wars of the Roses, and could make use of their appointments to office to affect the recruiting ability of all concerned. At the very top of the social scale was the King of England, and all appointments to office and land rights (or fees) were derived from him. These holdings and rights could then filter down through the families

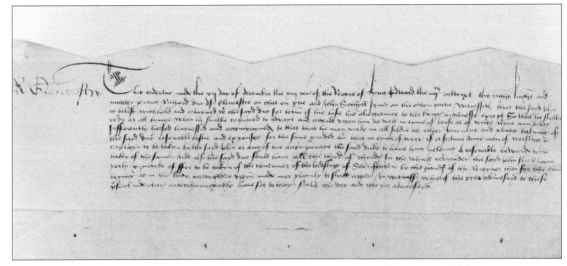

Indenture 'betwixt the right highe and mighty prince Richard duc of Glouestre and John Sothyll. John is 'retayned w[ith] the sayd duc . . . So that he shalbe redy at all tymes when he shalbe requyred to awayte and attend uppon him as well in tyme of pease as of werre, w[ith]out any delay sufficiently horsed, harnessed and accompayned'. (Nottingham City Archives)

of peers and nobles to their connections and tenants who worked their estates. There existed a complex social hierarchy, with peers, including the king's immediate family, at the top, supported by a substructure of dukes, marquesses, earls, viscounts, barons, knights, esquires, gentlemen, yeomen and commoners. Every man knew where he stood, taking his place in the complex neo-feudal (or as Charles Plummer described it, bastard feudal) system which regulated their lives, and laid down that they served their king in peace and war, taking up arms on his behalf when necessary, such as during local disputes, factionalism, and national civil warfare.[2]

The roots of feudalism in England were to be found in the Anglo-Saxon period, but it flourished after the Norman conquest, when it came to have a specific meaning: the holding of land as a 'fee' in return for service, usually military. Some twentieth-century historians believe that this basic form of 'legitimate' feudal system was replaced by the later form of so-called 'bastard feudalism', which consequently has featured strongly in histories of the Wars of the Roses right up to the present day.[3] The bastard feudal system could be, and was, exercised by kings and aristocrats alike, the latter creating small private armies for their own ends. K.B. McFarlane, a pioneer of modern thinking regarding bastard feudalism, traced the origins of this system back to the process of recruiting troops to fight in the Hundred Years War, but historians now generally agree that bastard feudalism was at work long before, perhaps as early as the year 1270.[4]

As the 'illegitimate' offspring of the more stable ancient feudalism, bastard feudalism used to be blamed by historians for having *caused* the Wars of the Roses.

This is no longer the accepted view, although certainly the bastard feudal ties between man and master through contracts of indenture enabled the nobility to raise the manpower to fight their battles (and in some cases to usurp the throne itself with their adherents' support). The proliferation of military service obligations during the Wars of the Roses affected almost everyone, down to the lowliest estate worker, the bond of allegiance to each man's overlord offering a simple mechanism to provide manpower. However, it is clear that such a system could easily run out of control without strong leadership from the crown. Small personal grievances between neighbouring lords could all too quickly escalate into something much more serious, with private armies being used without restraint to settle minor disputes. In such circumstances violence could erupt without warning, and these private wars could – and did – result in quite substantial casualties. In 1470 Viscount Lisle wrote a scathing letter to William, Lord Berkeley, which illustrates what could happen when private quarrels were taken to extremes:

> William, called Lord Berkeley,
> I marvel you come not forth with all your carts of guns, bows, with other ordinance, that you set forward to come to my Manor of Wotton to beat it down upon my head. I tell you, you shall not need to come so nye, for I trust to God to meet you near home with Englishmen of my own nation and neighbour, whereas you by subtle craft have blown apart in divers places of England, that I should intent to bring in Welshmen for to destroy and hurt my own nation and country. I was never so disposed, nor never will be; and to the proof here of, I require thee of knighthood and manhood to meet me half way, there to try between God and our two hands, all our quarrel and title of right, for to eschew the shedding of Christian men's blood, or else at the same day bring the uttermost of your power, and I shall meet thee.[5]

The long-standing grievance between Lisle and Berkeley concerning property rights erupted into private war on 20 March 1470 at Nibley Green. Lord Berkeley won the battle outright and Lisle was killed. There were approximately 150 casualties (more than at St Albans in 1455) and in the aftermath Lisle's manor at Wotton was sacked.

In such a dispute or affray it was up to the king, as supreme overlord, to intervene in the strongest possible way before any confrontations of this kind could take place. Similarly, it was each noble's duty to sort out disputes between his tenants. However, if the king or noble was weak and unable to control his subjects, there was nothing to prevent escalation and a general degeneration into lawlessness. Thus control and mediation in private disputes became a continual concern to the higher classes and contributed to the polarising nature of the Wars of the Roses conflict. Contemporaries, especially theologians, knew this and saw it as being very dangerous to the structure of medieval society: 'Every lord beholdeth another, how he is arrayed, how he is horsed, how he is manned; and so envieth the other . . . the squire is not satisfied unless he lives like a knight; the knight wants to be a baron; the baron an earl; the earl a king.'[6]

The bond, or 'indenture' of service laid down the retainer's duties and obligations to his lord. Interestingly, there was more emphasis on civil rather than military obligations, although both types of bond employed similar terminology. For example, such indentures were used to employ lawyers to handle a lord's legal affairs, and thus it is true to say that to a certain extent bastard feudalism also had a stabilising effect on medieval England. It was an essential part of everyday medieval life. Of course, disputes could also be solved with bribery, threats or violence, and even civil retainers could be called upon to provide military service when necessary.

As the Wars of the Roses developed it became clear that nobles with private armies posed a potential threat to the crown, and at various times the monarch attempted to regulate the practice of giving liveries. The privilege of 'livery and maintenance' (the giving of uniform clothing and the maintaining of an individual's interests in return for services) was granted to trusted nobles for the term of their life only, thereby curbing the dangers of occasional paid military service for war, which was in essence the real threat of bastard feudalism. However, such restrictions failed to become permanent legislation and retainers continued to be employed in large numbers by all classes of society and for varying periods of paid and unpaid service. Edward IV, and later Henry VII, tried to regulate bastard feudalism through Parliament and imposed fines on offenders, but the very infrastructure of the aristocracy demanded its survival in some form. Indeed, such acts of Parliament were but hollow gestures, for the king could not afford to throw away his ability to raise a national army if necessary: only through this system was the vast pool of English soldiery available to him.

The document setting out the details of a retainer's life or annual obligations was sealed with wax using the lord's arms, badge, cipher or monogram, then physically 'indented' (perforated) along its length or width and then torn into two pieces. One part was kept by the lord while the other was 'retained' by the lord's man as proof of connection, and hence the term 'indentured retainer' came into use. Retainers could be called upon at any time, as Lord Neville was in 1483 by his overlord, Richard, Duke of Gloucester: '. . . and my lord do me now service, as ye have always before done, and I trust now so to remember you as shall be the making of you and yours'.[7] Richard, Duke of Gloucester, had called upon his indentured retainers to supply the manpower to support his usurpation of the throne in 1483, and to provide him with military protection against his enemies.

The noble's 'household' retainers acted as his bodyguard, accompanying him to jousts and other events, moving with him around his other manors or estates, and supporting him as he fulfilled his own obligations to the crown; in extreme cases this might include going to war. 'Households' in the Wars of the Roses varied in size according to the power and status of the individual lord, but in almost all cases men would be required to serve on a domestic level, as pages, yeomen or grooms, while being trained in arms. Such men wore their lord's livery and protected him at home as well as on the battlefield. The *Black Book of Edward IV* laid down the regulations concerning households: the king was allowed 600 retainers, a duke no more than 240, a marquis 200, an earl 140, a viscount 80, a baron 40, and a knight 16.[8] However, numbers could fluctuate considerably when,

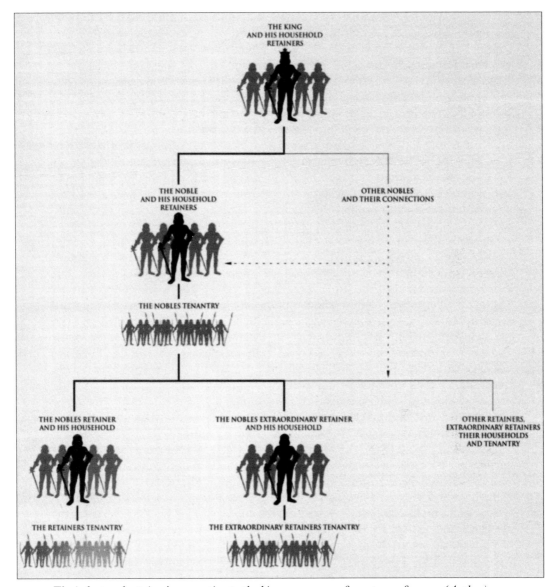

The indentured retainer's connection to the king as a source of manpower for war. (Author)

for example, retainers were away on their master's business, or when another retainer and his household came to stay with his benefactor. Thus it was very difficult for the numbers to be controlled. Moreover, it was not uncommon for those household retainers closest to their lord not to have contracts or written indentures, their loyalty to their lord being based on more than simple duty or obligation. Such 'indentured retainers' might live on one of the noble's estates, or have only a distant connection to the household (so-called 'extraordinary' retainers). It was also possible for men to be liable for service with more than one overlord: John Paston, for example, was 'employed' by both Lord Hastings and the Duke of Norfolk. So-called 'well willers' who enjoyed the 'good lordship' of several lords could supply important additional manpower when necessary, but the noble's immediate household retainers and 'feed men' were obviously the most dependable in a desperate situation. Such households were important bulwarks of strength for the nobility on the Wars of the Roses battlefield when all else had failed, and their true worth was shown in several battles of the period. The chronicler 'Gregory' watched them in action at the second battle of St Albans in 1461 when 'the substance that got the field were the household men and feed men'[9] of the nobles who on this occasion appear to have won the battle almost singlehandedly. Similarly, in Richard III's last charge at Bosworth against Henry VII, his most trusted household men rode beside him.

Dressed in the lord's livery – usually a jacket in his heraldic colours 'per pale' charged with a symbolic badge sewn on front and back, household retainers presented an impressive sight both at court and on the medieval battlefield, but their effectiveness depended to a large part on trust. The importance of livery jackets with regard to the uniformity and control of soldiers is highlighted in the Duke of Norfolk's request to his retainer Sir John Paston in 1485. Called upon to produce a contingent for military service, Paston was instructed to 'bring with you such company of tall men as ye may goodly make at my cost and charge, besides that ye have promised the king, and I pray you ordain them jackets of my livery, and I shall content you at your meeting with me'.[10] However, on this occasion Paston did not comply with the summons to arm and clothe his men, and Norfolk, his overlord, was killed leading the vanguard of Richard III's army at Bosworth a few days later.

Liveries were part of the heraldic symbolism which marked out a man serving a particular lord, and were the forerunner of the more modern conventional army uniform. Livery jackets were worn by the retainer and potentially the men he brought with him. Sir Thomas Montgomery, as a Knight of the King's Body (Edward IV's bodyguard), was given a gift of crimson 'cloth of gold' for the covering of his brigandine.[11] In the poem about the Bosworth campaign entitled 'The Song of Lady Bessy', Sir William Stanley 'made anon ten thousand coats readily, which were as red as any blood thereon the hart's head [his badge] was set full high'.[12] Badges were generally sewn on to livery jackets and references to 'white fustian' cloth suggests that simple designs in cheap material provided an effective way to mass produce livery badges for large numbers of men. Such mass production was at work in 1459 when the young Edward, Prince of Wales, distributed a 'livery of swans'[13] among the troops commanded by his mother Queen Margaret. It seems that uniformity in the Wars of the Roses was extremely important. It may even be fair to say that on this occasion a uniform common to all members of the queen's army was created, with the 'swan' badge being displayed on the various livery jackets worn by nobles and their retainers. At a practical level, such symbolism simply made recognition of units in battle easier, but it also served to create a sense of common purpose and patriotism among the disparate contingents.

When a retainer put on his livery jacket, and gathered his armour and weapons in anticipation of battle, it is fair to assume that he must have had some knowledge of the cause for which he was to fight. The fact that he was bound by indenture meant that his lord's quarrel was effectively his own, and that his fortunes would rise or fall alongside his lord's. When called upon to do so, he would ride in his immediate overlord's small retinue, accompanied by his own supporters, to an agreed destination or muster point. Small contingents gradually linked up, finally joining the main 'army' of a leading noble, such as Richard, Earl of Warwick. Such gatherings faced various problems which meant that recruiting was not a simple process. These problems are interrelated and had some effect on each unit's role in battle.

For instance, when the call to arms came, did all the retainers follow the drum with all their tenants, or were some men left behind to protect their lord's vacated estates and farm the land while they were away? What problems did this cause the retainer with a view to the number of recruits he had promised to bring to his lord? If some retainers failed to answer the call to arms, or failed to bring the required number of men, what would happen to them? Were the types of 'soldier' each retainer brought entirely random so that, for example, the lord might find himself with all longbowmen at his command and nothing else, or was the retainer expected to plan the composition of his force in some way to provide a balance? Did all the retainers on the same side tolerate and help each other, or were they rivals at a local level? Did this ever jeopardise army unity on the battlefield? To only some of these questions can we supply accurate and plausible answers.

The numbers of retainers who went to war could be affected by a number of factors, such as the seasonal aspect of warfare and the speed and duration of particular campaigns. It is a fact that only a very small proportion of the total male population of England actually took part in the Wars of the Roses. At this time, the total population in England was around two million people, of whom around 600,000 were men of fighting age. But in a conflict that lasted on and off for thirty-five years, only some 50,000 soldiers took part at any one time.[14] Campaigns during the wars were usually of short duration, and generally involved only small numbers of soldiers. Thus the seasonal aspect of warfare was rarely a consideration because the low figures left plenty of men on a noble's estates who were able to take responsibility for farm management and other matters, even during summer campaigns.

The speed and intermittent nature of the campaigns of the Wars of the Roses is an important consideration which must be taken into account in any examination of recruitment practices and their effect on normal life. The duration of the various campaigns has been thoroughly examined by historians, particularly W.H. Dunham and A. Goodman; they conclude that even if the majority of a retainer's tenants joined him on the march, disruption to estates would still have been minimal. Some retainers and common soldiers were also paid wages to cover their obligatory service away from home. In his work, *Lord Hastings' Indentured Retainers*, W.H. Dunham estimates that 'actual fighting [in the Wars of the Roses] probably occupied less than twelve weeks between 1450

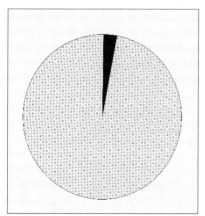

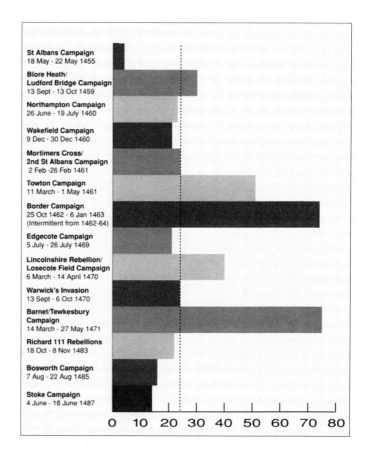

Above: The percentage of active campaigning in thirty-five years of conflict, and, right, the length of campaigns in the Wars of the Roses showing the average number of days served by soldiers in England. (Author)

and 1485'.[15] However, even if this were true, it does not mean that this was the length of time each soldier was away from home on campaign. According to this estimate the medieval soldier was hardly ever absent in thirty-five years and as Dunham points out 'normal life for 95% of the people for about 99% of the time' was not disrupted.[16] Perhaps more accurate is Goodman's assessment of 428 days' fighting in thirty-five years,[17] but even this is a very low figure when compared with foreign wars where an English soldier might serve for much longer periods.

The prolonged campaign of 1460–61 saw the largest numbers of men in arms. Beginning with the battle of Wakefield in 1460 and including the battle of Towton and the subsequent capture by the Yorkists of Newcastle and York, this bitter campaign raged intermittently for well over three months. Militarily, the duration of the conflict was not exceptional in itself, but the five armies involved in the campaign were continuously being mustered, or on the march and hence 'in arms' for a very long period when compared with other campaigns of the Wars of the Roses. The two main Lancastrian armies (Queen Margaret's northern army and the Earl of Pembroke's Welsh and mercenary contingents) and the three Yorkist armies (the Duke of York's force, the army led by Edward, Earl of March, and the

Earl of Warwick's southern muster) fought four battles between them in this period. Retainers were ordered to bring in their men at the last possible moment to a specific rendezvous, and the large-scale recruiting before the battle of Towton on 29 March 1461 drained the country of its best fighting men more quickly than any other medieval encounter in England.

Rapid recruitment was another common feature of the Wars of the Roses, mainly because the cost of finding supplies and wages for the soldiers in the long term was so expensive. The shorter the time the soldier was in arms, the cheaper it was for his overlord. However, a retainer's military service was expected to last as long as necessary, no matter what this involved. Having signed a contract to serve his master at all times, the retainer did just that, marching and fighting whatever the weather and conditions. However, this was less clear-cut for the retainer's men, who were a constant source of worry, especially during long and unseasonal campaigns, but there were penalties for desertion. Sir John Paston, fighting in the north with the Yorkist army in 1462, alludes to this in a letter to his brother:

> We have enough people here [Newcastle]. In case we stay longer I pray you see that money is sent here by Christmas Eve at the latest, for I cannot obtain leave [from the Duke of Norfolk] to send any of my waged men home. No one can depart – unless, of course, they steal away without permission, but if this were to be detected they would be sharply punished.[18]

The northern castles were at that time under siege by the Yorkists, and Paston was well aware that his men would not relish a prolonged stay in the north-east, and that if large numbers of his men deserted this might create difficulties in his own relationship, with his overlord, the Duke of Norfolk. Punishments meted out to retainers for non-attendance included the non-payment of wages or annuities, while in those cases where there was no contractual payment, the threat of forfeiture of land or other property was used as a deterrent. However, such punishments, when applied, rarely lasted; reinstatement soon followed the reprimand for non-attendance. Even kings 'forgave' individuals for this behaviour in order to retain their further support and manpower, rather than risking alienation in uncertain times.

The composition and size of retainers' forces are also discussed by W.H. Dunham in *Lord Hastings' Indentured Retainers*. In this instance, a structured force of individuals was documented. Ninety of Hastings' indentured retainers (with 69 extant documents) are recorded between 1461 and 1483. This number was made up of 20 gentlemen, 59 esquires, 9 knights and 2 peers of the realm, only two of whom were paid in cash for their services. These men agreed to 'ride and go' with Hastings when needed and they promised to bring their men 'defensibly arrayed' to an agreed meeting place. In return Hastings promised to be a 'good and favourable lord' to his retainers, meaning that aid, favouritism, support and preferment could be expected in due course.[19] A typical indenture during the Wars of the Roses is the one binding John Bonington esquire to Lord Hastings and dated 20 April 1474.

This indenture made the twentieth day of April the fourteenth year of the reign of King Edward IV between William, Lord Hastings, on the one part and John Bonington, esquire, on the other part, witnesseth that the said John of his own desire and motion is belaft and retained for the term of his life with the said lord afore all other, to ride and go with the same lord and him aid and take his part against all other persons within the realm of England, his ligeance only except. And at all times shall come to the said lord upon reasonable warning accompanied with as many persons defensibly arrayed as he may goodly make or assemble, at the costs and expenses of the said lord. For the which the same lord promiseth to be good and tender lord to the said John in all things reasonable that he hath to do, and him to aid and succor in his right as far as law and conscience requireth. In witness whereof the foresaid parties to these present indentures interchangeably have set their seals and signs manual. Given the day and year abovesaid.[20]

Thus it seems that the composition of a retainer's force could vary considerably in the Wars of the Roses because of class status and availability. The documentation for Hastings' men allows us to examine the numbers of men he and his retainers supplied for Edward IV's expedition to France in June 1475; this shows a balance between men-at-arms and archers and tells us much about the composition of contingents for service abroad. In the case of this 1475 muster the word 'archers' almost certainly means a mixture of longbowmen and infantry armed with poll-arms and other weapons although, as always in wars against the French, the archers made up the greatest numbers, a fact confirmed by Philippe de Commines.[21] In 1475 Lord Hastings personally supplied 40 men at arms and 300 archers for Edward's invasion force. Comparing these figures to the number of knights, esquires and gentlemen known to have been in Hastings' service in 1474–5 (according to Dunham, only about six are identifiable), this shows quite clearly that his indentured retainers were able to call upon additional men-at-arms for military duty, as well as supplying a complement of 'archers'. In other words the retainer recruited the well-armed men from his own family and household, and archers and billmen from his lands. Lord Hastings' contingent for the invasion of France in 1475 consisted of his own indentured retainers and their tenants as follows:

Lord Hastings 40 Lances. 300 Archers.
Sir Ralph Hastings (his brother) 8 Lances. 100 Archers.
Lord Grey of Codnor 10 Lances. 155 Archers.
Sir Robert Tailboys 12 Lances. 80 Archers.
Sir William Trussell 6 Lances. 60 Archers.
Sir Nicholas Langford 8 Lances. 60 Archers.
Sir Simon Mountfort, according to Dugdale, supplied 5 spears (men-at-arms) and 60 Archers. Receiving 2s. per day for himself, 1s. 6d. per day each for the other 4 spears, and 6d. for each archer.[22]

The important point to remember is the number of men recruited by each of Hastings' retainers (his personal retine) and the actual composition of his total force (904 men). This figure gives us reason to question the overall size of medieval armies. Certainly most of Hastings' other indentured retainers (knights, esquires, gentlemen, and so on), documented as being in his service in 1474–5, accompanied their 'good lord' on the invasion, and are included, although not listed by name, in the totals for 'lances' or 'spears' given above. A 'lance' was the continental system in which men were grouped around a knight to fight with him in battle, and each unit usually comprised a mixture of troop types, averaging out at one man-at-arms, a squire, and three archers. Occasionally seven men were included in the unit in continental armies. However, the 'lance' system was not the normal form of recruitment in England during the Wars of the Roses. In fact here the word 'spear' was generally used for a single man-at-arms, or a man in armour, who could fight on foot or on horseback. Indeed, the English word 'spears' rather than 'lances' is used to describe the sum total of soldiers in the 1475 muster. Thus we can say that the term 'lance' in this muster is representative of one man-at-arms, rather than a group of five or seven men.

In the 1475 campaign Hastings' retainers would have 'taken his lord's part' in the quarrel chiefly because of the support and preferment they would receive in return. John Morre, a retainer of the Yorkshire knight Sir Robert Plumpton, assured him of his willingness to serve in a letter which is indicative of the humble – even cringing – relationship that existed between man and master in this period:

> I recommend me unto your mastership, thanking your mastership heartily of your kindly and hearty mastership showed unto me, undeserved of my part as yet. I beseech almighty Jesu that I might do that thing that might be pleasure to your mastership; you shall have my service. I have many things to thank your mastership for.[23]

Most men lived in fear of their overlords, and would do almost anything in return for favour or preferment. Thus it is hardly surprising that this aspect of service during the Wars of the Roses has been likened to a kind of 'medieval gangsterism', although it was certainly a legal and legitimate form of service at the time.

Retaining was practised on an immense scale in England during the Wars of the Roses and many men served more than one master at a time. Lord Hastings may have been able to call upon a very large number of men-at-arms and tenants (the figure of 3,000 men may, however, be an over-estimate) who were gathered from his estates and local areas of influence with the exception of some 'well willers' who lived further afield and served primarily other more immediate masters. This territorial aspect of retaining enabled recruitment to proceed much faster in times of need, and produced a close-knit contingent of men which was easier to control and organise – and punish if the need arose.

Retainers generally served more than one master, including the king at the highest level, to increase their own protection, not to mention the rewards that could be obtained from favouritism. Because of this dual service retainers

The seal of William, Lord Hastings, c. 1461. (Geoffrey Wheeler)

continually excused themselves from taking their overlords' part against certain men. Lord Grey of Codnor, for example, served Lord Hastings against 'all men' but 'my Lord of Clarence and Sir Thomas Burgh, knight, only except'.[24] Occasionally, however, some indentures were purposely well-worded to take into account the dangers of dual service. An indenture between Richard Duke of Gloucester and the Earl of Northumberland in 1474 illustrates this: 'And also the said duke shall not accept nor retain into his service any servant or servants that was at any time sith hath been, with the said earl retained of fee, clothing, or promise according to the appointment taken betwixt the said duke and earl by the king's highness and the lords of his council'.[25]

In Lord Hastings' case the bond between man and master was extremely close: he had been knighted on the battlefield of Towton in 1461 by Edward, and later he was created an English baron in repayment for his services to the Crown. But above all this Hastings was Edward's retainer. It is apparent from surviving contemporary indentures that the special relationship between Edward IV and Lord Hastings was not uncommon. Although a closely bonded relationship without payment in coin was a common feature of retaining during the Wars of the Roses, this was only one form of 'good lordship'. In the fifteenth century military service could be paid for through bastard feudalism for short-term use, especially for a retainer's men (his tenantry) when called upon to 'ride and go' with him. In this way some retainers were retained for life with annuities amounting to £10 or even as much as £40 per annum. Hastings, however, made the supreme sacrifice and took his special bond with King Edward so far as to procure his own execution at the hands of Richard Duke of Gloucester in 1483 rather than betray his sacred oath to his overlord's son, the young Edward V, then under the threat of losing his inheritance. Most retainers were not as conscientious as this, however: according to a friend of the Stonor family, Hastings' own retainers soon went over to the Duke of Buckingham's protection after their lord's execution.[26] Ironically Buckingham met his end soon after this, which meant that Hastings' original retainers were once again looking for protection and preferment from another master. Such were the risks taken by an indentured retainer in the service of a leading noble.

COMMISSIONS OF ARRAY

The fact that all men between the ages of sixteen and sixty owed allegiance to their rightful king by law, regardless of whom they served as a local superior, gives us reason to question the haphazard nature of recruitment through Commissions of Array in the Wars of the Roses. Edward I's Statute of Winchester (1285) called for all able-bodied men to serve for forty days a year, and commissioners were appointed to muster men from both towns and shires for military duty. The appointed commissioners, usually knights and sometimes men from the king's own household, would inspect and record twice yearly the state of military readiness in such districts to prevent either fraud or deception. This continued to be the case in the Wars of the Roses.

John Fitzherbert, a Derbyshire commissioner in the reign of Henry VII, was given the task of raising the subsidy to provide the means of 'defence against the cruel malice of the Scots' who had received Perkin Warbeck as 'Richard IV';[27] James Blount esquire was given 'the rule and governance' of the town of Derby in Lord Hastings' absence in 1474.[28] Both men were duty-bound to provide finance and recruit troops, but at different extremes of military importance. Fitzherbert was a commissioner acting on behalf of the King against a common enemy, while Blount was given 'the rule' of a town and its military catchment area, with Lord Hastings' consent, for use in local matters.

Similarly, Lord Neville received a commission from Richard Duke of York in 1460 to provide men for his forthcoming campaign to curb the increasing Lancastrian threat in Yorkshire.[29] Lord Neville dutifully fulfilled his commission and raised men from York's lands, but instead of delivering these troops to his master he used them against the Duke of York by 'treacherously' taking his newly raised recruits over to the Lancastrians, then based at Pontefract. These recruits were common soldiers, some of whom had served and worked on York's own estates, and therefore owed him local allegiance above any other. How Lord Neville managed to persuaded these men to fight at the battle of Wakefield against their benefactor, or why in other campaigns some men inadvertently found themselves on 'the wrong side', has much to do with the haphazard ways the common soldier was recruited through Commissions of Array.

As explained above, all the methods of recruitment examined in this chapter overlap each other considerably. The locality of operations was one of the most important considerations, as the loyalty of a medieval soldier also depended on his livelihood at a local level. A shire levies muster roll would almost certainly include in its catchment area a retainer's estates, towns, villages and manors where his own tenants lived and worked the land. What then occurred when unfriendly commissions were imposed on a town or district in the Wars of the Roses, or when a man had to choose between his king or a rebellious but dependable lord?

As we have seen, the king was able to call upon a universally understood method of recruitment to raise the 'commons' in a show of force, whenever the need arose, through his network of nobles and retainers. It was this bulk of manpower that the king had in mind when indentures were drawn up between man and master. The system of bastard feudalism provided the machinery that enabled the king to tap the accepted quantities of men required to form English armies. However, as with the case of the unscrupulous Lord Neville, sudden changes of allegiance could cause major disasters in the Wars of the Roses. This occurred not only when a noble turned his coat (Lord Neville's sympathies were staunchly Lancastrian through his family ties), but also when the common soldiers' hearts were turned against a benefactor without warning and under false pretences. A pretended Commission of Array in Neville's case proves that a common soldier's promised fealty to his king (in this instance Henry VI) far outweighed local obligations to his master (the Duke of York). In short, it was a question of the greater loyalty and the locality of operations deciding the issue.

In unfamiliar counties, where a dubious individual's influence might not be so effective for recruitment purposes, the pretence of a lawful commission to array troops might be enough to secure men for political propaganda purposes, but this might not last when a battle was imminent – unless genuine grievances were held against an opponent. Someone who had offended the county, for example, could very easily be used as an excuse for effective recruitment, or alternatively a personal blood feud might be used to persuade an individual to take up arms against another. In Lord Neville's case the Duke of York was many miles away from Yorkshire in 1460, controlling the captured but rightful king of England (Henry VI) in London. Local patriotism and propaganda, encouraged by the fact that a large-scale 'rescue' army was being assembled at Pontefact to reinstate the king, and, above all, Neville's authority as a commissioner to act, enabled the recruitment of troops to proceed (8,000 men according to one account).[30] Once mustered and amalgamated with other soldiers almost anything was possible; at the very least local men were denied to an opponent's army. This is exactly what occurred at the battle of Wakefield in December 1460, when the Duke of York was cut off in 'enemy' territory without sufficient support troops.

Large-scale efforts to recruit soldiers for the Towton campaign were put into action when the Earl of Warwick received a commission from the newly acclaimed King Edward IV to muster levies from Northamptonshire, Warwickshire, Leicestershire, Staffordshire, Worcestershire, Gloucestershire, Shropshire, Nottinghamshire, Derbyshire and Yorkshire. However, some of these expected recruits, especially the troops from Yorkshire, had already been gathered in by the

Lancastrians when Henry VI issued his own Commissions of Array as King of England in March 1461. Indeed, the Yorkist act of attainder after the battle of Towton includes the names of many soldiers from all parts of the country, which highlights the fact that problems of duplicate kingship made recruiting a very haphazard and variable operation during the period.[31] Securing troops depended on the loyalty of a commissioner, and, as one might expect in the Wars of the Roses, dealing with an appointed noble's loyalty was not always the surest route to take. It is for this reason that trusted local individuals from towns, and in some cases whole districts, were appointed as commissioners. Sheriffs and other local officials presided over the shire levies muster in person to make sure proper procedures were adhered to on behalf of the king. In a signet letter from Edward IV to the City of Coventry in 1469 the King warned against fraudulent behaviour on 'pain of death': 'in no wise ye make any rising or assemblies with any person whatsoever he be, nor suffer any of our subjects within our said City of Coventry to do upon the said pain, without that we under our Privy Seal or signet or sign manual command you to do'.[32] What was feared was the pretence of a commission by the Earl of Warwick to muster Coventry men in the King's name against the King. The authenticity of Commissions of Array during the Wars of the Roses was a serious enough problem to make some commissioners wary of official documents which could be used to raise city levies for war.

When a Commission of Array was empowered by the shire a prepared list of expected recruits was produced by town and village and a description of the militia's weapons, if they had any, was documented. This was usually organised locally and, because of the relatively small population at the time, large portions of England had to be involved to form effective armies. The arrayers would appoint the necessary officials to secure all able-bodied men from every city, town, village and hamlet, warning them to be ready – 'horse and harness competent, and weapons convenient' – to serve when called upon to do so.[33] If the local contingent did not have enough weapons or equipment, other soldiers, who either had duplicates or paid money in lieu of service (scutage), were to provide the required quota or money to supplement or supply the levy, but no one was left out who was between the ages of sixteen and sixty.

In 1450 the Oxfordshire village of Ewelme responded to the king's commission. The community was part of the muster to array seventeen villages in the Ewelme half-hundred, of which Ewelme itself supplied six men for military duty:

> Richard Slythurst – harness and able to do the king's service with a bow
> Thomas Staunton (the constable) and John Holme – whole harness and both being able to do the king's service with a bill
> John Tanner – a harness and able to do the king's service with a bill
> John Pallying – harness and not being able to wear it
> Roger Smith – no harness, an able man and good archer.[34]

The seventeen Oxfordshire villages together supplied eighty-five soldiers, seventeen of whom were archers, but the evidence suggests that, in this district at

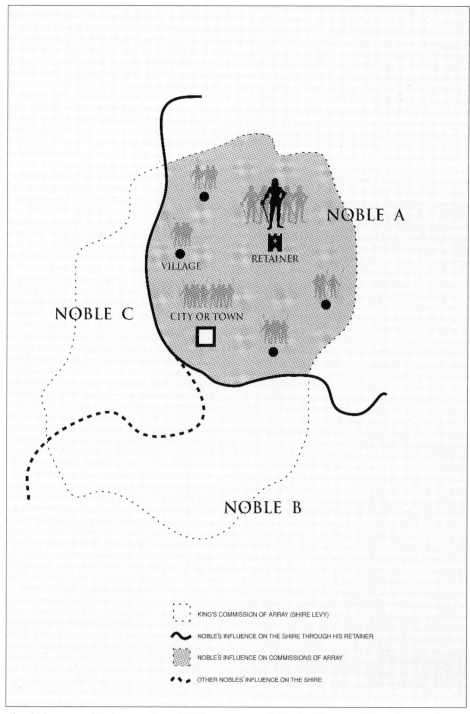

NOBLE A

RETAINER

VILLAGE

NOBLE C

CITY OR TOWN

NOBLE B

KING'S COMMISSION OF ARRAY (SHIRE LEVY)

NOBLE'S INFLUENCE ON THE SHIRE THROUGH HIS RETAINER

NOBLE'S INFLUENCE ON COMMISSIONS OF ARRAY

OTHER NOBLES' INFLUENCE ON THE SHIRE

A noble's geographical connection with his retainers and the significance of Commissions of Array in the shire. (Author) least, equipment and men were sadly lacking. Harness, meaning armour, was in short supply and only owned by those individuals who could afford to pay for it, had acquired it in some way, maybe from previous service, or had perhaps inherited it through family ties. Interestingly, archers are deficient in the muster, which lists an average of only one longbowman from every village. This undermines the popular perception of 'a nation of archers' (see also p. 82 below). The Ewelme levy seems to have had to excuse itself by recording that other men without harness and weapons were 'able with a staff': the 'staff' probably referring to other offensive poll weapons such as the bill and glaive.

The penalty for English soldiers not turning out to serve when required to do so was in some cases extreme, but despite this some Commissions of Array experienced resentment, shirkers and even desertion. Shire levies were generally untrustworthy soldiers, and these were the most numerous part of any large Wars of the Roses army. Various episodes during famous battles of the period attest to this lack of discipline, training and unwillingness to serve. It was because of this that commanders were forced to issue commissions 'under pain of death' rather than relying on volunteers to serve out of loyalty. Even so, arrayers acting on behalf of King Edward himself, especially in the crucial years of 1469–70, had great difficulties when calling upon their tenantry to comply out of goodwill and traditional loyalty to age-old recruitment practices.[35] Warwick's nephew, the Bastard of Fauconberg, found this when he tried to levy troops in Kent in 1471, even though this was an area that had been previously well tuned to popular discontent and rebellion:

> Other of Kentish people that would right fain to have sitten at home, and not to have run into the danger of such a rebellion . . . they were compelled, by like force, to lend them their array, and harness: and as such were unharnessed, aged, and unable, and of honour, they were compelled to send men waged, or to give money wherewith to wage men to go to the said Bastard's company.[36]

Fauconberg's rebellion was a turning point in the Wars of the Roses with regard to Kentish thoughts of rebellion, but even so, the Bastard's uprising was a great threat to Edward IV's regime, and was serious enough in the end to necessitate King Henry VI's death.

Jack Cade's rebellion in 1450, in contrast to the above, highlights what could be achieved through propaganda when calling upon an armed shire levy to act against oppression, and in this case corrupt county officials. Popular sympathies, coupled with the resentment and hatred of certain individuals who had offended the county of Kent, had dramatic results. There was always a volatile mixture of grievances in any shire, which periodically opened up old wounds and consequently helped individuals to muster large amounts of men during the Wars of the Roses. In 1460 when the 'three earls' (Warwick, Salisbury and March) invaded England from Calais, Kentish troops were once again raised in popular revolt, which allowed them to reach London unscathed and later capture King Henry at the battle of Northampton. With a new king's commission, which was again levelled against King Henry VI, Kent also supplied thousands of troops for

Edward IV's campaign in the north where many later fought at the battle of Towton for the Yorkist cause.

The high authority of a king's commission, therefore, could sometimes be undermined by a particular noble's influence, to the extent of threatening the very foundations of Commissions of Array. If the noble 'had the rule' of a particular shire through his retainers' connections and was in rebellion against the king, then the king's commission could simply be ineffective. Some shires could also be geographically split or partitioned by several nobles' affinities, all of which might affect the king's Commission of Array. In the Wars of the Roses potential soldiers were exposed to various different influences, all of which affected their local recruitment; their loyalties were thus bound to become divided in a more complex way than might at first be imagined.

The noble's local interest in the shire meant that a Commission of Array was generally an ineffective and outdated way of mustering loyal support. It was a noble's connection within the shire that dictated recruitment, because locally the shire levy's attachment to the noble's retainer was immediate and bound by immediate service, whereas the king's commission was only a distant reminder of the shire levies' ancient commitment to military service. A noble's complete monopoly of a certain area therefore gave him an effective way of gathering manpower and of deploying it wherever the noble wished, against whoever opposed him and whenever the need arose.

Occasionally in the Wars of the Roses the levy was unwilling to leave its own county to fight elsewhere, but overwhelming evidence in all existing indentures suggests that a noble's retinue always rode with him to war with as many tenants 'defensibly arrayed' as possible. As we have seen, all contracts of indenture required this compliance of service, and because tenants were also bound by a similar, but largely unwritten, obligation to their immediate master's 'connection', the tendency was for a noble to take control of a shire's manpower. Many towns and cities had similar affinities with local lords, as well as to the king himself, through various urban 'captains'. Musters of these troops could also be used against the reigning monarch when a contending noble controlled the area in question. In this respect Commissions of Array were largely controlled by the aristocracy during the Wars of the Roses, not the king.

Other problems could occur in the shire when troops were left leaderless and on 'standby', expecting to be used for some purpose in the near future. In January or February 1461 John Paston wrote of the disaster that befell the Norfolk shire levy immediately before the second battle of St Albans. He warned that:

> people should not come up [to London] till they were sent for, but to be ready at all times. This notwithstanding, most people out of this country [Norfolk] have taken wages, saying they would go up to London, but they have no captain, nor ruler assigned by the commissioners to await upon them, and so they straggle about by themselves, and by likeliness are not likely to come up to London half of them. And men that come from London say, they have not passed Thetford, not passing 400. And yet the towns and the country that have waged them shall think they be discharged, and therefore if these Lords above

[the Earl of Warwick] wait after more people in this country, be likliness it would not be easy to get without a new commission and warning. And yet it would be thought right strange of them that have waged people to wage any more, for every town hath waged and sent forth, and are ready to send forth, as many as they did when the King [Henry VI] sent for them before the field at Ludlow [the 'battle' of Ludford Bridge, 1459].[37]

During the winter months of January and February 1461 the Earl of Warwick was badly in need of troops in order to confront the Lancastrian army which was then sweeping towards London after their victory at the battle of Wakefield. He therefore issued Commissions of Array, with Henry VI's authority, to his chief captains, who were ordered to recruit in their areas of influence. Paston's letter indicates that troops were mustered and 'waged' in Norfolk, but were without a captain to lead them, and thinking they were needed immediately in London they marched off without a leader. Some, according to the letter, were aimlessly wandering about the countryside like sheep, and it is obvious that good organisation was sadly lacking in the shire at this time.

   Timing was a crucial factor in effective recruitment because levies were only paid for a certain period of military service, usually only a few weeks, by the communities they belonged to. The commissioners, and indeed the nobles who took advantage of Commissions of Array, therefore left this waiting period as long as possible before the order was given to march. The above disastrous array, by contrast, seems to have been effected prematurely, perhaps out of the panic caused by Warwick's own scaremongering propaganda campaign. This sort of disaster, along with the more important problem of late summonses, had drastic effects on the campaigns and battles of the Wars of the Roses. The lack of recruits from Norfolk, for example, may have contributed to Warwick's defeat at the battle of St Albans (1461); it may also, for a different reason, have been the deciding factor in explaining the Duke of Norfolk's late arrival at the battle of Towton a few weeks later.[38]

URBAN MILITIAS AND GARRISONS

Central to shire recruitment through Commissions of Array were the town and city militias, where the English population was obviously at its most dense. The much-quoted, but partially defective, Bridport muster roll of September 1457 provides us with a very detailed account of the names of certain soldiers who were expected to serve in its town militia, as well as listing the weapons and military equipment they possessed.[39] We cannot, however, use the information from this muster roll to draw up a picture of all the town and city militias in England during the Wars of the Roses. The amounts of men that were supplied by English towns and cities varied enormously depending upon population. Troop types and weapons also varied from area to area; northern troops, for example, were much more seasoned to warfare, and indeed violence, than their southern counterparts because of their repeated experience of border warfare with Scotland. We must therefore conclude that some militias were better equipped for combat than others in the wars.

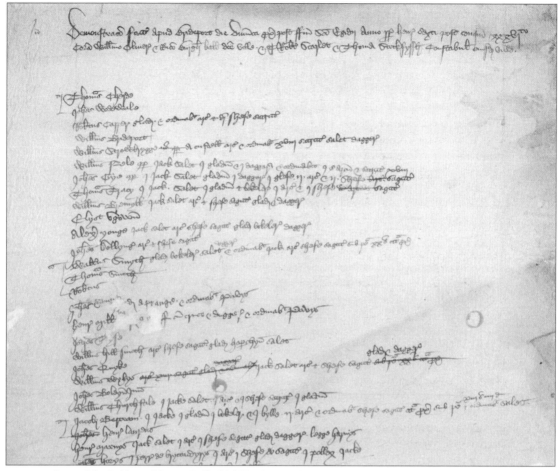

Part of the Bridport Muster Roll of 1457. (Dorset County Record Office)

The threat of French raiding parties on the south coast of England in 1457 prompted the Dorset coastal town of Bridport to act immediately upon Henry VI's commission to array the southern shires in anticipation of a foreign invasion. Out of 197 named men that were mustered at Bridport, approximately half had no equipment at all listed after their names, which suggests that either these men failed through death, illness or desertion to turn up and be checked by the commissioners, or alternatively that they did not have any military equipment in their possession. The commissioners obviously thought the militia defective because they ordered that arms and equipment were to be procured and made, and in some instances those individuals who had duplicate arms and armour were expected to surrender them to those who were deficient.

The two bailiffs and two constables who presided over the Bridport muster must have reminded the assembled levy of their ancient obligation to serve their sovereign through Commissions of Array, and ordered them to be ready 'at all times' and to await further instructions. The local officials then delivered the sum totals of men, and the general information about Bridport's state of military readiness, to the shire commissioner, who in turn placed the total information with commanders. (The total southern muster amounted just over 12,000 men in 1457.)[40]

From the surviving evidence of Commissions of Array it is quite obvious that towns and cities were expected to pay the immediate cost of the muster, hence their reluctance to pay soldiers for long periods of service. However, some communities paid in lieu of service, not only because local finance was linked with civic pride and esteem, but also because by providing troops and standing the cost a subtle lever could be applied in the future when government funding was needed for urban repairs, building work and so forth. Cities and towns followed this principle time and time again throughout the Wars of the Roses. Here, for example, the Mayor and Aldermen of York are writing to Henry VII:

> Most humbly and piteously shewith unto your highness, your true subjects and most humble orators, the Mayor, Aldermen and Commoners of your City of York, how in the time of the reign of the prince of famous memory, King Harry the sixth, your uncle, they were sure and fast in disposition towards him, their natural sovereign lord, to their duty ever ready to receive and aid his grace and other nobles of the north parties, taking his lawful and true part against his adversaries in those days and to their great charge and cost not only sent unto his battle of Wakefield 400 armed and well arrayed men to do him service, contenting afterwards the Queen's grace then being, and the famous prince Edward their son, unto the battle of St Albans, with other 400 of like men to the assistance of their said sovereign lord, but as well after the same field kept his grace and the said Queen and prince and other the true lords and liegemen at all times during their pleasure within your said city, relieving them with vitals and other goods to the uppermost of their powers; unto the lamentable battle of Towton, called Palmsunday field, where there were of your said city at their own cost above 1000 men defensibly arrayed, of the which many were slain and put into exile.[41]

It is apparent from the above extract that loyalty, funding and preferment are all intermixed with the fact that military service had been given generously in the past by the city of York. At heart the city was staunchly Lancastrian for much of the Wars of the Roses, hence the reassurance of the city's continuing loyalty to Henry VII. A city or town had to move with the times during civil war, however, often serving several different monarchs and sending troops where authority and the politics of the time dictated. The Duke of Gloucester's summons to the city of York in June 1483, for example, supports the fact that soldiers from cities and towns could be called upon incessantly to give military service. The assembled muster of troops at Pontefract, including men supplied by the Earl of Northumberland, Lord Neville and others, was sufficient to cause concern among Richard's enemies, even though these troops were in fact delayed by Gloucester for about a week.

It is logical to assume that towns and cities provided both billmen (including other poll-arms) and archers when mustered together, chiefly because these were the main types of weapon that were available during the Wars of the Roses. However, there is contemporary evidence to suggest that the law of Edward IV which prohibited the playing of football and other games in towns caused a resurgence of archery practice at town butts. We can therefore assume that there had been a shortfall of longbowmen during the early years of King Edward's reign at least, and partly as a result of the Act their numbers approached those of other troop types (such as those supplied by Commission of Array and nobles' retinues). The shortfall of longbowmen was also blamed on the high price of bowstaves, which were then being imported from abroad; an Act of Parliament of 1472 lamented that 'archery was greatly discontinued and almost lost'[42] because of the scarcity and high price of Mediterranean bowstave timber.

King Edward is said to have paid for 3,436 archers out of a total force of 6,000 men for the Tewkesbury campaign, which also suggests a more equal balance of both archers and billmen during this particular period. And although the Bridport muster roll indicates that longbowmen amounted to 73 per cent of the total force, only half of the total muster turned out for service on this occasion, and other troop types may have helped form a more equal balance of archers and billmen. To take another example: in 1449 the troops recruited from seven manors in Westmorland for the Earl of Salisbury by his retainer, Sir Walter Strickland, included 69 archers and 74 billmen with mounts, and 71 archers and 76 billmen without mounts.[43] We cannot argue for a national standard from these examples alone, however: the variable numbers and percentages of billmen compared to archers in battles must be interpreted on a more local and regional basis rather than as a national average.

As well as supplying troops to fight, towns and cities had occasionally to protect themselves against advancing armies. Closing the gates of a walled town was one way of prompting enemies to move on because sieges were extremely costly and impractical for commanders. Such delays in military operations could lead to soldiers deserting in droves, either through want of victuals, or because of the effects of bad weather or through lack of wages. Such urban protection in towns and cities during times of local and national rebellion was provided by the militia. When a town was situated on a hostile border, its garrison was supplemented by further support troops which were supplied by the Wardens of the Marches. With the king's authority large armies could be recruited by the Marcher lords for the defence of the realm, for example against Scottish raiding parties; alternatively, a town's local militia could be used to meet a local threat to urban life. *Gregory's Chronicle* records the day before the second battle of St Albans in 1461 when Queen Margaret's northern Lancastrian army had been ravaging the countryside near Dunstable:

But the day before that battle [St Albans] there was a journey [battle] at Dunstable; but the kings men [the local town militia] lacked good guiding, for some were but new men of war [raw recruits], for the chiefest captain was a butcher of the same town; and there were the kings men over thrown by the

Northern men. And soon after the butcher, for the shame of his simple guiding and loss of the men, to the number of 800, for very sorrow as it is said, hanged himself.[44]

As with the unfortunate butcher of Dunstable, who is mentioned above, local levies could be vastly inexperienced troops, especially when confronted by battle-hardened, victorious and renegade soldiers in search of loot. The swiftness of the Queen's invading Lancastrian army in 1461 indicates that local militias had to be hastily raised, and if they were badly led by inexperienced local captains the result could be disastrous. If the quality of Dunstable's militia is typical, then we must conclude that towns were not normally attacked, or indeed needed no troops in order to protect themselves, during the Wars of the Roses.

Even so, the battle at Dunstable does highlight the rawness of shire levies and the inexperience of the 'new men of war' that are so often mentioned in the chronicles of the period. In 1461 the Earl of Warwick was only relying upon token resistance in an effort to gain time to muster the main Yorkist army in London which would ultimately face the oncoming Lancastrian threat. He certainly did not place too much reliance on town levies stopping the northerners' unruly *chevauchée* southwards. Only when town militias and shire levies finally amalgamated together with other sturdier troops could any semblance of order be achieved on the battlefield.

Coventry was more deeply involved in the fortunes of York and Lancaster than any other English city except London during the Wars of the Roses. Coventry's location at the heart of the kingdom was very important to strategic military campaigning at the time, and later it was to provide a firm base for the Lancastrians against an increasingly hostile capital. The invaluable *Coventry Leet Book* provides a vivid insight into urban troop involvement during the Wars of the Roses. It shows that towns and cities were expected to provide soldiers time and time again for ruling monarchs. In 1455 Coventry equipped 100 archers for Henry VI; in 1460 the city sent forty men to be defeated at Northampton, within Henry VI's fortified camp on the banks of the River Nene; and in 1461 Coventry sent 100 men with Warwick to fight in the snow at Towton. Forty more Coventry men marched off to aid Yorkist operations in Northumberland and fifty soldiers were sent to help Edward IV in 1469. In 1470 Coventry again raised troops for King Edward in order to help put down the Lincolnshire rebellion, and forty men were sent in pursuit of Warwick and Clarence in the same year. In 1471 Coventry was again used as a base of operations, but this time it was occupied by the Earl of Warwick, who rejected King Edward's offers to engage in open battle. When Edward made his dash for London, twenty footmen and twenty horsemen from Coventry went in pursuit and were among Warwick's defeated forces at the battle of Barnet in April of the same year. When Edward beat the Lancastrians at Tewkesbury in 1471 he forced Coventry to pay £200 to restore the city's civic liberties because it failed to send men to his aid. In 1485 the city once more scoured its wards for troops and supplied a contingent to fight for Richard III at Bosworth, then afterwards welcomed Henry VII on Richard's defeat.[45]

The 'Coventry Sallet', c. 1480. (Herbert Art Gallery and Museum, Coventry)

Clearly both towns and cities played an important part in the Wars of the Roses by supplying urban troop contingents as part of a general commission to array troops in various shires. Coventry apparently did not suffer drastically because of the conflict, and we can suppose that the wars affected other towns in much the same way. Over a period of approximately thirty years Coventry's officials spent only about £600 on equipping and paying their troops; such payments and recruitment presented no drastic threat to municiple life for a population of about 9,000 people. However, the presence of city, town and shire levies, under their respective banners and captains, in the battles of the period proved to be an unknown quantity. Before the battle of Towton in 1461 many towns responded to Edward IV's commission of array:

> The Wolf came from Worcester, full sore he thought to bite,
> The Dragon came from Gloucester, he bent his tale to smite,
> The Griffon came from Leicester, flying in as tight,
> The George came from Nottingham, with spear for to fight,
> Blessed be the time, that ever God spread that flower.[46]

The political poem 'The Rose of Rouen' echoes what civic pride was all about in medieval England. Town recruits sometimes marched off in resplendent new livery jackets, such as those furnished by the Nottingham chamberlains to their troops in 1463–4.[47] Similarly, the contingent supplied by Coventry in 1455 were well uniformed and better equipped than most.[48] However, in isolated instances some recruits never went into action at all and returned home, as did Coventry's contingent in 1455. Civic pride was no substitute for experience and professionalism in a whirlpool of swords, bills and axes. In this respect, against well-equipped retinue troops the less experienced and generally ill-equipped levied soldier was more at risk on the battlefields of the Wars of the Roses than any other.

Important towns on the English Marches had semi-permanent garrisons during the Wars of the Roses. The manpower for a garrison was, for the most part, provided by the Wardens of the Marches who were given the task of dealing with the king's enemies on the borders of his kingdom. The warden was the king's retained military commander, and in the East March of Northumberland he was also castellan of the royal stronghold of Berwick upon Tweed, receiving an annual income of about £2,500 in peacetime and £5,000 in time of war. The size of the garrison at Berwick during the Wars of the Roses is difficult to specify, because its fluctuating manpower depended on how active Scottish troops were on the English border. In time of great need the eastern garrison could be substantially augmented to deal with an immediate border problem. To the west, however, in the important northern outpost of Carlisle there was an equally volatile area of Scottish border activity. The garrison at Carlisle consisted of five men-at-arms and a hundred archers who acted as a permanent garrison against such Scottish raiding or invasion – hardly an army at all. After 1411 the warden of the West March received £1,000 a year for maintaining these troops; the Berwick garrison may therefore have been twice as large as that employed at Carlisle, judging by the warden's double wages there. By the end of Henry VII's reign the garrison totalled 150 men at Berwick in peacetime and double this when at war with Scotland.[49]

The garrisons of the Northumbrian castles played an important part in the unusual 1461–4 border campaign simply by prolonging the conflict, due to their very existence, against the non-committal of Edward IV's artillery. These garrison troops were, for the most part, the retainers and tenants of the nobles who happened to be given the task of securing border strongholds during the campaign. In 1463 Lord Montagu received £6,000 in wartime to retain troops 'extraordinarily' for service in the North, which amounted to six times his normal income.[50] The Nevilles and Percies before this, who were the traditional fifteenth-century wardens of the West and East Marches respectively, were equally well rewarded by the king in return for a secure border. From their powerbases in the north of England each of the great northern magnates could command a vast following of soldiers in the Wars of the Roses, which could be used for defence in the service of their king against his enemies, or for private war. In this way, a warden of the Marches had a distinct recruitment edge over his counterparts elsewhere in the kingdom.

This factor, however, could not only spell trouble for the king, but also become a great potential threat to northern equilibrium, as the warden of the East March could gather troops to act against his counterpart in the west. The king's policy was thus to try to keep both wardens well apart, and so prevent any one noble from gaining absolute control of the North of England. In this way a kind of order was maintained during the first half of the Wars of the Roses when both the Neville and Percy families were feuding against each other. The king was well aware that it was far easier for northern lords to deploy much larger numbers of men than their counterparts in the South, and so monarchs aligned themselves accordingly. This, of course, had a direct influence on the Percy and Neville families in that parts of the North of England were forced into taking opposite sides during the conflict.

On a number of occasions during the reign of Henry VI, Wardens of the Marches found it very difficult to secure payment for their services, both because of the sporadic political upheavals in the government and because of the lack of ready money in the Exchequer. Not only had wardens to pay their soldiers, but defences also had to be maintained against attack. In 1451 Berwick's defences were dilapidated, and in 1483 Norham Castle's walls were ruinous. Norham retained a fluctuating garrison of around thirty men, which indicates that permanent garrisons, apart from those mentioned above, were rare. That of Berwick dates from as late as 1482.[51] Therefore we may conclude that as far as pitched battles are concerned, experienced garrison troops were of little tactical use because their numbers were insignificant.

The exception to this was the English outpost garrison at Calais where more than a thousand permanent soldiers were in paid service under the command of the king's appointed captain. Four-fifths of all wool that left England en route to Flanders and Holland during the fifteenth century went through the port of Calais and was processed by the Merchants of the Staple. Not only had the wool to be protected in warehouses until it was sold, but the strategic position of Calais called for a garrison of troops to protect it and its outlying march against the French. The march of Calais also included the strongpoints of Guisnes and Hammes and in repayment for protection the garrison expected prompt payment. The *Cely Letters* document how important it was for the soldiers to be paid on time, as well as the problems that could arise when these troops 'called sharply for their wages'. In the following case even a change in currency was a worry to the captain of the garrison:

> and they [the garrison] demanded all sterling money to be paid at Calais, but Master Lieutenant and the Fellowship [the Staple] at Calais hath agreed with my lord and the king's council and to be fully concluded upon the same; that they shall pay this half year's wages, half sterling money in England to be paid the last day of July, and the other half to be paid at Calais by Midsummer in Flemish money.[52]

Shortages of cash during the Wars of the Roses occurred when political upheavals took place. Between June 1451 and June 1454 the Calais garrison cost £17,000 in contractual payments to soldiers and £9,300 in improvement and rebuilding costs.[53] The appointed captain of the Calais garrison had to make sure his soldiers were appeased even when finance was not forthcoming from government sources, for fear of all out mutiny. When the Earl of Warwick was captain, he desperately embarked upon various buccanneering activities in the English Channel, raiding foreign shipping in an effort to secure the garrison's loyalty. Success in controlling the garrison helped to further Warwick's own political ambitions, as he was then able to give effective support to his Yorkist friends with garrison troops, especially in the decisive 1460–61 campaigns.

It appears that the garrison were a law unto themselves if badly treated. In 1460 they vented their anger by raiding the wool warehouses in Calais to secure their wages by force. By dictating their continued employment themselves the garrison was, in effect, a very powerful military arm in itself. As long as its soldiers were paid on time the garrison would respond and respect orders, whoever issued them; in this sense the Calais garrison were mercenaries loyal only to their paymaster. However, at the 'non-battle' of Ludford Bridge in 1459 we hear of an unusual display of 'loyalty' by the Master Porter of the Calais garrison, Andrew Trollope. Trollope and his men had been recruited by the Earl of Warwick (the Yorkist captain of the garrison) for service in England against King Henry VI. However, Warwick's association with the Duke of York meant that the garrison had inadvertently found themselves on the wrong side. The King, who was in effect the garrison's traditional paymaster, proceeded to line his army up for battle in the fields some distance away, while the Duke of Somerset formulated a plan which gave Trollope's men a chance to redeem themselves by changing their allegiance and deserting the Yorkist battleline at the first opportune moment. Money as well as the Yorkists' precarious 'rebellious' position dictated the garrison's next move: Trollope dutifully complied with the royal offer of pardon by leading his men over to the King's camp during the night. This action by the Calais garrison was directly responsible for bringing about the collapse and dispersal of the Yorkist forces in the field at Ludford, and consequently their commanders' later attainders for treason.

MERCENARIES AND FOREIGN ALLIES

Scotland in the fifteenth century, although in theory owing fealty to the English king because of his ancestors' previous successes there, had its own monarchy and interests, including a traditional ally in the French. Wales and its March, also owing allegiance to England, had much in common with the North of England at this time, but the great nobles in the south and east of Wales operated with near-regal powers. These Marcher lords held 'liberties' whereby they personally superintended the legal system in their own areas of influence. They marshalled the Welsh Marches from their own castles and were rewarded by the King of England for their services in much the same way as the Nevilles and Percies were in the North of England. However, as also in the North, infighting was common and the Welsh lords aligned themselves with the factions who fought the Wars of the Roses. Ireland was a different matter: the English king's control extended no further than the Pale (the area around Dublin). Outside this area were the Anglo-Irish lords and their troops, who played vital roles in the Wars of the Roses but

A mercenary handgunner prepares to fire from behind a pavise. (Paul Lewis Isemonger)

maintained their independence virtually as kings in their own lands. Further out lived the Gaelic chieftains where the king's authority was completely rejected. Because of this territorial and administrative split in Britain during the fifteenth century, and because of the close involvement of foreign powers in English politics, troops from all these sources could be recruited to fight for one side or the other.

Mercenaries and foreign allies were sought out to provide an alternative source of manpower when it was needed, or when a specialist skill or military 'edge' was required. Nobles' connections either through their appointment to office, or through their support of foreign powers, meant that both paid mercenaries and foreign troops could be recruited to fight on the battlefields of the Wars of the Roses. Varying amounts of these soldiers were used in the wars, but, as we saw in Chapter 1, the great majority of English armies during this unstable period had in their ranks allied or mercenary companies fighting under their own banners and captains. Some battles, indeed, hinged on their military performance and thus their recruitment was an important feature of the power politics of the time.

Before the battle of Mortimers Cross in February 1461 the Lancastrians recruited Breton mercenaries who were amalgamated with Welsh, Irish and English contingents against Edward Duke of York's much more experienced army of the Marches. The Earl of Warwick at the second battle of St Albans placed his 'goners and borgeners' (gunners and Burgundian?) mercenaries in a crucial position on the battlefield, although in the end they were outflanked by the Lancastrian army.[54] Many nationalities fought on both sides at Towton, including Scots, Welsh, French and Burgundian troops, the latter fighting under the Dauphin's banner. Yorkist specialist handgunners were also provided by Seigneur de la Barde for the Towton campaign, although their small numbers must have reduced their effectiveness. Because of the atrocious weather conditions which prevailed at Towton, many such guns were probably rendered useless, if we are to believe the comments made in Gregory's chronicle that they exploded prematurely on their mercenary owners at St Albans a month earlier.[55] During the border war of 1461–4 Scottish troops were in constant use by the Lancastrians; they were paid for by the forfeiture of Berwick upon Tweed. French mercenaries under the command of the famous mercenary captain Pierre de Brézé fought for Queen Margaret in her bid to take back Yorkist strongholds in the North. The Flemish troops who landed with Edward at Ravenspur in 1471 were bought by the friendship and political connections of Edward's Burgundian allies during his exile there. Most of these troops would also have fought in Yorkist ranks at the battles of Barnet and Tewkesbury shortly afterwards.

Alienated Scottish lords provided some troops for King Edward IV's French invasion of 1475, and Edward's allies in Burgundy, through the fortuitous marriage of his sister to Charles the Bold, once again supported the English king in the abortive military operation which followed. In 1485 Edward's brother, Richard III, was faced with Henry Tudor's motley force of English, Welsh, Scottish and French troops at the battle of Bosworth, and at Stoke Field, in the last pitched battle of the Wars of the Roses, Irish troops, under the command of Thomas Geraldine, were involved with English retinues and German mercenaries captained by Martin Schwartz. At Stoke the 'naked' (meaning ill-equipped) Irish troops found themselves at a great disadvantage, and were slaughtered by the effects of the longbow. Mercenaries could also be paid for by certain individuals, such as Dr Morton, the Bishop of Ely, who had the financial means to be able to hire a contingent of handgunners to protect his cathedral, and presumably himself, against the threat of Queen Margaret's northern army in February 1461.

We can see from this brief survey of specific campaigns that mercenary troops often featured in battles of the period; but it was chiefly after 1460 that their involvement in numbers became more telling on Wars of the Roses battlefields. The need for additional troops during the dynastic struggles of the 1460s was critical for pretenders and usurpers, and when factions were isolated or ousted from the country into exile. To be able to carry on the fight effectively political connections had to be sought out, or foreign money had to be employed – often both – in an effort to win back forfeiture, or indeed the crown of England itself. One result of this was that the political differences of countries such as France and Burgundy were played out on English battlefields, and the recruitment of countries onto opposite sides in the conflict obviously deepened the rifts between them.

The age-old alliance of France and Scotland against their common enemy England, or more correctly pro-Yorkist England, also made military recruitment more complicated in the Wars of the Roses. In the case of the unusual Lancastrian alliance during the border war we may wonder at the mix of troop types when they amalgamated. How were such troops kept under control, not only on the battlefield but also when they were in close proximity to each other? What occurred when such nationalities were encamped or garrisoned together? Language and dialect must have been a great problem to common soldiers and commanders alike, and they would have had to rely heavily on the trilingual basis of their education in order to converse effectively with foreign captains fighting for them. Translators would have been useless under such circumstances, especially when giving orders in battle.

The problems of foreign troops are highlighted by Philippe de Commines, who describes the 'standing army' of Charles VII:

> They [the French soldiers] live off the country continuously without paying for anything, committing other crimes and excesses as we all know. For they are not content just to live, but in addition they beat and abuse the poor and force them to go look elsewhere for bread, wine and victuals, and if any good man has a beautiful wife or daughter he would be very wise to protect her carefully.[56]

According to Philippe de Commines, who had been a soldier himself before turning historian, the French troops supplied by Charles VIII to aid Henry Tudor in 1485 were 'three thousand [of] the loosest and most profligate persons in all that country' that could be found.[57] The threat of these 'unruly foreigners' in English ranks prompted Henry Tudor to issue stern orders that any violations of English property, or abuses levelled at the population in general, would be met by harsh penalties. Foraging was carried out before the battle of Bosworth by the Tudor army, but the food taken was paid for by the king when he came to power.[58] As always, the prompt payment of mercenary soldiers usually stifled such unruly behaviour; the fickle and threatening nature of mercenaries and foreign troops, however, was an important factor in the Wars of the Roses.

By far the worst excesses of such unruly behaviour by mercenary troops occurred when Queen Margaret's army pillaged its way southwards towards London, then back to Yorkshire, in the midwinter campaign of 1461. It was an unusually harsh winter that year, and Scottish contingents in Lancastrian pay had allegedly been promised that all land south of the River Trent could be pillaged at will in lieu of wages. Whether or not this was true, soldiers under the Queen's command eventually got totally out of hand to the extent that only the better trained Lancastrian troops actually fought at the second battle of St Albans, while others went off in search of loot. According to John Whethamstede, the main chronicler and eyewitness of both battles of St Albans, on each occasion troops became unruly after bloodshed.[59] In general, however, there were only isolated instances of pillage and England does not seem to have been like the France described above by Commines, where *chevauchées* were far more serious on land and people.

Descriptions of mercenary troops are limited, and muster rolls documenting troop strengths are all but non-existent, but it is clear that some mercenaries, as opposed to other hastily recruited foreign troops, had specialist skills which included experience with handguns and artillery pieces, in pike 'training'

Foreign troops equipped with pikes, halberds and artillery fight at the battle of Murten, 1476. (Royal Armouries)

(particularly the Flemish or Swiss type) and in the making of innovative field defences. This is how Londoners described the mercenary troops Edward IV had brought with him from Flanders in 1471: 'And about two of the clock at afternoon came King Edward into the city with a fair band of men, with a black and smokey sort of gunners Flemings that were foremost to the number of 500 and so rode unto [St] Pauls.'[60] The *Arrivall*, Edward IV's official chronicle detailing the reclamation of his throne in 1471, states that these troops were also carrying pikes – a weapon unfamiliar to the English in the Wars of the Roses.[61] However, it is hardly surprising that the Flemings who entered London in 1471 had them as standard equipment, considering that both the Burgundians and the Swiss were already well versed in combat with the weapon on the continent.

The Swiss and German mercenaries in the Earl of Lincoln's army at Stoke Field also probably wielded pikes and handguns; these were, after all, their tried and tested national weapons. During this last pitched battle of the Wars of the Roses we are told that approximately 1,500 to 2,000 of these troops fought bravely, and probably very effectively en masse, under the command of their highly reputed Swiss colonel (and former Augsburg shoemaker) Martin Schwartz – a rare occurrence for mercenary troops under the pay of a foreign power.

Some foreign troops employed in the Wars of the Roses had also learned how to construct innovative devices to defend a battlefield position; others had acquired a specialist knowledge of ordnance weapons. The troops manning the unusual, and moveable, defensive field fortifications and contraptions on Barnards Heath at the second battle of St Albans in 1461, for instance, were probably the ones who built them in the first place – in other words the Earl of Warwick's paid mercenaries of Burgundian 'gunners'. Although they provided a novel defensive net of linear and self-standing devices between contingents of soldiers, handgunners and artillery, they were marked out in Gregory's 'Chronicle' for ridicule and criticism because they failed to achieve any advantage whatsoever over the enemy.[62] Military innovations of this kind, however ineffective, were tried out by both sides in the Wars of the Roses in an effort to gain some advantage over armies of similar weaponry, manpower and tactical skill.

In conclusion, the evidence that we have cited on methods of recruitment in the Wars of the Roses suggests that the vast majority of soldiers were not conscripted into a standing army, and therefore that they were ill-disciplined, ill-experienced and untrained. The nucleus of any army that fought in the wars, on the other hand, were the trained men-at-arms, comprising the small households of retainers and 'extraordinary retainers' of the nobles, gentry and knights who lived for fighting and saw it as a chance for advancement.

These leaders of men must have greatly feared for their contingents' loyalty, especially when the questions raised in the next chapter are taken into account. However, in theory at least, loyalty held retainers and their tenants to their lord, and Commissions of Array bound the subject to his king with official documents and well-tried military machinery. Hence some semblance of order prevailed for recruitment to proceed before an actual battle was contemplated. What occurred then, we may ask? We must first consider what the Wars of the Roses soldier endured before he encountered the enemy.

CHAPTER 4

'Iron smiteth not so sore as hunger doth if food fail'

FINANCING THE SINEWS OF WAR

One of the greatest problems faced by English medieval armies during the latter years of the Hundred Years War was one of lack of finance. This problem was highlighted when nobles such as Richard Duke of York were forced into standing the costly business of warfare until they were eventually paid back (or not, in York's case) by the king either in coin or with royal favours such as gifts of land and titles. Henry VI's unpaid financial debt to Richard Duke of York was a serious breach of faith with a leading noble; in York's case this fuelled a host of grievances which later played their part in the outbreak of the Wars of the Roses.

The difficulties inherent in military finance and expenditure in Henry VI's reign were familiar not only to English kings, but also to the English people who had, after all, to stand the full weight of increased taxation when the country – or, more correctly, the king – was at war with his enemies. On a number of occasions during the Wars of the Roses the king had no other option but to levy huge taxes upon his subjects in order to pursue warfare at home and abroad. The northern chronicler John Warkworth, writing in the first decade of Edward IV's reign, pondered upon the broken promises of the Yorkist regime, the injustices of the King's military budget and the plight of the common people because of it:

> when King Edward IV reigned, the people looked [forward] to all the aforesaid prosperities and peace, but it came not; but one battle after another and much trouble and great loss of goods, amongst the common people; as first the XV [fifteenth] of all their goods, and then an whole XV, and yet at every battle they had to come far out of their countries [shires] at their own cost; and these and such other things brought England right low.[1]

Other contemporary writers confirm that during the fifteenth century such persistent high taxation contributed to a degree of unrest among the English population, which in turn caused a great number of the more serious revolts against the monarchy. In the reigns of Henry VI and Edward IV these rebellions

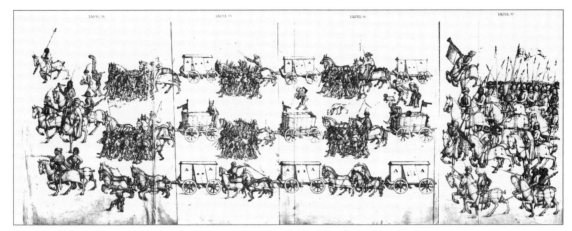

Fifteenth-century army on the march from Das Mittelalterliche Hausbuch *showing contingents of troops marching alongside their wagons of supplies. (Royal Armouries)*

in Kent, Yorkshire, Lincolnshire and elsewhere were deeply rooted; their discontented populations sometimes actually forced pitched battles to be fought because of faction-backed revolt. During the early years of Edward IV's reign the problem of high taxation came to the fore, especially in the years 1461–4 and 1469–71 when increased Lancastrian, then later pro-Warwick, military pressure forced desperate measures upon the King's government to tax the English people in order to finance the Yorkist war effort.

All army commanders, be they kings or rebel nobles, understood the problems that were inherent in supplying food to their soldiers while on campaign. However, this was only one of the many problems faced by commanders in the field. For instance, their soldiers' horses and draught animals had to be provided with fodder while they were on the march; soldiers had to be found suitable camping areas and billets for the night; and in some cases they needed furnishing with other military supplies such as livery jackets, badges, weapons, armour and ammunition when these were deficient. Shortages of any of the more vital supplies, such as food, could spell disaster to commanders when campaigning, but this did not stop leaders from going to war. To minimise the risks of supply problems, therefore, certain personnel were employed to deal with such logistical matters long before the outbreak of the Wars of the Roses, and particularly when English armies fought overseas.

When Edward IV invaded France in 1475 he employed professionals to oversee logistical matters for him. The Controller of the Ordnance, William Rosse, was commissioned to take carpenters, stone cutters, smiths, plumbers, shipwrights, coopers, sawyers, fletchers and other workmen to support the King. Rosse was also responsible for the King's guns, gunpowder, cannon balls, crossbows and bolts, bows and arrows, and arrow and bowstave timber (so that replacement bows and arrows could be made if they were needed). He was also in charge of all English ships of 16 tons or over and all of their crews; clearly Rosse had a job of some importance. Indeed, kings could not do without this kind of organisational backing when on campaign. Rosse's service later led to a more permanent military appointment when he was given charge of all food supplies at Calais, with the title of 'Vitteler of the town of Calais and the March of the same'.[2]

Men such as William Ward and Edmund Gregory ensured that the army of 1475 was well supported with technical know-how. Their engineering skills could be used for supervising the digging of trenches, constructing dykes, building bridges, undermining castle walls, erecting redoubts and providing a host of other military services while the army was in the field. Thirty-five foremen managed such operations under Ward, while the actual manual work was carried out by soldiers and others who were pressed into employment. Ward also superintended the making, collecting and paying for good and sufficient longbows and arrows from the southern shires of England, which must have brought him into contact with William Rosse as the King's Controller of the Ordnance.[3] Even the King's tents had to be looked after and erected in the field each night; in 1475 this task was managed by an indentured retainer of Edward IV called Richard Garnet, who was also expected to fight as 'a man at his spear' for his King if required to do so. In 1475 Garnet had with him 'twenty-four yeomen well and sufficiently habillied, armed and arrayed', not only to help him with the King's tents, but also to fight alongside him on the battlefield. Garnet's appointment as 'Sergeant of the King's Pavilions' dates from July 1461, which probably means that he was employed by the King in this capacity during the Wars of the Roses as well.[4]

All the above positions, and many more besides, had to be financed in some way, along with the vast amounts of material and supplies that were necessary to put an effective army into the field. Army logistics in England during the Wars of the Roses, however, presented new and greater problems. One of the pressures brought about by civil war in England was the need for commanders and their organisers to employ shrewd bargaining methods with their suppliers; at the same time they had to be able to appreciate the importance of precise timing and prompt delivery of goods to the armies that would ultimately fight. This important job fell to the paid bands of victuallers, harbingers and scourers, who were continually about the army's business in the field collecting supplies and scouting ahead of the column. In England such men did not have the luxury of ravaging basic army requirements from enemy territory if stocks ran out: everything necessary for armies that passed through English shires had to be paid for and properly requisitioned.

At the top of the list of financial burdens placed on the king's or nobles' 'purse' in time of war was the payments to his soldiers on campaign. Aside from contracts of indenture for paid and unpaid service, for most soldiers, willingness to fight depended on wages. During Edward IV's 1475 invasion of France the standard payment for English soldiers fighting abroad was as follows:

> Duke, 1 mark per day
> Marquis, 10 shillings per day
> Earl, 6 shillings and 6 pence per day
> Baron, 4 shillings per day

> Knight, 2 shillings per day
> Esquire, 1 shilling per day
> Scourer, 12 pence per day
> Archer, 6 pence per day.[5]

Edward's muster roll provides us with a typical scale of payment for English medieval armies while serving abroad in the late fifteenth century. During the Wars of the Roses, however, other factors applied at home which forced alternative methods of payment and service to be considered by commanders. In exploring these factors, one must be aware that armies during this period were formed and disbanded much more quickly than when English armies fought in France, which forced costs of supply and payments down for army commanders at home.

As we have seen, retainers were not always paid in coin for their services, and communities often paid for their own troops from their own coffers. This did not mean, however, that putting an army into the field during the Wars of the Roses was a relatively simple and cost-effective operation, because food and supplies had to be bought legitimately and not pillaged 'chevauchée style' in England.

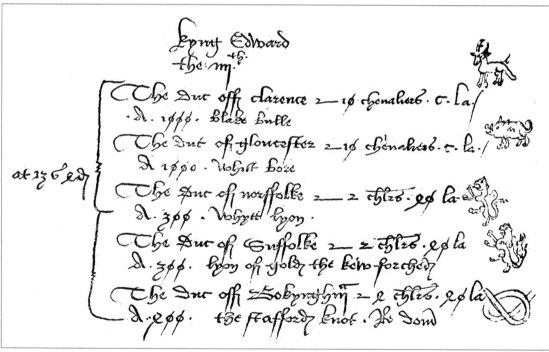

Part of the muster roll of Edward IV's French expedition of 1475. The list is headed by the Duke of Clarence (black bull), followed by the Duke of Gloucester (white boar), the Duke of Norfolk (white lion), the Duke of Suffolk (double-tailed lion), and the Duke of Buckingham (Stafford Knot). (Geoffrey Wheeler)

Such indiscriminate pillaging of the English countryside could, and did, lead to fear and distrust of the army, and adversely affected future recruitment. As pillaging by soldiers was attempted only 'on pain of death', large numbers of carts and oxen carrying food, fodder and supplies were provided for marching armies to minimise such unruly behaviour in the ranks. But because an army's wagons could only carry a very limited amount of supplies while on the march, large sums of money had to be raised through loans and taxes to pay towns and cities for bulk supplies.

What, then, are we to make of a marching and camping Wars of the Roses army? How much did it cost to pay and supply? How many miles could it travel in a day? What occurred when a town was asked to provide supplies to a starving or thirsty army? Where did troops find lodgings for the night? Was all food taken legitimately, or did some scourers and soldiers take what they needed, when they wanted, ignoring the risks and penalties of looting? How were supplies managed in winter, and did some soldiers and animals die on the march before ever reaching the enemy through lack of food, proper tents or insufficient clothing?

As we have seen, an overlord's personal retainers were always in his constant paid and unpaid service; these soldiers were a ready-made source of manpower, without the need for any further expenditure on them in time of war. The retainer's armour and weapons were standard equipment, and were bought, or provided by him personally, as befitting his knightly or gentlemanly status. Mounts were also already in the retainers' stables in expectation of travel, hunting and warfare, primarily because of the retainer's oath to his overlord to 'ride and go' with his master whenever the need arose.[6] Food supplies were not a problem to him either because of his affluent lifestyle: ready money enabled him to purchase goods more easily while the army was on the march. He could also rely on the service of his household servants, who provided for his needs and secured lodging for the night, by paying for the best available billets and field tents or by supplying his own personal camping gear.

The lifestyle of a retainer's tenants in the field was very different, both in financial status and personal comfort. These men formed the bulk of a Wars of the Roses army, and they had to be paid and supplied during their military service from a noble's personal funds with the noble's retainer acting as middleman. Billeting outdoors, without proper tents and in all weathers, was accepted as a fact of everyday army life: it was clearly the common soldier who had to suffer the real hardships of war and stand the sacrificial cost of battle, rather than his employers or paymasters.

As only about 10 per cent of the annual income of nobles went on fees for their retainers,[7] it has been assumed that the numbers of indentured retainers were never very large.[8] This is confirmed by contemporary documents and musters describing the size of a noble's immediate retinue, not including his tenantry. Household retainers were also regulated to a given figure, as detailed in Edward IV's 'Black Book'. The financing of a retainer's tenants for war was a different matter. It is documented, for example, that John Howard, Duke of Norfolk, could call upon 700 tenants from 44 different manors,[9] and if we are able to believe the '2,000 Stafford knot' badges made for the livery jackets of the Duke of

Buckingham's men in anticipation of military action in 1454,[10] then it is clear that substantial funding was required for a retainer's tenants on campaign, to provide both food and basic wages – the all important extra incentive for them to fight well for their masters on the battlefield.

During the Wars of the Roses Edward IV was granted huge sums of money in the form of loans from individuals, gifts from the clergy and taxes levied by Parliament. He received huge loans for the Towton campaign in March 1461, for example, and in the Parliament of 1463, which was prorogued in York on a number of occasions because of Edward's involvement in the North, the King was granted the sum of £37,000 to defend the realm against the Lancastrian army which was then firmly entrenched in the powerful Northumbrian castles.[11] The majority of this money, in two instalments, was to be raised by payment of the last fifteenth and tenth of shires, cities and boroughs, and by all persons receiving above ten shillings a year from their lands or rents (much as the chronicler John Warkworth described, see p. 93 above). People earning below ten shillings per year were exempt from payment providing their goods and chattels were valued below five marks. As the impoverishment of certain localities meant ineffective taxation for war, quite apart from providing the potential for local and national rebellion, the financing of war was an object lesson in accounting and budget management.

An example of the cost of English armies on campaign is given in 1482–83 when Richard Duke of Gloucester raised men for his forthcoming Scottish campaign and rewarded them afterwards for their 'good agreeable service' in the field:

Easter, Anno 22 Ed, IV, To Sir John Elrington, Knight, the King's Treasurer at War, by the hands of Richard, Duke of Gloucester: viz. for the wages of 1,700 fighting men, retained by the said Duke to accompany him in the war against the Scotch; viz. from 11th August until the end of fourteen days the next following – £595.
To Sir John Elrington, Knight, the King's Treasurer at War, in part payment of the wages of 20,000 men-at-arms, going upon a certain expedition with the Duke of Gloucester against the Scots; paid to his own hands – £4,504 11s 8½d.
To the same Treasurer, as a reward given unto divers soldiers, as well in the retinue of the Duke of Gloucester as in the retinue of the Earl of Northumberland and others, for their expenses in going from the town of Berwick to their homes; viz. by the hands of the abovesaid Duke – £350, and by the hands of the aforesaid Earl – £94 13s 6d. And by the hands of John Brown of the kings household 16s, £345 9s 6d.[12]

As always, the strength of this large force is debatable; it has in fact been estimated at only 2,000 men by some historians, only a fraction of the above figure. However, bearing in mind that there was always a much smaller proportion of men-at-arms (retainers) compared with the abundance of tenants required to form Wars of the Roses armies, then we may be sure that the 20,000 additional troops requisitioned by Gloucester were not all men-at-arms, as the letter above suggests, but were tenants carrying longbows and poll-arms, probably in the service of the Earl of Northumberland, who was clearly retained by the Duke of Gloucester at this time. Similarly, the 1,700 men retained by Gloucester cannot all have been men-at-arms either. The above payments are therefore useless in calculating an individual soldier's wages.

Furthermore, Gloucester's 1482–3 Scottish campaigns can be treated in much the same way as any other foreign war: it was quite normal for English soldiers to live off the land in Scotland. In contrast to a Wars of the Roses army fighting in England, foreign war commanders knew that their budget for food and supplies would be extremely low. We must therefore look at different examples to assess the cost of a standard Wars of the Roses soldier.

English towns and cities were expected to finance their own troops in the Wars of the Roses, or to pay a sum of money in lieu of this service to the king. In 1459 the Lancastrians commissioned the Mayor and Sheriffs of Coventry to 'assign and tax what number of able men might be had out of the said city at the costs of the same city to attend upon our sovereign lord's person [Henry VI]', against the Yorkists. The Mayor was compelled to scour Coventry's wards for men to fight, and forty men were sent to join Margaret's army in the Midlands, but no pay is mentioned. However, in April 1470 forty men were again raised at 12*d* a day for a month's service to go with King Edward into the South. Ten wards collected £100 to pay them with, which gives us some idea of a soldier's wages during this

A mail shirt, similar to the type worn by footmen during the Wars of the Roses. (Royal Armouries)

period.[13] The payments made to local soldiers by many other town councils confirm this figure; in the York Civic records, for example, we find the same average cost of waged soldiers in the Wars of the Roses, as well as an indication of how this particular council recruited men within its city limits and paid them for their military service. The resulting small contingent of York men made an attempt to join Richard III's army which was preparing to march out from Leicester in an effort to resist Henry Tudor's invasion force of 1485:

> Friday after the feast of the Assumption etc, that is 19th August, in the third year [of King Richard's reign],
> Wer assembled in the councaill chambere, where and when it was determyned upon the report of John Nicholson, which was commen home from the kinges grace from Beskwod, that 80 men of the citie defensible araiyed, John Hastings gentilman to the mase being capitayn, shuld in all hast possible depart towards the kinges grace for the subduying of his ennemyes forsaid, wheraton evere parish in the citie was sessid as it appereth hereafter. And that eevere sogiour shuld have 10s for ten days being furth 12d by day. And also that the concaill shuld mete at two of the clok at after none the same day at the Guild Hall ther to poynt such personnes as shuld take waiges and therto receve the same.[14]

It is doubtful whether the York militia reached King Richard's Yorkist army in time to fight at the battle of Bosworth on 22 August 1485 unless they were mounted troops. Considering that the rate of pay for a mounted scourer during Edward IV's 1475 invasion of France was also 12d per day, it is clear from this that some kind of standard seems to have been set in the Wars of the Roses for paying certain types of soldiers. The common soldier probably had to pay for his own food out of the daily wages paid to him by the contingent's paymaster, who held on to an agreed amount of money for the duration of his contingent's service. However, this payment only applied to a given period of military service: after this period more money had to be found or soldiers could lawfully leave the army and return home without notice.

The numbers of men who marched off to fight in the Wars of the Roses fluctuated dramatically in civic records, and generally decreased as the wars progressed. For example, the city of York sent 1,000 men to the battle of Towton in 1461, but only 80 men to the battle of Bosworth in 1485, even though Henry VI and Richard III were both well supported politically by the city.[15] Urban troop strengths were not all that dependable during the period, chiefly because of the shrewd and thrifty financing of soldiers by town and city officials. The existence of troop deficiencies in a noble's contingent, through financial and territorial recruitment problems, is one of the reasons why campaigns during Wars of the Roses were generally short-lived. Taking all the wars into account, an average of only twenty-three days in the field can be calculated (see p. 68). Longer campaigns were only possible because of the replenishment, or the efficient 'refreshing', of armies, which enabled them to continue marching or sustain pressure during siege warfare. It was therefore essential that commanders effected swift recruitment and movement during Wars of the Roses campaigns, and that they could refresh their troops while on the march. If this balance of finance, speed and replenishment of supplies was achieved by a commander he could minimise desertions through of lack of pay and victuals.

Commanders who fought in the Wars of the Roses, and especially those who had a limited source of income, knew all too well the financial problems of recruitment. Only the noble's personal household and 'feed' retainers were dependable for an indefinite period of military service, which amounted to a very small nucleus of military support. If his finances dried up because of long drawn out campaigning, a noble could rely neither on his own tenants, nor his own retainers or 'well willers', nor the shire and town militias supplied to him under Commissions of Array, nor even hired mercenaries. Similarly, even the King of England could not count on his own nobles for military support unless they were adequately rewarded for their service. And it was always possible that a retainer's promised troops did not muster, did not fight or deserted him. The retainer was thus a very important pivot on which all military matters impinged. If he failed to bring the required quota of troops he was in breach of his contract and was responsible for breaking his sacred oath of allegiance to his lord. If he succeeded, he could be well rewarded and the Wars of the Roses could continue.

SUPPLIES AND TRANSPORTATION

The author of the fifteenth-century military manual entitled *Knyghthode and Bataile* reminded medieval army commanders of the importance of adequate food supplies for both soldiers and animals while on campaign.

> Have purveyance of forage and victual
> For man and horse; for iron smiteth not
> so sore as hunger doth if food fail.[16]

The warning is obvious: not heeding the warning was an important factor in many of the disastrous marches, lost battles, unprepared armies, short sieges, fainthearted pursuits, army desertions and cases of isolated pillaging that occurred during the Wars of the Roses. We must now explore this issue further. After all, how soldiers coped with food shortages is at the very heart of understanding the morale of an army both when marching and on the battlefield.

The precautions taken against food shortages during military campaigns are frequently documented for earlier medieval armies, such as those that fought in the Hundred Years War. For example, it is recorded that these invading English armies were well supplied with food when they left English ports for the continent, but soldiers were still forced, and indeed encouraged, into pillaging enemy territory to solve food shortage problems. By riding into French-held lands, and by both raiding and laying waste to the countryside as they went, an English *chevauchée* could achieve two important things: first, it could deprive the enemy of its supplies, and second, it could supply itself with what it needed to continue campaigning. In England, of course, this was not the case.

As regards the supply problems faced by larger armies of the period, the Burgundian chronicler Jean de Waurin remarked upon the great number of wagons with victuals (and ordnance) parked in the fields outside the city of London during the first week of March 1461 in preparation for Edward IV's northern campaign against the Lancastrians.[17] The campaign culminated three weeks later at the battle of Towton in what is now North Yorkshire, some 200 miles away from the capital, so it was abundantly clear that before marching off the Yorkist army would need a vast amount of supplies, not only from London but from many other outlying towns and villages around it. Several towns were ordered to support the war effort by sending food and supplies to the city in wagons at the King's request in an effort to make absolutely sure that Edward's army was well sustained during their long march 'to the journey of York'.[18]

Apart from thousands of sheaves of arrows (in themselves a great burden to transport on the march), bowstrings, camping gear, artillery and powder (if we are to believe de Waurin's account), armour and spare weapons, the Yorkist 'quartermasters' had to make sure that more basic supplies were loaded into wagons. These wagons, pulled by teams of oxen and horses, were loaded with food and drink (ale and wine) for the soldiers, and in some cases fodder would be provided for riding retinues. However, if the Yorkists were so well furnished with supplies at the start of the Towton campaign, why does de Waurin state that they were impoverished by the end of it? 'It was so cold with snow and ice,' he reports, 'that it was pitiful to see men and horses suffer, especially as they were badly fed.'[19] The Yorkist line of march northwards illustrates the importance of good logistical planning during Wars of the Roses campaigns.

As was customary in the Wars of the Roses the chief captains of the Yorkist army, in this case the Earl of Warwick and the Duke of Norfolk, had been sent out to recruit troops in their own 'countries' some days before the main body and Lord Fauconberg's vanguard was assembled and ready to leave London for the North (11 March 1461). The Earl of Warwick's recruiting drive probably took him on a western route, through his domains in the West Midlands, to Lichfield, and then to Coventry. An eastward route was then taken towards Doncaster where he hoped to rendezvous with King Edward and the main Yorkist army. The Duke of Norfolk hurried to secure troops and supplies in East Anglia, and after recruiting his men he hoped to link up with all the Yorkist contingents somewhere in Yorkshire, possibly at Pontefract Castle. We can trace these marches because we know that the Earl of Warwick was in possession of the necessary documentation which gave him extensive powers of Commission of Array to muster troops in several English counties to the west and north, and there is also evidence that the Earl was at Coventry by at least the middle of March where he had the Bastard of Exeter tried and executed for his father's death after the battle of Wakefield in December 1460. Norfolk's pool of troops were to the east, and according to more than one chronicle he was badly delayed, resulting in his late arrival at Towton on 29 March 1461.[20] The delay was caused because Norfolk's troops were so dispersed by the Commission of Array to muster troops before the second battle of St Albans on 17 February 1461. Indeed, the *Paston Letters* suggest that it may have taken several days for Norfolk's retainers to re-recruit their men and convince the Duke's 'country' to wage more troops.[21]

Ralph Neville and his twelve children. Traditionally the Nevilles were Wardens of the West March of England, although some members commanded in both the east and west Marches during the Wars of the Roses. (Bibliothèque Nationale)

The vanguard of the Yorkist army was commanded by the experienced sixty-year-old captain Lord Fauconberg. He left London on Wednesday 11 March with approximately 10,000 'footmen' and presumably the cumbersome Yorkist supply and baggage train. Two days later King Edward, with his household men, servants and riding retinue, galloped through London's Bishopgate to follow Fauconberg's vast and unwieldy force with its long line of wagons which were gradually winding their way up the Great North Road.

The Yorkist army must have quickly been struck by the devastation caused by the Lancastrian army which had retreated that way only a few weeks previously. After being denied food and supplies from London, the Lancastrian army, or what was left of it, had been forced into retracing their steps back to York over the same scoured countryside they themselves had burned and pillaged before the second battle of St Albans in February 1461. Devastated crops and butchered herds of animals must have worried the Yorkist commanders considerably, and to counter this problem Edward's army probably turned eastwards along the Cambridge road in order to find better refreshing there.

Even though the Yorkist army carried emergency supplies, it was customary for the army to purchase food and supplies for its soldiers as it went. This was achieved by using its bands of victuallers, harbingers and scourers to alert targeted towns in front of the army's proposed line of march. Moving a Wars of the Roses army was like uprooting the whole population of a large town or city: it was just not possible for an army to transport all its supplies in its wagons. However, the further north the main Yorkist army marched, the less they could rely upon much needed supplies from unfriendly, or already ravaged, areas. Thus the more dependent the Yorkist soldiers became on their own wagons of emergency food supplies.

Oxen were probably butchered and eaten during the sixteen days it took for the Yorkist vanguard to reach Pontefract Castle, but once they arrived in Yorkshire, according to Jean de Waurin, supplies were exhausted, and the bedraggled Yorkist army probably resorted to living off the land, even though pillaging had been warned against on 'pain of death' by Yorkist propaganda. To make matters worse, the Earl of Warwick's contingents (approximately three to five thousand men) had also linked up with King Edward's main army. The Yorkist command now had to act quickly or cope with a gradually deserting and unruly army through lack of food and supplies.

The food shortage problem was compounded by the weather conditions in March 1461, which were miserable, wintry and icy with a whiff of snow in the air. We are also told by both Edward Hall and Jean de Waurin that morale was at a low ebb, especially among the common soldiers. On one occasion they were only persuaded to stay put by some desperate theatrical measures on the part of the Earl of Warwick soon after the surprise skirmish at Ferrybridge on 28 March. His ritual killing of his own horse in front of the Yorkist army symbolised that he for one would not retreat again, as he had been forced to do at the second battle of St Albans a month earlier, and he expected his men to follow suit.[22] The incident shows that from this point on the Yorkist army had to be encouraged, and probably even pushed, up the road towards the Lancastrians at Towton, some eight miles away, at the point of a poll-axe.

After the battle of Ferrybridge the Yorkist army became disjointed as the vanguard pressed on to the village of Saxton; the main Yorkist 'battle' was forced to encamp at Sherburn with what was left of their precious supply wagons. King Edward's large and unwieldy force was very lucky indeed to be thrown into action the next morning at the battle of Towton, because the fighting 'teeth' of the Yorkist army were becoming increasingly dependent on the supplying 'tail'. The Lancastrians had been very unlucky that their plan to harrass and stall the Yorkist army at Ferrybridge did not work better. If Lord Clifford's troops had not been forced to retreat at Ferrybridge then the Lancastrians might have succeeded in causing wholesale desertion in Edward's army, with inevitable and premature defeat to follow.

The difficulties described above were not by any means isolated occurrences during the Wars of the Roses. Soldiers in larger armies could not be trusted to march or pursue enemies without adequate 'refreshing'. In the case of Towton, Yorkist soldiers were more than likely fighting for food and supplies as well as for their lives when they advanced upon the Lancastrians during that fatal Palm Sunday morning in 1461. In other instances armies would not even budge because of a lack of supplies. An anonymous royal servant chronicling the events in March 1470, later known as the Lincolnshire Rebellion, illustrates this problem more clearly. After the rebels were defeated at 'Losecoat Field', Edward IV pursued his brother Clarence and his cousin Warwick northwards towards Yorkshire:

> [King Edward] put his whole host in noble order of battle, advancing his banner to Chesterfield understanding that none other but that they [Clarence and Warwick] should be there, and then their aforeriders were come to Rotherham to take their lodging, therefore the night following he [Edward] came to Rotherham, where he lodged that night, and there he had certain tidings of their departing, and that knowledge had forasmuch as it was thought by his highness, his lords, and other noblemen there being with him, that he might not conveniently proceed with so great a host, for that the said duke and earl, with their fellowship had consumed the vitaile afore him, and the country afore himself was not able to sustain so great a host as the king's highness had with him without new refreshing.[23]

King Edward had to seek better 'refreshing' for his army in the city of York, which aided Clarence and Warwick's escape over the Pennines into Lancashire and then eventually to France and safety. Thus lack of supplies on the march in the end enabled the Kingmaker to enlist further Lancastrian support on the continent and return in triumph to free Henry VI from captivity.

Shortage of food could also affect much smaller forces in the Wars of the Roses. The Duke of York's 'meagre army' of 5,000 men at Wakefield in 1460 used up its food supplies at Sandal Castle during the Christmas period. Foragers were sent out in desperation at the end of December to secure food from the town of Wakefield and the surrounding district, only to be intercepted on their return and attacked in the fields below the castle by a large advancing Lancastrian army commanded by the Duke of Somerset. The Duke of York's attempt to rescue his

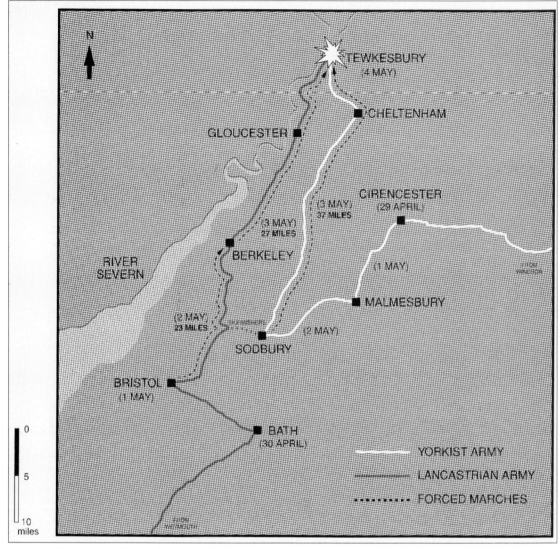

The march to Tewkesbury. (Author)

scourers and their much needed wagons loaded with supplies in the fields below
Sandal Castle resulted in the battle of Wakefield and the death not only of the
Duke but also other members of his family and half of his entire force.[24]

Foraging took time to complete, and, as at Wakefield, it was sometimes costly
and dangerous, and occasionally disastrous. Therefore not only was food
requisitioned legitimately from towns on the march, but also some was carried by
the army itself, that is to say individually by soldiers or pulled in carts and wagons
by draught animals. In Edward IV's 1471 campaign, which culminated in the

battle of Tewkesbury on 4 May, food was available from the Yorkist supply
wagons for emergencies, because there was none in the countryside through
which the Yorkist army was marching. On Friday 3 May 1471 the Yorkist army
was in hot pursuit of the Lancastrians heading for Tewkesbury. The *Arrivall* gives
us a glimpse of a medieval forced march and the hardships of the Yorkist soldiers
who had to endure it:

> and so, in fair array and ordinance, he [Edward] took his way through the
> champagne country, called Cotswold, travelling [with] all his people, whereof
> [there] were more than 3,000 footmen, that Friday, which was a right-an-hot
> day, thirty miles and more; which his people might not find, in all the way,
> horse meat, nor man's meat, nor so much as a drink for their horses, save only a
> little brook, where there was full little relief, [because] it was so soon troubled
> with the carriages that passed [through] it . . . So, continuing that journey he
> came, with all his host, to a village called Cheltenham, but five miles from
> Tewkesbury, where the king had certain knowledge that, but little afore his
> coming there, his enemies were [at] Tewkesbury, and there [they] were taking a
> field, wherein they proposed to abide, and deliver him battle. Whereupon the
> king made no longer tarrying, but a little comforted himself and his people,
> with such meat and drink as he had [caused] to be carried with him, for
> vittaling of his host.[25]

Another three or four miles were covered by the end of that hot day in May,
making a total of well over thirty-five miles in all, until Edward was satisfied he
was close enough to the enemy to make their escape unlikely. The parallel
Lancastrian forced march to Tewkesbury was just as grim and relentless, and by
all accounts it totally exhausted their troops who had passed through 'a fowl
country, all in lanes and stoney ways, betwixt woods, without any good
refreshing'.[26] After completing about thirty-six miles in one day, and at least fifty
miles in the previous thirty-six hours with only one short rest, the Lancastrians
had no other option but to stand and fight the next morning.

The extract above implies that the supply wagons were in front and mixed in
with the Yorkist army, where they unfortunately churned up the various streams
and rivers at the expense of King Edward's thirsty soldiers following on behind
and alongside them. Other contemporary accounts show that this order of march
was a normal occurrence in medieval armies. An illustration in *The Hasbuch*
military handbook shows that the carts and wagons of a fifteenth-century
Burgundian army were also in front of the main column of cavalry and infantry.
Making sure that an army remained in close contact with its supplies was a
constant worry to army commanders and precautions had to be taken to protect
wagons, which were always prone to enemy ambush, loss or damage. Contingents
therefore marched with their own food and supply wagons, with the consequence
that, first, the army was only able to move as fast as its supply wagons, and
secondly, because of this, a screen of scourers and flank guards was essential.

To this end scourers, aforeriders, prickers and spearmen protected a Wars of
the Roses army on the march, while also searching the countryside for additional

food supplies if needed. They reconnoitred the proposed route the army would take and, most important of all, they informed chief captains about the whereabouts of the enemy. Riding into towns and villages before the main army arrived, they could also warn of its approach march and requisition food and supplies to be made available when the army reached its gates. Prime billets within the town could be found and paid for by scourers acting on a noble's behalf, and suitable fields outside the town could be pointed out in advance, enabling soldiers to camp with the minimum amount of confusion, and with the least disruption and annoyance to the inhabitants of the area. As scourers were very important to the army, they were well paid for their services (12d per day – double that of an average footman or longbowman); they were also well appointed with horses, generally better equipped than footmen and consequently jeered at by the common soldier because of such preferment and mobility. In the chronicle normally attributed to William Gregory, while describing the events of February 1461 the author reveals the kind of jealousy that could occur within the ranks: 'As for spearmen they be good to ride before the footmen and eat and drink up their victuals, and many more such pretty things they do, hold me excused though I say the best, for in the footmen is all the trust.'[27]

Scourers did, however, continually let armies down with bad intelligence, as at the second battle of St Albans in 1461, when the Earl of Warwick was left in the dark about the whereabouts of Queen Margaret's army which was then advancing south towards the town, pillaging as it went. Even in the last crucial hours before the battle the Lancastrians' last reported position could not be estimated by Yorkist scourers as being any more accurate than nine miles distant, which in the end proved too vague for Warwick's planned defensive strategy. As a result, the Yorkist line was forced to hold its dispersed battle formation, in order to protect all the various converging routes into St Albans. Warwick's dismal defeat was inevitable.

Although an army's wagons were a great burden on the march, needing constant protection and marshalling on the road, they could also be useful for defence. When arranged into a 'laager' formation by astute commanders, transport vehicles could be used to protect the army when it was encamped; wagons could also provide additional cover for soldiers, or anchor a battleline, on the battlefield. The illustrations in *The Hasbuch* show what could be achieved by dragging carts into a defensive circle to protect a camp. At Blore Heath in 1459 wagons were used to protect the Earl of Salisbury's exposed right flank when it was confronted by a much larger Lancastrian army under the command of Lord Audley.[28]

Immediately after the battle of Blore Heath a similar defensive line was also constructed at Ludford Bridge by the Yorkist commanders, this time with 'guns, carts and stakes' protecting their unsteady and uncertain troops. Other examples of major field fortifications in the Wars of the Roses are recorded at Dartford in 1452, when the Duke of York and the Earl of Salisbury were in charge of operations, and also at Northampton in 1460, when the Duke of Buckingham was in command. All these nobles had seen service in the Hundred Years War: their experience of the defensive tactics used against the French led them to employ similar methods at home during the Wars of the Roses.

A late fifteenth-century medieval camp and wagon laager from Das Mittelalteriche Hausbuch
(Royal Armouries)

When legitimate means of securing food supplies failed in the Wars of the Roses, instances of pillaging inevitably occurred. Bouts of bloodlust also occurred after certain battles. Immediately after the battle of Wakefield in December 1460, for example, Queen Margaret's 'northern army', which then also included some Scottish troops, went on the rampage. They first attacked and sacked the town of Beverley, then advanced south 'like a whirlwind' on a wide front passing through Grantham, Stamford, Peterborough, Dunstable and other towns, pillaging as they went.[29] The fear and panic recorded by contemporary chroniclers suggests that this Lancastrian *chevauchée* was unusual in England at this time, especially on such a large scale and in the southern part of the country. In this case, others who were not associated with the Lancastrian army had joined in with the looting, which contributed to the scarcity of food and supplies in the Lancastrian army. Food supplies were so bad, in fact, that Lancastrian emissaries had to be sent to

London in an effort to requisition supplies in the name of the king: 'And the Mayor ordained both bread and victuals to be sent unto the queen, and a certain sum of money withal. But when the men of London and commons found out that the carts should go to the queen, they took the carts and departed the bread and victuals amongst the commons.'[30]

The Earl of Warwick's propaganda of early 1461 had been aimed at alienating the advancing Lancastrian army and undermining its attempts at recruitment, but the panic caused by this propaganda in southern England was to have a far-reaching effect. Warwick's propaganda campaign may have been the saviour of London, but it was also responsible for causing an irreparable north–south divide which led to the South fighting the North of England at Towton on 29 March. Widespread scaremongering flung the Lancastrian army into even more disarray than it had been in before the second battle of St Albans, and consequently into retreat and more pillaging on its way back to Yorkshire. Even though the Lord Mayor of London himself had ordered the refreshing of the Queen's army, then encamped near Dunstable, the Londoners themselves would have none of it. They knew that if they had been more sympathetic towards the Queen's northern army, then the Lancastrian rampage would have continued uncontrollably through the streets of London. The idea of Scottish troops in the capital was unthinkable; Queen Margaret was well aware of this, which is why she decided to keep her army well out of the city in the first instance while she negotiated for food and supplies to be brought out to it in wagons. Lancastrian victory, and Henry VI's reinstatement as a puppet monarch, was always going to be just beyond the Queen's reach as long as she had a supply problem and a renegade element in her starving army.

Alcohol was a major factor in the bad discipline and pillaging by soldiers during the Wars of the Roses. Excessive drunken behaviour occurred after both battles of St Albans in 1455 and 1461, for example. But the common soldier's preoccupation with ale and wine in the medieval period was no different from that of any other era: it was how soldiers dealt with danger and fear. However, even after the 'non battle' of Ludford Bridge in 1459, where no blood was spilt, we hear of a serious breach of discipline in Henry VI's Lancastrian army, as well as a 'minority's' drunken behaviour in Ludlow, the Duke of York's lordship in the Welsh Marches: 'The misrule of the king's gallants at Ludlow, when they had drunk enough wine that was in taverns and in other places, they full ungodly smote out the heads of the pipes and hogs-heads of wine, that men went wet-shod in wine, and then they robbed the town, and bare away bedding, cloth, and other stuff, and defouled many women.'[31]

The sack of Ludlow in 1459, St Albans in 1455 and 1461, Beverley, Grantham, Stamford, Peterborough and Dunstable in 1461, Tadcaster in 1487, and all the other less well documented incidents of drink-related violence, theft and in some cases rape during the Wars of the Roses, indicate clearly that commanders had serious problems controlling their soldiers' behaviour when they were near centres of population. Ale and wine was consumed daily by soldiers, and therefore carried with the army while it was on the march. Most armies and contingents got a good send-off with alcohol, and it was also given copiously before battle commenced. Beverley's contingents in 1460–61 were given alcohol free of charge as an incentive to go and fight for the Queen, and Coventry's troops in 1470 got 16*d* each for their service, a gallon of wine and 6*d* worth of ale, which had to be carried in wagons along with everything else the army needed.[32] Contemporary chronicles tell us that soldiers invariably drank to the very limit and extent of their supplies before going into action; alcohol, and the supply of it, was therefore crucial to a soldier's morale.[33]

All these supplies, and many more besides, had to be transported along with a Wars of the Roses army. Many historians have consequently tried to calculate the length of medieval baggage trains, and work out how fast (or how slowly) an army must have travelled because of such transport restrictions. There are simply too many variables, however, for anything other than conjecture: the weather and road conditions which prevailed at the time; the speed differences of certain draught animals and their actual physical condition; whether troops were mounted or unmounted; the size of the army; how much food, drink and fodder an army might consume over a certain period of time; how much of this was actually carried on transport, and what proportion was carried by the soldiers themselves. Edward IV's army of 'footmen' during his Tewkesbury campaign was able to cover more than thirty-five miles in one day, even in very hot weather, whereas the average speed of a medieval army on the march was more like fifteen miles per day.

A Wars of the Roses soldier was expected to carry his own gear and equipment on the march: this included his own rations of food and drink for the day, his personal weapons, enough ammunition (forty-eight arrows, if he was an archer) to fight immediately if necessary, possibly his own rudimentary camping gear or blanket slung over his shoulder, and any other spare armour he had with him as well. This would amount to a lot less than the sixty pounds or so carried by an average infantryman today on campaign. Mounted troops, including many longbowmen who rode with the army, could carry far more weight with greater ease, and move faster (as they were required to do on occasion).

The baggage train was responsible for carrying an army's extra weight. Each contingent would have had its own wagon, loaded with spare arrows (several hundred per wagon), spare bows, bowstrings and weapons, the armour worn by the contingent's captains and men-at-arms in battle (not usually worn on the march unless battle was imminent), the contingent's own food supplies for a limited period of time, barrels of wine and ale for its soldiers, and lastly tents, including camping gear, for the more well-to-do. The king and his nobles had many more wagons in order to transport their tents, pavilions, desks, chairs, armour, food, drink and valuables. The king also had an array of secretaries, helpers and servants to cater for his every wish and personal well-being on the march.

The long lines of vehicles needed to transport all these goods on campaign can only be imagined. The resulting column could be as much as a day's march from head to tail. Therefore a commander had to act quickly and decisively during a campaign and he must have tried to keep army supply wagons to a bare minimum.

ARMY CAMPS AND BILLETING FACILITIES

On 5 June 1487 Henry VII at the head of a large army confronted the Earl of Lincoln's rebels who were advancing south in support of a Yorkist pretender. A herald or pursuivant to the king's court gives the following report of Henry's tentative and troublesome march towards his enemies who were eventually brought to battle at Stoke Field some days later. The various places where Henry's army pitched camp are described in some detail, the condition and morale of the King's soldiers are referred to, and a host of other issues are documented.

> From Coventry the king removed to Leicester, where, by the commandment of the most reverend father in God the Archbishop of Canterbury [Dr Morton], then Chancellor of England, the king's proclamations were put in execution, and in especial voiding common women and vagabonds [who were then mixed in with the army], for there were imprisoned a great number of both, wherefore there was more rest in the king's host, and the better rule. And on the morrow, which was on the Monday, the king left there the aforesaid reverend father in God and rode to Loughborough, and the said Lord Chancellor's folks [the Archbishop's contingent] was committed to his nephew, Robert Morton, unto the standard of the Earl of Oxford in the foreward.

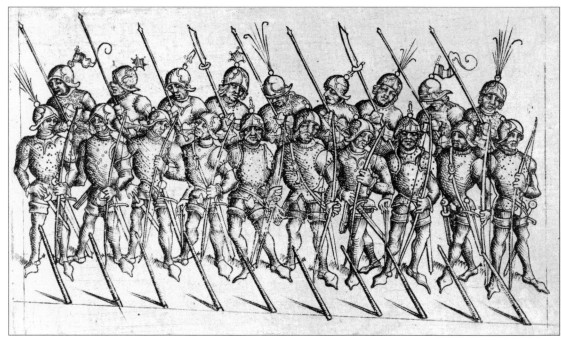

'A bow and a bill at his back'. Fifteenth-century Burgundian soldiers in sallets and brigandines positioned behind stakes as illustrated in the Bartsch Chronicle. (Graphische Sammlung, Austria)

Henry rid himself of even more of these so-called 'common women and vagabonds' which had been drawn into his army at Loughborough by putting them into the stocks and in the prisons there, and on Tuesday he had his force encamp in the open near a wood called Bolney Rice, but on Wednesday, while advancing towards Nottingham, the King had further problems to contend with: 'on the Wednesday the king's marshals and harbingers of his host did not so well their diligence that way, for when the king removed there was no proper ground appointed where the king's host should lodge that night then following'.

However, according to the herald's report it was a fine night and the army wandered about searching for a place to camp until they came to 'a fair long hill, where the king set his folks in array of battle, that is to say, a bow and a bill at his back', obviously for protection against the Earl of Lincoln's still unlocated army. The King then left his vanguard at the hill, which was close to Nottingham, and rode with a 'battle' of his army a further three miles to a village where he lodged in a 'gentleman's place'. His soldiers encamped near the village and in a 'bean field' close by. Henry's army was now split into two battles separated by three miles, and to make matters worse, rumours were rife that the King had fled. The next day the King reappeared to hear Mass in a nearby church. He then made another bad decision, to compound the rumours that had been spreading through the army:

> the king, not letting his host to understand his intent, rode backward to see, and also welcome the Lord Strange, which brought him a great host . . . and all were fair embattled, which unknown returning to his host, caused many folks to marvel. Also the king's standard and much carriage followed after the king, unto the time the king was advertised by Garter king of arms, whom the king commanded to turn them all again, which so did them all in battle on the hither side of the great hill on this side of Nottingham, unto the time the king came.

After Lord Strange and his contingents had been amalgamated into Henry's main battle, this force was turned around by the King and marched back to encamp for the night in different locations near Nottingham. That night 'the king's host lay under the end of that hill toward Nottingham to Lenton ward, and his foreward before him to Nottingham bridge ward. And the Earl of Derby's host on the king's left hand to the meadows beside Lenton.' It is not surprising that during this evening and the next day there was a certain amount of unease and confusion in the Tudor army with regard to the King's intentions. Some of the royal army actually deserted, which forced the King to array his 'true men' quickly as a deterrent to any further action of this kind. Henry was very lucky indeed that his whole army did not desert him, especially later that day when word came of the rebel advance. In fact many more 'cowards', to use the herald's words, fled after the King's army had encamped at Radcliffe, nine miles from Newark, the following day.

Apparently undaunted by the problems that were rife in his army, and unaware that his own actions had contributed to his soldiers' distrust of him, on Saturday the King heard two Masses and found some trustworthy men of the district to show him the best way to approach Newark. Even now, at this late stage in the campaign, it seems that the King and his captains still had no idea of the exact location of the Earl of Lincoln's army, but from this point on hired guides with their local knowledge seem to have helped the King's forces considerably:

> they knew well the country, and showed where marshes and where was the river of Trent, and where were villages or groves for bushments, or straight ways, that the king might conduct his host the better. Of which guides the king gave two to the Earl of Oxford to conduct the foreward, and the remnant retained at his pleasure. And so in good order and array, before nine of the clock, beside a village called Stoke, a large mile out of Newark, his foreward reconnoitred his enemies and rebels, where by the help of Almighty God, he had the victory.[34]

The herald's report goes some way towards explaining the problems involved in moving large armies from camp to camp during the Wars of the Roses. Over a space of only a few days in the summer of 1487 Henry VII experienced at first hand the trouble that camp followers could cause medieval armies, what confusion could result from split forces, how unconcentrated troops could breed discontent in armies, what dangers could arise from the surprise arrival of new forces, the inconveniences of badly reconnoitred objectives, and above all, how unreliable communications and planning could be during a campaign. The King compounded the problem by showing himself to be an absent and unsure commander, so it is hardly surprising that morale was affected and troops deserted. If these problems could occur over a campaign of only a few days, what dangers beset armies that were in the field for many weeks?

The billeting of soldiers in the Wars of the Roses is often taken for granted by historians, but contemporary evidence proves quite conclusively that proper camping and billeting played an important part in many of the military campaigns of the conflict. For example, sieges could be very short affairs if proper tents and camping facilities were not provided, especially when attacking soldiers experienced harsh winter campaigning, as the Earl of Warwick's men did before Alnwick in January 1463.[35] If suitable areas for army camps could not be found by harbingers on the march, lost time, indecision and anxiety could have a disastrous effect on troops before an important battle commenced. Immediately before the battle of Edgecote in 1469, for example, a quarrel over billeting arrangements affected the Yorkist army's performance on the field of battle:

> there was a great insurrection in Yorkshire, of divers knights, squires, and commoners, to the number of 20,000; and Sir William Conyers knight was their captain, which called himself Robin of Redesdale; and against them rose, by the kings commandment, Lord Herbert Earl of Pembroke with 14,000 of Welshmen, the best in Wales, and Humphrey Stafford [Earl of Devon], with 7,000 archers of the west country; and as they went together to meet the northmen at a town [Banbury], they fell in a variance for their lodging, and so the Earl of Devonshire departed from the Earl of Pembroke with all his men.[36]

Hearne's Fragment provides us with more details regarding this strange disagreement over billeting conditions at Banbury, by stating that it was the quarrelsome 'harbingers' of these two allied forces that actually forced the issue, which then escalated into a more serious problem between two major nobles when they quarrelled over their lodging.[37] As a result of a simple dispute between the two Yorkist forces, the Earl of Pembroke's forces were not only instantly deprived of numbers, but more important, they had suddenly lost their valuable complement of archers. When Redesdale's army finally encountered only Pembroke's Welsh contingents at Edgecote the following day, the result was always in doubt for the Yorkists. During the subsequent battle they were shot to pieces by far superior northern fire power, and the campaign fell in favour of the chief instigator of Redesdale's rebellion, the Earl of Warwick. This victory enabled Warwick to isolate Edward IV and temporarily imprison him. Clearly, the harbingers' role in a Wars of the Roses army was so important that any bad planning or complacency on their part could affect army unity in the field.

Armies were kept on a short leash during the Wars of the Roses. Discipline was difficult to maintain at the best of times, even in a partially unified army with a common cause to uphold. For this reason, most army commanders on campaign tried to billet their soldiers outside towns and cities, in an effort to keep them well away from the temptations of inns and taverns. Soldiers could easily melt away into the streets, or even overrun a whole township, if let loose in a drunken stupor. Commanders therefore tried to make sure that scourers and harbingers selected good and strategic places to camp, where trouble might then be kept to a minimum.

Contemporary chronicles document that before most battles of the period soldiers were billeted well away from areas of population. At Ludford in 1459 the Duke of York's troops pitched their defensive camp some distance away from Ludlow in the fields beyond the bridge over the River Teme. When the Lancastrians fortified their camp at Northampton in 1460 they did so across the River Nene close to Delapré Abbey, and the Yorkist army at Wakefield selected the area around Sandal Castle for their billets rather than the town itself. In 1461 the Yorkists, under the Earl of Warwick, chose to fortify and camp in areas north of St Albans to await the arrival of Queen Margaret's 'hordes' from the north. A large triangular piece of land at Bubwith Heath near Pontefract on the Knottingly road was chosen by the Yorkist commanders in March 1461 before encountering the Lancastrians at the battles of Ferrybridge and Towton. Later in the wars the Earl of Warwick's army was kept in check at Hadley Green, half a mile outside Barnet in 1471, where Edward 'would not suffer one man [of his army] to abide in the same town, but had them all to the field with him, and drew towards his enemies, without the town'.[38] The *Arrivall* also describes many instances in the Tewkesbury campaign where King Edward marched his men through towns, and had his soldiers encamp away from urban areas to speed up his various forced marches. In the same campaign Margaret's army eventually camped in 'The Gastons' to the south of Tewkesbury where the following day they were defeated by Edward's forces. Similarly, in the campaign that ended with the battle of Stoke in June 1487, Henry VII was very keen on keeping his troops well outside Nottingham and other towns, so as not to interfere with urban life and detract from his still uncertain kingship.

'The Infantry Tent'. A stylised depiction of army life in the Bartsch Chronicle, which was far removed from reality. (Bibliothèque Nationale)

When troops were billeted in towns and cities there was always trouble. Rival contingents tended to engaged in gang warfare and paraded their allegiance to a particular noble to the full, using their uniform livery jackets as symbols of power and affiliation. London saw this to a greater extent than any other place, when rival factions were at court or were summoned to Parliament. In the years leading up to the outbreak of the wars, and later the civil war which was to escalate in 1458, billets in London were positioned well apart to avert trouble, and watches had to be continually kept on soldiers until the charade known as Love Day was over and the contending factions dispersed to their own territories.[39]

Armies and supplies were mustered outside major towns and cities such as London, York, Coventry and Leicester both to minimise confusion and to facilitate the marshalling and ordering of various troop contingents when they arrived. St John's Field, for example, outside the City of London, was used for this purpose throughout the Wars of the Roses. In 1461 Edward IV mustered his contingents 'outside the town wall' at Hereford before encountering the Welsh Lancastrian army at the battle of Mortimers Cross.[40] Army mobilisation also depended on contingents arriving at a specific destination which was usually mentioned in signet letters from the king to his nobles, and consequently a noble to his retainers, depending on the urgency of the campaign he was involved in. Thus the commander could march and encamp with a relatively small body of men, wagons and supplies, while his other captains recruited simultaneously along the way according to their own particular status and troop strengths. While on the march, therefore, an army encampment might not be very large; in fact many Wars of the Roses armies were probably in a state of flux for many days until the main mustering point was reached and the army was finally amalgamated for concerted action.

We can see this process in operation on numerous occasions during the Wars of the Roses, for example when the Duke of Norfolk was ordered to come to the aid of Richard III in 1485 against Henry Tudor. As we have seen, Norfolk wrote to Sir John Paston, his retainer, to bring his men to Bury St Edmunds, the East Anglian mustering point, as quickly as possible. From here Norfolk's troops, minus Paston's contingent who did not reply to the summons, were marched to Leicester where further contingents from London, York, Nottingham and elsewhere were finally concentrated after all mustering separately in their own local districts. The whole Yorkist army was therefore only fully encamped at Leicester, and later at Sutton Cheney near Bosworth, for the minimum amount of time.

To come to a specific mustering point at the last possible moment was the best way to conserve supplies, deflect trouble in the ranks, avoid sprawling camps with burdensome camp followers, prevent large-scale desertions from occurring, and above all create speed when armies marched off again. These precautions did, of course, run the risk of affecting army unity by creating unfamiliar and separate contingents of soldiers. This in turn could cause treachery in the face of the enemy, and generally lead to confusion on the battlefield. If an army did not 'shake down' together in some small way before battle commenced then its contingents were bound to fight in an insular fashion; they would not maintain any cohesion with the rest of the army; they would only fight well at the side of men they knew and trusted; they would be wary of others because of treachery; and soldiers would separate and form small pockets of resistance under their own respective banners on the battlefield. This happened to a greater or lesser extent in all the battles of the Wars of the Roses.

CHAPTER 5

'With jacks and sallets clean'

DEFENSIVE PROTECTION AND OFFENSIVE WEAPONS OF THE WARS OF THE ROSES

So far we have seen how the Wars of the Roses soldier was recruited locally, we have followed his march to a particular destination, we have documented his arrival at various mustering points and camps along the way, and we have appreciated that his eventual amalgamation within a particular noble's contingent was a crucial part of a faction-based army. We have also established that a soldier's

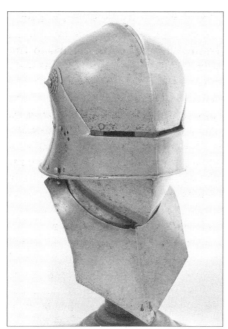

Sallet and bevor, German, c. 1480. (Royal Armouries)

service was at the behest of a certain knight, or noble, who in turn fulfilled similar obligations towards his king, or towards a leading peer whom he supported, and that both the structure of bastard feudalism and the accessibility of troops through Commissions of Array made all this possible. Proper funding and good planning oiled the wheels of such delicate military machinery. However, once an army was committed to battle, a soldier's fighting ability became the main factor working for success or failure.

The medieval soldier needed to have confidence in the protection afforded to his body. If blows to his frame could be deflected, or dulled in some way, then he might be able to strike back at his attacker. Vital organs were obviously the most vulnerable parts of a soldier's anatomy if he was attacked, but a soldier's head and limbs were just as important as, if not more important than, his torso when it came to being incapacitated by various medieval weapons. The head, arms and legs of a soldier were in fact the most exposed areas in an attack because, in the majority of cases, a soldier was not able to kill his opponent outright with one blow, without using his weapon to disable him first. The limbs and head of a common footman were also prone to being pierced by arrows, considering the vast amount of missiles launched in consecutive volleys during a battle. However, during the brutal hand-to-hand combat which inevitably followed the arrow storm, the medieval soldier gained a great advantage over his adversary if he was able to inflict head wounds, or hook his opponent to the ground by his legs. Thus it was the limbs, especially the legs and the head, of a soldier that were targeted first, with a view to moving in on the vital organs once an opponent was concussed or immobilised on the ground. That is, of course, if there was enough time to do this.

Armour underwent a number of significant changes during the medieval period; by the late fifteenth century the making of plate armour had become a fine art, while also providing the wearer with a great deal of protection against most offensive weapons. A complete 'harness', as it was called, could be very expensive, but this high cost was certainly not measured in weight of metal. In fact, a full harness was certainly lighter, plate for plate, in the Wars of the Roses than its much heavier predecessors. This was primarily because the metal from which armour was constructed was being better forged, and also because once made, it was distributed more evenly over the body of the wearer than it had ever been before. Consequently, the better quality and placement of armour offered even greater protection to a soldier's anatomy, chiefly because of the addition of special built-in, curved, reinforced and fluted design features which not only helped strengthen armour, but also helped deflect offensive weapons away from the surface of the metal and thus away from the body. With regard to the protection afforded to the chest and back of a soldier, the breastplate had been complemented by a backplate at the beginning of the fifteenth century, and the gorget neck plate, or plates, had been superseded by the bevor in the Wars of the Roses to complete the full harness by protecting these previously vulnerable areas of the body. Medieval armour was also designed at this time to be more flexible, so as to allow more unrestricted movement – the main advantage to a medieval knight who might be fighting in a close-quarter mêlée. Finally, the general increase in armoured plates now meant that the knight was beginning to be totally encased in metal, which inevitably boosted his confidence on the battlefield.[1]

As one might expect from any important military innovation in any era, these enhancements in full plate armour made some old ideas of defensive protection obsolete. In the second half of the fifteenth century the knight, or man-at-arms, opted to discard his trusty 'heater' shield, which was previously only deemed necessary for defence when overall plate armour was lacking. Subsequently it was only used by him at the tourney or when other ceremonial occasions dictated. Only the more common footman now used the medieval shield as part of his own personal defensive equipment. His buckler, as it was called, was small, round in shape and could easily be slung from a belt, sword hilt or strap around the soldier's waist.

A further reason for the absence of the traditional heraldic shield on the battlefields of the Wars of the Roses was the nature of the weapons the knight used against his opponents' similar armoured protection. During this period, the armoured knight generally chose to dismount to fight his battles on foot; he also began to favour a two-handed approach to warfare in order to compete with the common footsoldier who carried similar two-handed shafted weapons such as the bill and the glaive. Further, the knight required a very heavy, powerful and well-designed two-handed shafted weapon to compete with the better metallic qualities and design features of the armour then being manufactured. With such weapons as the poll-axe, for example, he was able to crush the outer casing of an opponent's body armour and thereby fracture the bone and tissue beneath. The weight of the poll-axe could also distort armour plate to such an extent that it could force a joint to seize up and thereby physically incapacitate an opponent's arm or leg encased beneath it. Consequently, the shield became an encumbrance to this two-handed approach to warfare and it soon became redundant on the battlefield. From this point on the knight became increasingly dependent on his personal weapons, his household men and his own suit of armour for protection and survival in combat conditions.

In the clattering hell of thousands of falling arrows the armoured knight was generally safe in his *cap-à-pie* from long-distance shooting, unless he was very unfortunate and happened to catch a falling arrow, or an incoming crossbow bolt, between an unprotected joint in his armour. However, at short range he was not so invulnerable, and when advancing to close with the enemy, longbow arrows and especially crossbow bolts could actually penetrate armour plate at distances of up to eighty yards, if the trajectory was at a right angle to the surface of the metal.[2] If artillery or handguns were levelled at the man in armour, then the physical damage, and the effect on morale, were considerably greater. Nothing could withstand this power; when firearms became more commonplace on the battlefield they made the knight's presence obsolete amid the gunpowder clouds of sixteenth-century Renaissance warfare.

However, in the Wars of the Roses it was the lesser armoured footman who experienced a great disadvantage against the much improved armoured protection of the medieval knight and his heavy weapons. Nobles and knights on foot were obviously targeted for plunder – which was one of the main reasons why the common soldier fought in the first place. Only if they became isolated from their household men could wealthy nobles and gentry be sought out, outnumbered and pulled to the ground. If the armoured man could be restrained by others, even while still standing upright, then he could be attacked with greater ease through the visor of his helmet, or through the joints in his armour.

Contrary to popular opinion, various different armours from all medieval periods were worn by soldiers during the Wars of the Roses. It would be wrong to think that all knights, and some of the more affluent footmen, could afford the new fashionable designs. Therefore soldiers who participated in the Wars of the Roses equipped themselves with what armour they could lay their hands on – that is, if it was still serviceable or readily available from a noble's limited stocks. We can see this in documents where a soldier's name and equipment is recorded, such

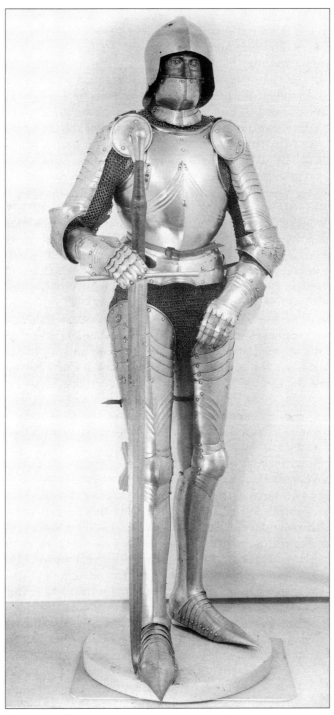

Composite 'Gothic' armour and an example of a two-handed sword of the mid- and late fifteenth century. (Royal Armouries)

as the Bridport muster roll.[3] From such evidence we discover the common soldier was not 'armed to the teeth' or so well equipped for battle as we might imagine, because his personal military equipment had to be either supplemented by others of his contingent or supplied by his immediate superiors. Most of the higher classes, however, invested in the most up to date and expensive styles of full harness from established armourers in Italy, Germany and the Netherlands. These new styles can be seen in existing 'composite' Gothic and Milanese armours of the fifteenth century.[4] With the addition of the gorget plate or plates, the backplate and the later introduction of the bevor and mail standard, such armours afforded much improved overall protection. However, the piece of armour most commonly associated with the Wars of the Roses soldier by the mid-fifteenth century was a new and more fashionable helmet called the sallet (see p. 129 below).

Footmen wore any type of plate armour and mail they could afford to buy, procure in some way, or strip from the dead on the battlefield. Armour was also passed down from father to son; various different types of harness and part-harness are mentioned in contemporary wills, mainly because of the value attached to such family heirlooms in terms of both money and prestige. However, as these pieces had obviously to be of the right shape and proportions to fit the wearer, leg harness, gauntlets, breastplates and every conceivable piece of the full suit of armour was altered, and in some cases 'mixed and matched' by soldiers, to complement any other defensive protection they had. This ad hoc acquisition of armour made the partially armoured, or badly equipped, soldier very vulnerable on the battlefield. Contemporary documents recording town, city and shire militias show quite clearly that some armour had been outgrown, was not serviceable or was badly out of date; some of it was not even owned by the stated individuals when districts were tested by commissioners for effective recruitment and the quick mobilisation of the shire levy.

Out of all the padded or 'soft' defences worn by the Wars of the Roses soldier the brigandine (a medieval form of the modern flak jacket) and the jack (a much lighter and more quilted version of the former) became the more common forms of upper body protection that were used during this period by footmen. Mail shirts and the more antiquated longer hauberk or harbergeon were also still worn by soldiers during the Wars of the Roses, as they had been for centuries before, and according to contemporary illustrations all the above might be worn in composite layers for added protection on the battlefield. Such protective overgarments as the jack and the brigandine could provide very effective defence against certain attack weapons, including even arrows, at extreme range. They also could afford some degree of protection against glancing strokes to the torso from many hand-to-hand weapons that were used at close range. However, serious damage and penetration could still result from a well-aimed blow, and the legs and arms of a soldier were generally not well protected by such garments.

Excavations carried out on medieval war graves, such as those at Wisby in Sweden and more recently at Towton in North Yorkshire, have shown that cuts and punctures to the skull (Towton) and cuts and fractures to the arms and legs of soldiers (Wisby) were the most common form of discernible battlefield injury, although in many more cases individuals must have died in battle as a result of various internal wounds caused by weapon thrusts to the abdomen, neck and groin, where wounds are not as apparent when examining skeletal remains alone. The horrific blows and punctures to the skulls of the unfortunate soldiers who took part in both the battle of Towton and the battle of Wisby pose many questions as to how well armoured the head of a common soldier actually was in battle.[5] It is inconceivable that soldiers of this period ventured into battle without some form of head protection, and therefore we may conclude that injury was sustained to the skull area because of the much documented, and frequent, removal of headgear in battle, the discarding and loss of helmets in the rout, the penetration power of medieval weapons and arrows, and also because of the forced removal by an opponent during hand-to-hand combat.

Protection from missile attack in medieval warfare called for a scaled up version of the shield to be used by those foot soldiers who needed greater protection than most. The 'pavise', for example, had been in use for a number of years for defensive purposes, especially by soldiers who were engaged in siege warfare, but this larger type of shield became particularly associated with the mercenary crossbowman during the fifteenth century. The pavise provided the crossbowman with a useful, and simply erected, defence behind which to crouch while he attempted to reload his weapon by the time-consuming windlass method. Mercenary handgunners and artillerymen also found a good use for pavises, while loading and shooting their innovative and temperamental gunpowder weapons.[6]

Much larger forms of defensive cover had been in use for many centuries, and long before the Wars of the Roses began, especially when armies were heavily involved in siege warfare; there were many forms of siege engines and wheeled mantlets with shooting windows, for example, which could be dragged into position before fortified buildings and castle ramparts to protect attacking soldiers from incoming volleys of arrows. Similarly, trenches and artillery emplacements with wooden palings and protective swinging mantlets had been in use for many years and would continue to be employed when armies were 'dug in' during the Wars of the Roses. Purpose-built

Footman's pavise, used chiefly by crossbowmen, but of the type mentioned several times in the Bridport Muster Roll of 1457. (Geoffrey Wheeler)

defences such as lattices, caltrops and spiked pavises were also used to protect vulnerable gaps between 'battles' in conjunction with many other innovative defensive measures which could be brought into place as and when the situation dictated the use of cover.[7]

Longbowmen still hammered their trusty six foot wooden stakes into the ground in front of them for added protection against any pre-emptive cavalry attack, and special redoubts were constructed by engineers with artillery positions to help protect exposed armies in the field. These fortifications, often with carts and wagons filling in the gaps between earthworks and stakes, formed quite formidable barriers against advancing armies, and were impenetrable when used in conjunction with artillery. The field defences at Dartford (1450), Ludford Bridge (1459) and Northampton (1460) were all constructed under the watchful eye of veteran commanders; all largely succeeded, but for the chance intervention of other external circumstances which rendered them useless.[8]

The defence of castles became a prime concern to both York and Lancaster during the northern border war of 1461–64, and in the Welsh and Calais Marches it was much the same story when the key to a important military area rested on its primary fortifications. However, this increased military activity in the Marches did not cause a revival in castle building on a grand scale during the Wars of the Roses. Defences were strengthened and added to, certainly, with towers and curtain walls, for example, but fifteenth-century nobles and gentry were more content to build themselves a private residence, or fortified manor house, rather than a castle in the traditional style that could withstand enemy bombardment from heavy siege cannon. Formidable northern castles such as Alnwick, Dunstanborough and Bamburgh fell repeatedly to sieges between the years 1461 and 1464, but only one (Bamburgh) was 'slighted' badly by heavy artillery fire, thereby forcing its defenders into submission. The other strongholds were either taken by starvation or as a result of long-drawn-out sieges, not to mention all forms of deception and treachery by defenders and attackers alike. More provincial castles such as Caister in Norfolk, for example, also became targets for attack during the period, but chiefly because of local and family feuding.

The defences of cities, towns, castles and even fortified manor houses provided some degree of welcome refuge for nobles and their soldiers, before they were able to fully concentrate their armies or put them into the field; similarly they afforded the inhabitants of towns and cities some degree of protection against contending parties who might try to force an entry for a particular strategic or political reason. The City of London was called upon many times to resist military operations, rebellion and general unrest in the Wars of the Roses, which ultimately focused on the heavily fortified Tower of London. The Tower, and indeed the city walls and defences of the capital, withstood three separate sieges in all between 1452 and 1471, which were repulsed for a variety of different reasons by the Tower garrison and in some cases by troops specially recruited for the purpose of protecting the capital. In 1460 Lord Scales captured the Tower of London and fired on the besieging Yorkist army then embattled on the outskirts of the city, to the extent that 'wildfire' and cannon balls overshot and fell among the streets and houses killing many citizens in the process.[9]

However, the amount of time, money and trouble it could take to carry out major siege operations, for what was often too limited a gain, was discouraging to astute commanders; thus other strategic and political methods were sought out to force the issue. The Wars of the Roses were primarily wars of movement, and as we have seen, speed was the crucial element to successful campaigning. Time and time again we read in contemporary accounts of castles and city walls being sought out to provide protection, and even a brief respite, when forces were under-strength, but only a limited amount of troops could benefit from this safe haven, especially when the associated problems of billeting soldiers in towns are taken into consideration. Castles were not generally equipped to house large armies behind their curtain walls, so camps were erected outside these buildings, and also beyond the urban population areas which provided them with food and supplies. As has been described, most commanders took great care to summon their contingents at the last possible moment, and in most cases mustered their troops on the march, to avoid being surprised when encamped in the field without adequate defence measures.

THE MAN-AT-ARMS AND HIS EQUIPMENT

As has been briefly described, by the beginning of the fifteenth century armour had reached a significant turning point in its development, chiefly because of new manufacturing techniques. 'White armour', as it became known, was being made from better quality iron and steel, and as a direct result of a new forging and carbonising process, which produced steel with a much higher carbon content, armour was generally far tougher and more resilient to the power of offensive weapons than it had ever been before. The later development of the blast furnace for mass production and the advantages realised in the processes of heating and quenching metals added greatly to this resilience, which was consequently to have a drastic effect on all armours and weapons of the period.[10]

During the fifteenth century tournament armour was much heavier than war armour, making it cumbersome and restrictive, mainly because of the greater protection a wearer needed during the 'controlled fight' which was such a feature of the chivalric displays of the period. War armour, however, had to be far more functional: it had to provide greater mobility to the man-at-arms on the battlefield, as well as giving him a certain amount of protection. A man-at-arms had, among other things, to be able to fight, mount his horse (unaided) and, to a certain extent, live in his armour while in close proximity to the enemy. The massive helms and additional heavy plates, lances and other accoutrements needed for the tournament were not worn or used on Wars of the Roses battlefields because of their great weight and restrictive nature. Indeed, even the more articulated and lighter war armours that were worn in the Wars of the Roses were heavy and restrictive enough to force individuals to discard certain items of the full harness as battles progressed.

Whether the man-at-arms was preparing for battle or the tournament he would require the help of his squire to put on his harness. This process of arming is typically illustrated and documented in a contemporary English manuscript

Holb a man schal be armyd at his ese
whan he schal fighte on foote

He schal haue noo schirte vp on him but a
dowbelet of ffustean lynyd with satene cutte
full of hoolis. the dowbelet muste be strongeli bounde
there the poynttis muste be sette aboute the greet of the
arme. and the b ste before and beshynde and the gussen
tis of mayle muste be sowid vn to the dowbelet in
the bought of the arme. and vndir the arme the ar
mynge poynttis muste be made of fyne twyne suche
as men make strynggis for crosseboives and they

*'How a man shall be armed at his ease when he shall fight on foot.' (The Pierpont Morgan
Library, New York, M. 775, f. 122v. Photograph: David A. Loggie)*

entitled 'How a man shall be armed when he shall fight on foot', where armour, dating from around 1480, is briefly described and depicted in an unusually dissembled form. First, the man-at-arms was fitted with his arming doublet, which was worn under his armour. This form of doublet had replaced the earlier medieval aketon, and it is particularly interesting how this, and the accompanying hose and shoes of the man-at-arms, are described by the writer of the manuscript:

> [the man-at-arms] shall have no shirt up upon him, but a doublet of fustian lined with satin cut full of holes [for ventilation]. The doublet must be strongly bound there, the points must be set about the bend of the arm and the rest before and behind, and the gussets of mail must be sewn on to the doublet in the bow of the arm and under the arm. The arming points must be made of fine twine such as men make strings for crossbows and they must be twisted small and [be] pointed as points. Also they must be waxed with cordwinder's cord and then they will neither stretch nor break. Also a pair of hose of (stamin sengill?) and a pair of short bulwarks of thin blanket to put about the knees for chaffing of his lions. Also a pair of shoes of thick cordwine and they must be fret with small whipcord, three knots upon a cord and three cords must be fast sewn onto the heel of the shoe, and fine cords in the middle of the sole of the same shoe, and that there be between the frets of the heel and the frets of the middle of the shoe the space of three fingers.[11]

The gussets of mail mentioned above were pre-sewn onto the arming doublet and were strategically placed at the most vulnerable and exposed parts of the body (i.e. the insides of the arms, at the elbows, armpit and sides of the upper body) where metal joints in the armour were not practical as they would restrict movement in battle. As the writer points out, the fifteenth-century arming doublet had strong wax cords attached to it (arming points) so that all the separate plates of armour might be secured by these, especially on those parts of the body where gravity, movement and the natural inclination of the human frame would have forced such plates to simply slip off. The typically English mail standing collar (standard) was also worn on, or sometimes attached to, the arming doublet for added neck protection, and as described above the man-at-arms would have then put on a heavily padded hose, without the addition of any mail gussets or arming laces, primarily to stop armour from chaffing the skin in these vulnerable areas of the body. Lastly leather shoes, with further cord laces, would have been put on his feet, and mail covers (mail sabatons) were strapped over these, and to the greaves, by the means of further laces attached to this and the leather under-shoe.

Articulated plate shoes (sabatons) were then attached to the man-at-arms' feet and clipped onto his greaves, and then the greaves (or jambs), which were made in two halves and hinged vertically, were attached and buckled to the lower half of his legs, completely encasing his shins and calves. The upper legs were protected by the cuisses, which were specially reinforced at the front, and extended only to the top of the thigh. These were then attached to his legs in a similar fashion to the greaves by buckles and straps, although unlike the greaves the cuisse did not always encase all the upper leg area at the back, and thus in some armours left the rear of the thigh highly vulnerable to weapon attack. Knee pieces with shaped wings (poleyns) then covered the gap between these upper and lower leg defences which were attached to the greaves and cuisse by means of rivets or turning pins.

The man-at-arms was then fitted with a pair of mail shorts (fauld) which protected his backside and genitalia. Alternatively a mail skirt or corset covering his thighs could be worn. The main body armour, which was hinged vertically at one side, consisted of both breastplate, lower breastplate (plackart) and backplates, metal skirt and tassets. This was then put on and buckled at the side and over the shoulders. The tassets, which hung from straps on the metal skirt, partly protected the more exposed areas of the lower body at the front, side and sometimes the back of the dismounted man-at-arms, and could be buckled to the lower half of the skirt, or alternatively, in the English fashion, halfway up it. However, for obvious reasons, it is clear that this lower part of the body was far more open to weapon attack than anywhere else, especially in the groin and bowel regions which were only covered by various layers of mail and cloth. (Weapons specifically designed to cause maximum injury by gaining entry through these exposed gaps in the lower body armour will be described later.) Armourers had to take into consideration the mobility and practicality of armour while aiming at maximum protection. A man-at-arms had to be able to mount and sit on his warhorse, for instance (removing his rear tassets in this case), he had to be able to move freely at the waist when swinging his weapons in battle, and he had to be able to bend, get up if knocked down, run if the need arose and even relieve himself when nature called. All these functions would have been restrictive in the extreme if steel had been introduced to these areas of field armour, so compromises had to be made at the expense of a certain amount of exposure to danger on the battlefield.

The plate armour which encased the knight's arms was put on next. First the vambrace, enclosing the whole of the lower portion (cannon) of the arm was tied and buckled onto the arming doublet by means of laces, then the upper plate (rerebrace), similarly enclosing the arm completely, was also tied and buckled into position. The angled elbow-cop (cowter) was buckled and attached by laces over these two pieces, and then the shoulder guards (pauldrons) were strapped on and tied to the top of the shoulders and arms, both front and back. Lastly the gauntlets, covering hands, wrists and cuffs, were fitted over the vambrace; with the added protection of mail mittens these sections of the armour gave protection to the arms and hands, although again the joints, and more particularly the knight's armpits, were still exposed to a certain extent, with only the arming doublet's mail gussets providing some minimal degree of protection. Because this was another vulnerable entry point which could be exploited by an opponent's offensive weapons, the left pauldron was made slightly larger than the right for added protection in combat. However, this extended pauldron was only fitted when the knight was mounted or participating in a tournament, and, more precisely, when using his lance in the couched position. When dismounted on the battlefield, both the right and left pauldrons were made symmetrical, thus leaving both armpits slightly exposed to attack. An opponent's weapon striking the left pauldron while the man-at-arms was using his own weapon in a right-handed or two-handed fashion, could more often than not be parried effectively by the surface of the curved metal plate, but both armpits were still largely exposed to danger underneath the pauldron if the man-at-arms could be disarmed or brought to the ground in some way. The knight was therefore prone to injury from various weapons through holes in his armour; the correct weapon could pierce into his chest cavity, lungs and even into the heart region itself.

The last piece of armour to be put on by the man-at-arms was his helmet, or more commonly in the Wars of the Roses, his sallet and bevor (mentonièrre), which when worn together covered the lower part of his face, the front part of his neck and completely enclosed his skull. Alternatively the armet could be worn, which covered the whole of his head and neck, at the expense of greater discomfort in battle. The sallet consisted of a rounded metal skull, curving in and out again at the nape of the neck to form a small tail, and as it only afforded protection to the head and upper part of the face, a bevor was usually worn with this in battle (see illustration on p. 118). Sallets were generally made from a single piece of iron with holes pierced on a line corresponding to the wearer's skull for attaching a lining. Rivets fixed the lining into position, but a padded arming cap was invariably worn under this, to help reduce impact blows and also prevent the chafing of the head in battle.

Armet of the type worn by some soldiers during the Wars of the Roses. (Royal Armouries)

There was a distinct difference between the Italian and German styles of sallet, as there was with the body armours of the period, in that the Italian style sallet was hemispherical, with a comb, the tail continuing the line of the skull. In the Wars of the Roses the tail was sometimes made of one or two lames (pieces) on loose rivets, fixed by pivots to the lower edge of the skull, and about this period a brow reinforce was also attached to the helmet for added protection. The German style sallet had a slightly flattened skull with a well-defined comb ending in a straight line over the brow. The tail was very pronounced and sloped outwards, while the sides of the skull, continuing the line of the tail, extended to cover the face to the chin. An eye slit with ridged edges was made in these much deepened skulls for greater visibility, and both styles of helmet were secured to the head by means of a strap buckled around the chin. The second half of the fifteenth century saw the introduction of the visored sallet with single or double eye slits, a modification of the Italian style which gave it more the appearance of the German version.

The bevor consisted of two or three plates, shaped to the contours of the face, which were joined together by pivoting rivets. The lower plate was shaped to the chin and extended to an elongated V-shaped plate at the front which was attached to the breastplate with a lock or with a leather strap and buckle. In the case of the armet, the more conventional bevor, which was used with the sallet, was replaced by very wide cheek pieces hinged along the skull of the helmet, while the lower edges were protected by either a gorget plate, mail standard or a metal wrapper. The armet was made up of skull, full visor, cheek pieces and rondel to protect the vulnerable areas at the back of the head, and a brow reinforce which was riveted to the skull. The armet was generally ogival or rounded in shape with a keel, but no comb, and it had the usual holes around the helmet in order to attach a lining to its interior. Both sallet and armet had a keyhole at the top of the ridge in the helmet where insignia could be located, and it is generally assumed that this was the only way of identifying knights in battle during the Wars of the Roses because the tabard or jacket, bearing the heraldic achievements of an individual, was not always worn over field armour.

Helmets, and in most cases the bevors that accompanied them, were extremely claustrophobic and uncomfortable when worn in battle, due both to the physical build-up of heat and perspiration which was generated while an individual was fighting, and also because of the psychological effect of the severe lack of all-round visibility. The main frustrating feature of these types of helmet was that both the sallet and the armet had very narrow eye slits and it is because of this that helmets were only put on, and visors closed, at the very last possible moment before battle commenced. Various examples of individuals being killed or injured when not wearing their helmets are recorded in contemporary accounts. Sallets were occasionally put on too late to prevent injury, and in some instances knights had to be reminded by their squires to apply their bevors. Helmets sometimes simply slipped off while fighting, bevors were purposely taken off because of severe chafing of the neck, and sallets were removed because of sheer discomfort when the need for air and water during the fight became too much to bear. The day before the battle of Towton John, Lord Clifford, was killed outright by a

Yorkist arrow because he had removed his gorget. The chronicler Edward Hall gives the details of this incident when Clifford and his contingent:

> met with some that they looked not for, and were attrapped before they were aware. For the Lord Clifford, either from heat or pain, put off his gorget, was suddenly hit by an arrow, as some say, without a head and was stricken in the throat, and rendered up his spirit. And the Earl of Westmoreland's brother and almost all his company were slain, at a place called Dintingdale, not far from Towton.[12]

Also at the battle of Towton, it is reported that Lord Dacre removed his helmet out of sheer exhaustion to drink a cup of wine, and was killed when an arrow struck him in the head.[13] Burgundian knights were renowned for leaving off their bevors in battle; in 1452 we hear that Cornelius, the son of Charles the Bold, was killed by a pike thrust in the face when he failed to wear his bevor with his sallet. Charles himself was wounded in the throat by a sword cut under similar circumstances at the battle of Montl'héry thirteen years later, when his sallet simply slipped off because of perspiration or because it had not been fastened on properly earlier that morning.[14] Such instances reveal that during a battle there was often a harsh choice between exposure to danger on one hand or death from exhaustion and dehydration on the other.

The cost of armour in the fifteenth century is recorded in various documents of the period and, as one would expect, transactions were regularly made between English knights and well-known armourers on the continent. In 1473 Sir John Paston received a letter from an armourer called Martin Rondelle in Bruges who signed himself 'Armurier de Monsire le Bastart de Bourgogne'. Paston was interested in purchasing a 'complete harness' from Rondelle, and more precisely a helmet, described as a barbuta (a conical-shaped helmet with a T-shaped opening), which was in fact far more commonly worn abroad at this time in countries that had warmer climates than England. Sizes had to be given so that Paston's armourer could work out an accurate price, but it is not known whether the sale took place.[15] However, in 1483 Lord Howard paid six shillings and fourpence to an armourer in Flanders just for his leg harness, which leads us to speculate on the cost of a full suit of armour which was fitted to precision and made to appeal to the most expensive tastes.[16]

Complete plate armours for men–at–arms were on the whole very expensive, and could be priced at as much as £33. In 1441 Sir John de Cressy of Northamptonshire bought a group of armours, probably for himself, his squire and his retainer John Savile. A complete Milanese armour cost him £8 6s 8d; the squire's armour cost him £5 16s 8d; and Sir John Savile's harness cost £6. Further purchases are recorded in the accounts of Nicholas Howard of Stoke by Nayland. In 1463–9 he paid £3 6s 8d for a complete harness, sallet and greaves; £6 16s 8d for a complete harness with an ostrich feather (presumably for the top of his helmet); and £6 13s 4d for two other harnesses.[17] Clearly different qualities of armour are indicated here, with possible reductions for more than one order. When compared to the 6d a day earned by an archer during the Wars of the Roses, we can see that the repercussions of such lost or damaged equipment in a battle were significant.

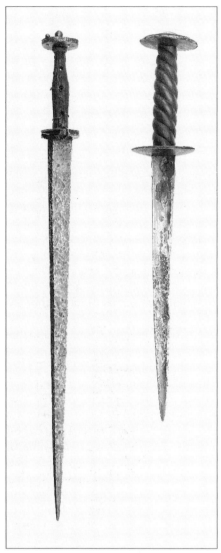

Two rondel daggers, possibly English, of the early fifteenth century. (Royal Armouries)

The knight's sword during the fifteenth century was still the popular dual-purpose cut-and-thrust version which varied from the very broad and rather short (28 inch) sword with single-handed hilt, to the narrower and longer (40 inch) long-hilt version which could be used with one or two hands (the bastard sword, or hand and a half sword). Purely thrusting swords were also used extensively during the Wars of the Roses; these were made with long narrow blades and long hilts. These weapons were provided with a blunt edge (ricasso) which was located 6 inches from the crossguard so that the blade could be gripped there by the left hand when the sword was being used at very close quarters. Crossguards were made straight, or curved inwards towards the blade, or sometimes formed a shallow S-shape, and once placed in the scabbard, which might be fitted with pockets near the top for both an eating knife and a steel for sharpening the weapon, the sword was slung from a hip-belt which took on a fashionable Y-shape. The lower part of the belt was attached to the scabbard about a foot from the top, which made it hang with the point a little to the rear to prevent the owner from tripping over it, and a dagger was slung from another belt at the opposite side of the hip to complement the knight's side arms.[18]

The preferred military weapon for exploiting gaps in armour was the dagger, and in the Wars of the Roses the man-at-arms equipped himself with a version known as the rondel dagger. It had a disc-shaped guard in front of the hilt and either a conical or a wheel-shaped pommel similar to the guard at the front, set on to the end of the grip. The rondel's distinctive hilt was accompanied by a straight slender blade which was triangular in shape for the purpose of stabbing rather than cutting. This type of dagger was usually very long, up to 15 inches in length, for maximum penetration of an opponent's body. Like the swords that accompanied them, the knight's dagger was sometimes very decorative for use both on and off the battlefield, using gilt, bronze, silver and even gold in its ornamental design work as befitting the status of its owner. (The swords and daggers used by the rank and file, which were very different from these more expensive versions, will be discussed later.)

Apart from the other one- and two-handed weapons that the man-at-arms might use in combat, the two-handed poll-axe was probably the most formidable 'knightly' weapon used on the Wars of the Roses battlefield. The word 'poll', meaning head, was used to refer to other similar shafted weapons of this period, such as the much longer bill and glaive. The word poll implies that these more common weapons could be head-counted; it has nothing to do with the long 'pole' which carried the head of the weapon itself.

The poll-axe was an extremely powerful weapon indeed, which was capable of inflicting immense damage upon the human body, even when the target was encased in full armour. Featured at the head of the shaft of the weapon, which was between four and six feet in length, was a vicious spike for thrusting at an opponent's body defences or joints in his armour, and at either side of this was both an axe-head and hammer, or alternatively a fluke (crow's beak) and hammer, for cutting, puncturing or delivering crushing blows to the body. An attacker's weapon could

A fine example of a fifteenth-century European poll-axe. (Royal Armouries)

also be parried by the shaft of the poll-axe which was protected from damage by two riveted metal flanges on either side of its wooden pole; on some designs a protective metal plate was added to deflect blows away from the hands which was similar to, but smaller than, that found on lances of the period. The poll-axe could also be used to hook an opponent to the ground, and it usually had a spiked metal end for stabbing, but above all, a full downward swinging blow could prove fatal to an individual on the receiving end of it. If not, then the damage caused to armoured joints, causing them to seize up, not to mention the effects of shock and concussion on an opponent's body when he received a blow, would result in giving an attacker a clear advantage over his enemy, whereby he could inflict further damage to his victim while he was immobilised or concussed on the ground. If the enemy was unprotected by armour then the poll-axe could be absolutely devastating in close combat. In these circumstances the trained knight with his poll-axe was quite capable of cutting a clear path of advance whereby he might not only survive the battle, but also more easily distinguish himself on the field in full view of his superiors.

Various examples of single-handed weapons survive to give us an indication that one's style of fighting was a purely individual choice, and a matter of taste, especially for the knightly classes. According to the contemporary poem 'The Ballad of Bosworth Field', during his last charge at Bosworth, Richard III carried a battle-axe into combat and not only killed Henry VII's standard bearer with it, but also unhorsed the formidable knight Sir John Cheyney before he was outflanked by his enemies and tipped out of the saddle when his horse floundered in the marsh.[19] Battle-axes, war hammers and maces were all in constant use during the Wars of the Roses, though unlike the poll weapon, which was only used when fighting on foot, all the above seem to have been primarily used on horseback (or as a mark of command on foot), in a one-handed fashion, the other hand being used to hold a horse's reins. The iron head of the war hammer closely resembled the head of the poll-axe, but it had no spike at the base of the shaft, and the axe head was replaced with a serrated hammer and fluke. A war hammer of this period might weigh only about two to five pounds and the mace was similar in weight, but the latter had a completely different head, which comprised either six interlocking serrated metal edges with spikes or a diamond-shaped multi-faced version of this. It could also be a host of other richly ornamented shapes and sizes which were generally individual and hence made to order.

On horseback the armoured knight demanded the full attention of all around him. Richard III's last charge down the slope of Ambien Hill accompanied by his household men must have been a sight to inspire the admiration of even the most treacherous of his subjects; it also proves that cavalry charges were still contemplated on the Wars of the Roses battlefield in desperate situations. Although English knights more often than not fought on foot during this period, we do know from contemporary sources of isolated incidents when cavalry were used to deliver 'shock' to the enemy for a variety of reasons, for example at Blore Heath (1459), Towton (1461) and Tewkesbury (1471). If placed well away from longbowmen, or if cavalry could charge when archers were already committed to the confusion of hand to hand combat, then a spirited cavalry attack could turn a battle upside down.

In the early fifteenth century the knight's war horse had been extremely vulnerable to arrow wounds, chiefly because of the lack of protection afforded to it by the material and leather caparisons that covered the horse's flanks, chest and rump. This lack of protection drastically changed for the better during the Wars of the Roses, and nobles who could afford the luxury of the 'barded' horse realised that greater protection against missile attack could bring about something of a resurgence in the much-beloved cavalry tactics of the previous century. The knight's war horse, which was usually a breed like the courser or destrier, could be covered with head protection, articulated neck harness with moveable lames, rump and chest protection. Even a horse's reins could be armour-plated to avoid enemies being able to sever them, thereby sending the horse out of control. With a special area set aside

Gothic armour for man and horse, German, c. 1480. (Royal Armouries)

in the horse's armour so that the spur could be inserted, the knight sat bolt upright in the much improved medieval saddle which, along with longer stirrups, angled his legs obliquely forward for greater support against collision and impact. Weighing as much as 333 pounds, fully armoured cavalry were in the minority during the Wars of the Roses, hence their limited use on the battlefield in large detachments. Expensively armoured mounts were owned only by the aristocracy, and were usually left tethered together behind the lines while their owners fought on foot with their household men in the front line. In short, the upper classes used their horses only for riding to the field, for better communication on the battlefield and, if they could, for escaping quickly in the event of a rout.[20]

A more important tactical advantage could be gained by deploying lightly armoured cavalry on the battlefield, loosely termed 'spears' or 'scourers' during the Wars of the Roses. These could be called upon to swiftly engage the flanks of the enemy, their riders wielding 15 foot lances. The 'spear' could be used most effectively against confused or crowded infantry who might be caught in a vulnerable position. Scourers – the mounted troops used in medieval armies for work on the march, such as flanking columns of infantry, scouting and foraging for supplies – have already been described. Fast, light and highly manoeuvrable, they were also used on the battlefield; in such battles as Towton, Barnet, Tewkesbury and at many others that are unrecorded, these soldiers had great success. At Barnet, for instance, Yorkist 'aforeriders' chased the Earl of Warwick's forces out of the town, and at Tewkesbury a contingent of 'spears' helped deliver a significant surprise blow to the Duke of Somerset's 'battle' when it was caught at a grave disadvantage. At Towton in 1461 they may even have routed a portion of the Yorkist left flank.

Wearing kettle helmets and various other forms of lighter body armour such as brigandines and jacks, the scourer was in fact a mounted infantryman of the better sort, sometimes equipped with leg harness and bits and pieces of the full suit of armour. Although various illustrations of the period show that light cavalry could be equipped with breastplates or plackarts and a lance, the light cavalryman could have far less protection than this; so much so, in fact, that only his job distinguished him from the more common footman or archer who could also ride to the battlefield on horseback, but ultimately fought there on foot. As the chronicler Gregory recorded, 'spearmen be good to ride before the footmen and eat and drink up their victuals' but he adds wryly 'in the footmen is all the trust'.[21] It was the thousands of footmen heavily involved in close-quarter fighting that characterised battles in the Wars of the Roses.

BOWS AND BILLS

The Italian writer Dominic Mancini made these observations on the northern and Welsh levies that had been recruited into Yorkist ranks by Richard Duke of Gloucester and the Duke of Buckingham when they arrived in London in 1483:

There is hardly any without a helmet, and none without bows and arrows; their bows and arrows are thicker and longer than those used by other nations, just as their bodies are stronger than other peoples', for they seem to have hands and arms of iron. The range of their bows is no less than that of our arbalests; there hangs by the side of each a sword no less long than ours, but heavy and thick as well. The sword is always accompanied by an iron shield . . . They do not wear any metal armour on their breast nor any other part of their body, except for the better sort who have breastplates and suits of armour. Indeed, the common soldiery have more comfortable tunics that reach down below the loins and are stuffed with tow or some other material. They say that the softer the tunics the better do they withstand the blows of arrows and swords, and besides that in summer they are lighter and in winter more serviceable than iron.[22]

In the absence of any other detailed evidence in contemporary letters or chronicles, this description of the arms and equipment of the more common Wars of the Roses soldier has become exemplary. All of the footmen, according to Mancini, possessed a helmet, a longbow and arrows, a sword, an iron shield (buckler) and a jack as standard equipment; according to contemporary musters, however, this was far from the case for all soldiers in the Wars of the Roses.

There is no doubt that Mancini actually described the men that he saw in London in 1483, and that he saw a generally well equipped Wars of the Roses soldier with a longbow as a main weapon. However, no plate armour was worn anywhere on the soldiers' bodies, except for on the head, and although the typical English protective jack is worn, which Mancini describes as being extremely tough and resilient against most weapons, the amount of protection they gave against the weapons used in close-quarter combat was limited. The defensive plate armour of the man-at-arms and his equipment gave him a marked superiority in close combat over the common footman, and a longer life expectancy on the battlefield.

The troops mustered by Gloucester and Buckingham in 1483 were predominantly northern and Welsh soldiers; can we therefore say that there were regional differences in weapons and equipment in England at this time? Further, where did the average billman fit into this equation, as Mancini's description suggests that only longbowmen were present in Gloucester and Buckingham's army? Were any bills used in the conflict, or any other weapons and poll-arms, such as the halberd and the pike, which were chiefly regarded as continental or Scottish weapons? Certainly, the number of soldiers who used the longbow as their main weapon during this period varied according to region, and, contrary to popular opinion, they were on the decline when compared with the number of archers mustered in the Hundred Years War.

We need also to examine not only the type of armour worn, but also how much it cost and who paid for it, and how widely was the livery jacket and its accompanying badge used in the Wars of the Roses? How many of these jackets were actually issued to common soldiers, and how many livery badges were worn without a livery jacket for short-term use? The issue of identification on the battlefield, when both sides more or less had the same equipment and wore the same clothing, is an important one.

The haphazard nature of recruitment in the Wars of the Roses has already been discussed. The speed of recruiting an army in this period had a direct influence on the quality, quantity and actual composition of a specific noble, town or shire's contingent. In emergency, without sufficient warning from commissioners, for instance, some contingents were bound to contain fewer men, or men who were badly equipped for warfare and therefore of limited use on the battlefield. Even specially raised forces were sometimes ill-equipped for war either because of recruiting problems or disunity in the ranks: the 'naked' Irish contingents at the battle of Stoke in 1487, for example, or the absence of archers and levies in King Henry's ranks at the battle St Albans in 1455.[23] Although an imbalance in weapon types might, to some degree, be redressed by a noble or town being able to supply limited private stocks of arms and armour for their troops, it is clear that most

A detail from 'The Martyrdom of St Ursula' by Hans Memlin showing an
infantryman wearing a jack with sleeves, c. 1468. (Royal Armouries)

men were expected to provide their own equipment as set down by Commissions of Array, and this is recorded in detail in local muster rolls. For example, in the Bridport muster of 1457, some men were absent from duty and most were ill-equipped, because more equipment was ordered to be made or procured by one means or another. The Ewelme muster also provides evidence of a badly equipped force, and the existence of 'naked men' in more than one army suggests pressed service.[24]

It is therefore a mistake to say that all common soldiers looked the same on the battlefields of the Wars of the Roses, equipped with jack, sallet, longbow and arrows, sword and dagger, livery jacket and buckler. Some contingents may have been very well equipped with duplicate sets of arms and armour, and some must have contained veteran soldiers who were hardened fighters, because they lived under the constant threat of border warfare, or had been previously involved in the Hundred Years War with France. To generalise is to be ignorant of the individual, his locality, his preferred weapon and his acquired armoured protection, not to mention the territorial and national differences that existed both between local contingents and even whole armies during the Wars of the Roses.

In common with all fifteenth-century men during this period, the medieval soldier wore shirt, doublet, woollen hose and boots as standard everyday clothes. The mail shirt or padded jack must have been the most common military possessions, although mail was certainly the more expensive of the two to make, and hence to acquire. Mail-making was an art form in itself, and thus it needed a professional craftsman to make it. Although no original tools survive, it is assumed that soft drawn iron wire was wrapped around an iron mandrel and was cut into links with a cold chisel. A simple punch and former may have been used to form the rings, another tool would be used to simultaneously flatten and shape the ends of each link, then a third tool would be used to pierce each link with a slot. Wedge-shaped rivets, facing outwards when closed, joined the links together when four of these rings were inserted through every one. This complex manufacturing process was complete when all these links were interlocked in the pattern of a garment which covered the whole of the upper body, the top part of the arms and the thighs. The soldier must have carried about 20 pounds of weight on his shoulders, comprised of approximately 30,000 links of iron.[25]

Gussets of mail, similar to those fastened onto the knight's arming doublet, could also be worn on the more exposed areas of the body instead of the full mail shirt. These mail pieces could be purchased at lower cost and had the added advantage of weighing less, but obviously did not give the same amount of protection as the more complete garment. Mail breeches might also cover the soldier's lower body and crotch area in the absence of any other thigh or lower body protection, and the typically English mail standard with all-round neck protection would give the common soldier a certain amount of defence against weapons aimed at his throat. However, as all forms of mail could be penetrated by arrows and crossbow bolts, as well as by other spiked poll weapons with any impetus behind them, mail shirts, gussets and standards were usually complemented by a padded jack or, for the more affluent soldier, a brigandine, which then formed several layers of protection, as well as keeping him warm in cold weather.

The English jack was a thick multi-layered garment which was made of linen folds stuffed with tow, wool or some other similar soft material so as to give it a quilted or padded look. According to Dominic Mancini, the soldiers he saw in 1483 boasted that the softer a jack was, the better it could withstand weapons, which presumably included arrows at long range. Therefore, as standard issue, these were probably the most typical protective overgarments worn by common soldiers during the Wars of the Roses. The more usual style of jack was fastened at the front with cord laces which were simply tied together, and the garment is sometimes depicted as having sleeves in it which were secured to the body of the coat in much the same way, using further cords at the shoulders to hold the arm pieces in position. Unlike the brigandine, however, the jack is always shown and described in contemporary manuscripts and accounts (including that of Dominic Mancini) as covering the thighs.

The household accounts of John Howard, Duke of Norfolk (1462–71) describe quite precisely that a soldier's jack was made out of eighteen folds of white fustian cloth and four folds of linen, which when stitched and sandwiched together would be made up into about thirty layers of material, one on top of the other.[26] Jacks were also made to order, and also modified, sometimes to include an inlaid layer of horn, or to incorporate metal plates which were secured by studs into the folds of cloth. Even mail was occasionally used to stuff the folds out, so as to give the wearer even better armoured protection at the cost of a much heavier jacket. However, these variants of the jack appear to be far nearer the description of the brigandine than the much lighter, and certainly more padded, common infantry jacket that was generally worn during this period.

Unlike jacks, brigandines were not only much heavier, but were also more expensive and therefore worn extensively by the higher classes of soldier, sometimes in preference to full armour, breastplates or plackarts. In the Howard accounts we read of brigandines costing as much as 16 shillings and 8 pence, which means that only the better off soldiers were able to afford them. Even more expensive brigandines were produced for the aristocracy, and were given by them to their followers in the form of gifts, which, when covered with costly materials such as velvet and studded with gilt nails (rivets), would command a great price.[27] It was therefore probably a noble's personal following and his retainers who wore this type of body armour under their livery jackets, and certainly large stocks of brigandines were always present in the personal armouries of the more affluent members of society. At his death John de Vere, Earl of Oxford, had the following in his 'armoury house': '175 sallets, 101 brigandines, 77 pairs of splints [leg harness], 16 corsets, 84 pairs of mail gussets [for the arms], 18 gorgets, 24 aprons of mail, 120 halberds, 140 bills, 120 bows'.[28] This list not only gives us some indication of the equipment that was available in a leading noble's stockpile, but also allows us to approximate how many men this noble could arm at a moment's notice as his personal household troops.

The brigandine itself was normally constructed of small rectangular lames of metal arranged in vertical strips which overlapped each other like roof tiles. These were then mounted on a supporting cloth or hide backing in parallel rows. The metal plates were attached to this backing by rivets whose heads were left visible outside the garment; other much larger L-shaped plates were occasionally inserted to protect the lungs and other vital organs. This defensive construction was then sewn onto the inside of a quilted jacket which gave it its final shape and distinctive studded appearance. Brigandines provided excellent protection against arrows; according to contemporary evidence they had to be literally smashed through, or broken up, by weapons at close quarters in order to inflict damage to the body.[29]

Thus we have good reason to question the defensive qualities of the more common footman's 'armour', the padded jack, and to conclude that a veneer of padding and mail, or mail and studded plates, would have provided the Wars of the Roses soldier with a good amount of body protection against the effects of the longbow at extreme distance. In addition, other areas of the soldiers' anatomy were left uncovered, and the legs and arms of a soldier were

Typical forms of 'acquired' protection used by a footman during the Wars of the Roses. Kettle hat, Italian (Milanese), c. 1480; bevor, Spanish late fifteenth century; brigandine, German, c. 1440–50; gauntlets, Spanish, c. 1470. (Royal Armouries)

generally exposed to the impact of various weapons. However, it is the vulnerability of the head that now concerns us.

The word sallet was used in the fifteenth century as a general word to describe the great variety of different styles of helmet that were worn by soldiers at the time. These ranged from the more expensive sallet with visor, which was worn by the higher classes and is described in detail above, through to the type known as the kettle helmet, and even described the less expensive simple skull cap derivative which was worn more by the rank and file of this period. The contemporary chronicler and soldier John Harding used jacks and sallets to stand for all the soldiers' equipment:

> In every shire, with jacks and sallets clean misrule
> doth rise and maketh neighbours war.[30]

Sallets are depicted in most illustrated fifteenth-century manuscripts as having a visor, even when worn by longbowmen. We should remember, however, that medieval illustrators were not depicting real life so much as

A scene from the famous 'Beauchamp Pageant' depicting longbowmen, crossbowmen and cavalrymen of the fifteenth century. Note the English longbowmen (left), wearing simple visorless sallets. (British Library)

generalizing the armour and weaponry of the period. In attempting to depict all classes of soldier at once, the amount of full armour used was grossly overstated. In fact, the rapid shooting of the English longbowman (now proved to be ten to fifteen arrows per minute) must have meant that a visorless helmet would have been preferred by archers, not only because it meant that a longbowman could view his target properly, but also so that he did not snag his bowstring on his raised visor when fully drawing it back towards his ear. The simple featureless sallet curving back over the nape of the neck, or the basic skull cap design, would thus have been standard for the vast majority of the men who fought the Wars of the Roses, assuming that archers made up about fifty to sixty per cent of the majority of armies that took part. The Beauchamp Pageant does in fact depict archers wearing visorless sallets and crossbowmen wearing kettle helmets.

Sometimes helmets were left black in a raw forged state, rather than being of a highly polished finish, and they were occasionally painted with heraldic devices in such a way as to be rendered more serviceable when rusting was almost inevitable, especially during unseasonable English campaigning. Even Edward IV is depicted wearing black armour in his personal history, the *Arrivall*: knights did not always wear immaculate shining armour on the battlefield.

The common soldier in the Wars of the Roses was always at the mercy of his own limited financial resources when it came to purchasing his own personal military equipment, and as John Fortescue points out in his *Governance of England*, written during Edward IV's reign, this personal budget was threatened during the wars:

> Some men have said that it were good for the king, that the commons of England were made poor, as be the commons of France. For then they would not rebel as now they do often times; which the commons of France do not, or may do; for they have no weapon, nor armour, nor good to be it withal . . . For so these folks consider little the good of the realm of England, where of the might standeth most upon the archers, which be no rich men. And if they were made more poorer than they be, they should not have the where with to buy them bows, arrows, jacks, or any other armour of defence, where by they might be able to resist our enemies.[31]

As Fortescue makes clear, there is no doubt that archers made up a good proportion of Wars of the Roses armies, the balance being provided by those who bore other weapons, especially poll-arms, and a nucleus of men-at-arms who were much better equipped in terms of both armour and weapons. The English archer, with his formidable weapon the longbow, had shown his prowess on many previous occasions in the wars against France. He had also been in action at home, against rebels fighting for the crown, and had been employed for centuries in the wars against Scotland. The early successes of the longbow against mounted troops can be read about in detail in many excellent works on the subject;[32] suffice to say that when used in great numbers, from a carefully prepared position, and with a certain amount of luck, the effect of thousands of consecutive volleys of arrows was absolutely devastating when unleashed against cavalry, and caused unprecedented disarray, panic and confusion among most infantry contingents. What we will discuss here is how the longbowman was equipped, and, in the next chapter, how he fought during the Wars of the Roses, which was in fact very different from his previous experience in France.

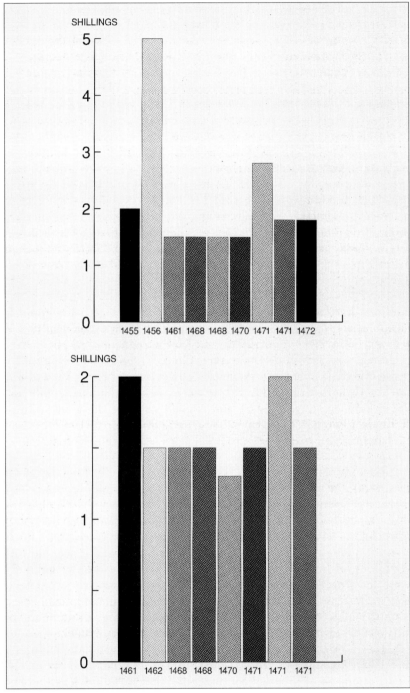

Top: yearly cost of longbows (each) and, bottom, arrows (per sheaf of 24) which were bought by the crown during the most intense periods of activity of the Wars of the Roses; information taken from Royal Armouries' inventories. (Author)

The English longbow was basically a stave of wood. The best longbows were made of yew, but in the Wars of the Roses they could be made from 'wych or hazel, ash, laburnum, or any other reasonable timber'. Out of the 1,359 bows which the Master handed over to the Controller of the Ordnance in 1475, all but 223 were made of yew.[33] Bowstaves of yew, as well as being made in England, were imported from Italy and Spain and they usually measured approximately 6 feet in length (described as 2 ells in the reign of Edward II). This standard issue was maintained in stockpiles; technically, however, an archer's own height and length of draw dictated a more efficient bow, and therefore a more effective shooting distance. It is difficult to imagine that all longbows were made to order, with exact specifications for individuals, and that all arrows were similary of different lengths, when thousands of both were expected to be used on the battlefield. Naturally, it was desirable for an archer to have his own personal bow and arrows, but this could hardly have been the case in war, when bows were damaged and lost, and arrows were spent in such abundance. Thousands of bows and arrows were standard issue, and, as can be seen in the amounts that were bought by the crown during the Wars of the Roses, they were preserved in stockpiles that were maintained in the Tower of London during this period. Therefore, it is almost certain that archers were expected to use what was available and adapt them accordingly to their own specifications. Heavy, powerful 150 lb longbows could shoot great distances, but this was not necessary if a standard issue bow and arrow could have the same desired effect at an effective yardage. Therefore, we may conclude that a longbow of 100–120 lb in draw weight would have been regular issue during the Wars of the Roses, as it had been in the past, and would be for some time to come.

The English longbow was shaped in D-section from a part of the wood that contained the dual properties of the chosen trees' natural heartwood and softwood, thus combining both strength and elasticity in a single bowstave. These special properties transferred as much of the bow's stored up energy as possible to the arrow, while retaining as little as possible itself, and the transference of energy was kept smooth while the arrow was being both drawn and shot into the enemy ranks. Horn nocks at the ends of the bowstave held a waxed linen bowstring in place, which was capable of launching an arrow approximately 250–350 yards.[34]

An archer was expected to carry spare bowstrings on his person, although many are recorded as being carried in barrels in wagons, along with the vast bulk of cloth-yard arrows and spare bows that were distributed to archers when battle was imminent. The medieval cloth yard (approximately 30 inches long) was the standard unit of measurement that was applied to an arrow's length during the Wars of the Roses (according to Edward IV's requirements). This length invariably matched the war bows that are described above. There were also various types of iron arrowheads in use during this period, designed to perform specific tasks on the battlefield against different targets. Long and short bodkin arrowheads of various weights were those most commonly used on the Wars of the Roses battlefield, as these were intended to counter infantry assault; the

Short and long bodkin arrowheads (actual size).
(Royal Armouries)

barbed type was used primarily against cavalry attack. At the other end of the medieval arrow shaft, three goose-feather flights were attached and bound into place with cord and glue, and two sheaves of these arrows (that is, 48) were usually stored in a canvas bag which the soldier would carry with him as standard issue. However, surviving musters indicate that some long-bowmen hardly had any arrows at all when they were recruited into their contingents, but supply from an army's baggage train would have been normal before battle commenced. Any additional war arrows would either be simply stuck into the ground, or tucked through the soldier's belt until needed.

The art of the longbow needed not only a keen eye for judging distances, but also great bodily strength, an immense amount of practice at village butts and also teamwork to achieve the desired effect on the battlefield. The longbow was useless if a lone company of archers happened to be caught forlornly in a field facing the enemy – longbowmen had to be, and invariably were, counted in thousands. As Philippe de Commines, who had seen and fought alongside English archers on the continent, wrote: 'In my opinion archers are the most necessary thing in the world for an army, though they should be counted in thousands, for in small numbers they are useless.'[35] Contingents of archers had to notch their arrows in unison, draw their bowstrings back in time, loose their arrows at the right moment and also be able to drop them accurately into the narrow width of ground they were aiming at 250 yards or so away from their position to cause the maximum amount of confusion among enemy contingents. This ability came from years and years of law-enforced practice at town and village butts and in open fields.

Although archers were used in great abundance during the second half of the fifteenth century, it appears that bowstaves were imported more frequently into English ports because of an apparent lack of adequate timber to make them from at home. An Act of Parliament of 1472 lamented that 'archery was greatly discontinued and almost lost'[36] because of a shortfall of bowstaves, which was in part due to the inordinately high prices that were being placed on them by Italian merchants. Further, it seems that training was also in decline, which explains why such games as football, dice, quoits and tennis were banned. By law, experience at the butts was essential to maintain this all-important and traditional military arm against the threats of invasion and national rebellion, and Edward IV had no option but to ban all such idle sports and pastimes in an effort to stem the rot which had obviously set in by the middle of his reign (1470). It is therefore clear that at certain times during the Wars of the Roses archery was appreciably on the decline, especially in those years when Edward IV introduced laws to curb idleness and enforce archery practice. Some contemporaries noted that archery was declining and that this *was* where the might of England had stood in previous years:

> By law every man should be compelled
> To use the bow and shooting for his sport,
> And all insolent play repelled,
> And each town to have butts for resort
> Of every creature for their comfort,
> Especially for all our defence
> Established before of great prudence.[37]

According to the evidence supplied in contemporary musters, longbowmen formed only fifty to sixty per cent of a whole army, the balance being those who used poll-arms. In the latter years of the Hundred Years War an average ratio of three archers to one man-at-arms was maintained as being the ideal balance to achieve maximum effect against continental armies. This high ratio was achieved again in 1475 when, because of Edward IV's legislation, longbowmen formed the majority of the troops when the King invaded France. However, this time they were used more as a threat than as the promise of Agincourt-style resurgence.

The crossbow was also used in small numbers during the Wars of the Roses, chiefly by continental troops who were employed by English nobles. The windlass crossbow was the most common type, so called because of the pulleys and levers (cranequins) which were inserted onto the back of the bow. When turned, these would pull the crossbow's string back so that a bolt, or quarrel, could be inserted in the stock. This process was aided by the presence of a 'stirrup' foot-brace whereby the bow was held in place by the insertion of the crossbowman's foot. The string would then be released by a simple trigger mechanism which would send the quarrel towards its target at a tremendous speed, achieving great distances and penetration power – arguably greater than the longbow ever could when it came to long-distance shooting.[38] However, the great disadvantage of the crossbow was in its rate of fire. It took far longer to reload the crossbow than the longbow, the latter being both instinctively loaded and rapidly shot. A competent longbowman could shoot at least six times as fast as a crossbowman with a reasonable degree of accuracy.

The Bridport muster roll of 1457 describes the weapons and equipment that belonged to the soldiers of a small Dorset coastal town immediately before the

Wars of the Roses began. The predominance of the longbow is evident, but it is clear upon closer inspection of the muster roll that most men had various other weapons besides, which could be used in battle when their trusty bows had been discarded in favour of side arms. Axes, swords, lead mallets, daggers and so forth were carried by most soldiers for use in the inevitable hand-to-hand struggle that most battles became after the preliminary archery duel had exhausted arrow supplies. The exchange of arrows was very short-lived in comparison to the final mêlée; thus the longbowman was only a longbowman for a very short time on the battlefield, and the acquisition of these other types of side arms was absolutely essential for him in order to survive.

Most of the Bridport men had the usual jack, sallet, sword, dagger and buckler as standard equipment, but the diversity of arms and armour is significant. Some common soldiers had poll-axes, bills and glaives, some had acquired brigandines; even part harness was owned. Various other weapons and pieces of equipment, including axes, cleavers, spears and pavises, were recorded, and more pavises were ordered to be made, but it seems that some equipment was outdated, if the bascinet owned by one man is anything to go by. However, a good percentage of the Bridport men either had no weapons at all or, according to some historians, may have failed to turn up for inspection. (The latter is hardly likely considering that serving the king was far preferable to forfeiture, or even 'pain of death' for desertion.)

One of the more common forms of weapon that could be used for protection at home as well as on the battlefield was the bill – a natural development of the agricultural billhook, which might have been found propped up against the door of many a medieval cottage and house in the fifteenth century. The Pastons of Norfolk recorded that this was standard practice against the increasing lawlessness that threatened them, and more than one bill was at hand near their door in order to tackle any unwelcome guests. The very fact that the bill was so accessible, and also that anyone could use it without much training, leads us to conclude that the numbers of billmen used during the Wars of the Roses were much larger than might be imagined at first, especially in cases when commissioners issued last-minute warnings to local communities who were deficient in archers. The bill itself could be anything ranging from the more common bill to the halberd, with glaives, partisans, guisarmes and even poll-axes falling into the 'bill' category when such multi-headed weapons were being described on muster rolls.

In many battles of the mid-fifteenth century the billmen were used in large numbers, mixed in with men-at-arms who were drawn up in close-order array. The weapon was raked and stabbed at the enemy in a similar way to most poll weapons of the period, apart from the halberd which had to be swung at an opponent in order to inflict the maximum amount of damage. All poll-arms could be stabbed at the enemy and they all had a long spike or blade at the head of a wooden pole, the latter being between six and ten feet in length. The difference was in the multitude of heads, blades, hooks and ferocious spikes that protruded from the main head, which gave rise to the various names of the weapons mentioned above. The sharp, concave hook of the bill was especially useful for

Fifteenth-century bill and halberd. The bill is English, early fifteenth century, and the halberd is Austrian or Swiss, c. 1450. (Royal Armouries)

bringing opponents to the ground, cutting through the straps and buckles of armour, thrusting up into the faces of attackers and causing horses to shy and leap out of control when attacked; it was also useful for ripping harnesses from horses. With most poll weapons a soldier, or, for that matter, a farmer on his land, could deal with several opponents at once, and poll-arms needed no special care to maintain, unlike the longbow which needed constant attention to prevent it from cracking or exploding when shot. Providing there was space to wield it, the bill was a formidable 'long reach' weapon; however, if space was limited, as it invariably was in close combat, other weapons might be employed by the common foot soldier.[39]

In the crush of close-quarter combat the common soldier was also equipped with a sword, dagger and buckler; he may also have possessed a short axe, and sometimes a maul, the latter being quoted by contemporaries as being a 'mallet of lead'.[40] Short, heavy, thick swords were popular during this period, but the falchion (much like the eastern scimitar) was also in widespread use by English foot soldiers during this period. The falchion had a single sharp curving edge similar to the more modern light cavalry sabre. However, straight swords with single-edged blades were also made to varying degrees of quality and length, similar to the sword that was found near the battlefield of Wakefield in 1966, which had a distinctive curved guard that was designed to protected the knuckles of the user. Many types of swords and falchions can be seen in the illustrations of the Beauchamp Pageant (produced between 1485 and 1490) where various types of soldiers carry all manner of side-arms as well as their preferred weapon, which might be either a bow or poll-arm.

Hand axes were also carried by soldiers for practical purposes, and were used as much for cutting wooden stakes and firewood as for beating someone's brains out on the battlefield. Mauls were used for digging pits and for hammering stakes into the ground, whereas all forms of dagger were used to cut and eat food with. Thus all these side-arms were to a certain extent more essential to daily life, especially daggers, and hence more common as military equipment than swords. Out of the 211 men who are mentioned in the Bridport muster roll most had daggers, which may have been the ballock or 'kidney dagger'. This form of ten-inch single-edged dagger had a very distinctive guard with two lobes –representing the shape of the kidneys to prudish Victorians, but to medieval man depicting a completely different part of the human anatomy. Double-edged quillon daggers were also popular during this period, when all forms of dagger were being used, as the rondel dagger was, for exploiting gaps in an opponent's body armour and thereby penetrating the mail beneath by means of a direct, straight, well-aimed thrust.[41]

The most eye-catching garment worn by the Wars of the Roses soldier was his livery jacket. This generally set him aside from other men, in that once chosen (or forced) to become 'connected' with a certain 'master', he was, to all intents and purposes, protected, unified and affiliated to a particular contingent through its symbolism. Livery jackets were worn over padded jacks, or any other armoured protection a soldier might wear, and three different designs seem to have been fashionable during the Wars of the Roses. The coarse woollen garment was produced from four pieces of cloth stitched together and the jacket was either sleeveless or half-sleeved or resembled a proper coat with full sleeves. Various lengths could be worn which were fastened up the front with ties or, for the more affluent or favoured members of society, with heraldic buttons. The material of a livery jacket was dyed in various colours per pale (two halves vertically separated), bendy (diagonally) or in any other heraldic fashion a noble might choose, and in colours ranging from gules (red), vert (green), azure (blue) and or (yellow) to mixtures like tawny and russet (various shades of brown). Black was also in common use, but was more difficult to produce.[42]

The design of the livery jacket was usually taken from an overlord's heraldic achievements, and more precisely from his personal standard which was split into two livery colours (per fess) with his badge, the standard of St George and the noble's family motto upon it as recognition devices. However, only the badge from the standard was distributed to the noble's men, and this was invariably mass produced, so that it could be sewn onto the front and back of livery jackets and be recognized in battle. Town and city liveries were also distributed in much the same way to varying degrees of design and material cost. In some instances only the livery badge appears to have been worn by individuals, which might be sewn direct onto a soldier's protective clothing, causing no end of confusion in battle, as all English soldiers looked basically the same. The Duke of Gloucester in 1483 had 8,000 white boar badges 'wrought upon fustian'[43] for his men; but on other occasions soldiers might not have any liveries at all. Illegal liveries were also commonplace during the Wars of the Roses, adding more problems to an already confused and gaudy battleline, which was often besmirched with dirt and filth from the march, resulting in further mistaken identity, treachery and possible defeat.

HANDGUNS AND ARTILLERY

Amid the clash of steel and the hiss of arrow shafts in flight, the sound of the handgun and cannon might also suddenly split the air on the Wars of the Roses battlefield, with a warning of an era of change to come. Edward IV's particular interest in artillery is illustrated in his frequent use of it during most of his campaigns, especially in 1471, where guns are mentioned as being present at the battles of Barnet and Tewkesbury. However, guns were also in place behind field defences or redoubts even before this, at the battle of Northampton in 1460, for instance, and also at Ludford Bridge in 1459, although they were not used to any great extent due to adverse circumstances. At the second battle of St Albans in 1461 mercenary handgunners and artillery pieces were yet again employed in a Yorkist army, and in the border war of 1461–4 great bombards were shipped northwards and used against the defences of Bamburgh Castle. At

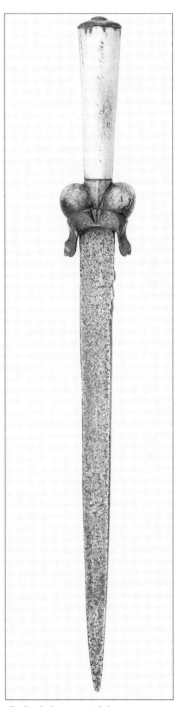

Ballock dagger with bone grip. Flemish, late fifteenth century. (Royal Armouries)

'Losecoat Field' Edward IV used his artillery to disperse the Lincolnshire rebels, and in the royal inventories of the King's army which embarked for France in 1475 various types of guns are mentioned, highlighting their importance during this period of their development. At Bosworth, according to Jean Molinet, and most probably also at Stoke Field in 1487, guns were again in evidence and deployed amid the ranks of archers and foot soldiers who probably now saw them as commonplace on the battlefield. The importance of artillery in the Wars of the Roses is also underlined by the fact that it was being constantly moved around the country, even though such weapons might not be used in the end for military action either because of bad weather or because other major strategic problems affected its transportation. However, the threat of artillery and handguns was there, and any commander who possessed such gunpowder weapons might use them to gain a limited political and psychological edge over the enemy.

The different types of cannon and handgun that were used during this period of innovation are described in many contemporary documents. For example, an inventory of Caister Castle, which was compiled by John Paston after the siege there in 1469, provides a clear indication of the diversity of firearms, and calibres of shot, that were used:

> Two guns with eight chambers shooting a stone seven inches thick, twenty inches compass. Two lesser guns with eight chambers shooting a stone five inches thick, fifteen inches compass. A serpentine with three chambers shooting a stone of ten inches in compass. Another serpentine shooting a stone of seven inches in compass. Three fowlers shooting a stone twelve inches in compass. Two short guns for ships with six chambers. Two small serpentines to shoot lead pellets. Four guns lying in stocks to shoot lead pellets. Seven handguns with other equipment belonging to said guns.[44]

The heaviest calibre siege guns (bombards) were fired from ground level through a touch hole in the barrel, due to the force of recoil which accompanied them when they were shot, but many other guns, including serpentines, were much more mobile and were mounted on their own wheeled carriages or 'carts'. These field guns could be multi-tubed contraptions, such as those described above, shooting various calibres of cannon balls, to guns that were breech-loaders, equipped with a movable section at the back of the barrel with a handle attached for lifting it in and out of the gun. This breech-block was filled with gunpowder, and when a stone or iron ball was placed in the barrel, the block was wedged back in place behind the main barrel and fired via a touch hole. Trunnions were adopted for raising and lowering the wooden stock of field guns so as to increase or decrease their range, which could be as much as 400 yards for field guns and over 2,000 yards for the heaviest unmounted siege weapons. However, field guns with movable stocks were undoubtedly the most useful on the battlefield because continuously moving targets could always prove a problem for any gun with a fixed position. These types of gun were in place when the Earl of Warwick faced Edward IV at the battle of Barnet in 1471, when King Edward 'suffered no guns to be shot on his side, all that night, or else right few, which was to him great advantage, for, thereby, they [Warwick's gunners] might have [estimated] the ground that he lay in, and have levelled their guns near'.[45]

The Earl of Warwick's gunners may have shot at the King's army all that night, but the rate of fire of these guns was extremely slow, to such an extent that chains, barricades, wooden stakes and in some instances pikemen were put in place to protect them from enemy assault. During a siege, cannon balls weighing as much as two hundredweight would have to be placed in the barrel, which had to be swabbed and cleaned out thoroughly after every discharge and new gunpowder prepared and loaded into the chamber. This could take literally hours to do. Field guns had to be treated in much the same way, although they could shoot much more quickly. Compared to the longbow, therefore, the gun was of very little tactical use on the battlefield at this time: most armies of the Wars of the Roses came to hand strokes very quickly indeed after an opening exchange of missiles.

Medieval gunpowder was a mix of saltpetre, sulphur and carbon (charcoal), and this mix was crucial, to the extent that an improper balance of ingredients was extremely unstable and could lead to premature explosions. The mix was also hindered by travel during the medieval period, as in transit the heaviest of the three intimate ingredients always sank to the bottom of the barrel. When transferred to the gun this volatile and disproportionate mix could cause guns to explode prematurely, although the problem was partially remedied with the introduction of wet-mixed powder at the beginning of the fifteenth century. Even so, guns still caused injury and death to their operators. King James II of Scotland was killed in this way in 1452, not to mention all the other gunners who are not so well recorded, but who persisted with the weapon.

Technical innovations in the fifteenth century caused the handgun, or 'culverine à main', to become more powerful and accurate than ever before. Some handguns were little more than a simple wrought-iron tube with a touch hole, but most by this time had a wooden stock in order to support the gun's barrel and also to place against the operator's shoulder when it was fired. The S-shaped lever, called a serpentine (snake), was another innovation which simplified the use of the handgun by allowing the operator to focus on the target while balancing the stock and holding its trigger mechanism in a similar way to a modern rifle. The serpentine was equipped with a smouldering match that, on pulling the lower lever upwards towards the stock, would deposit the match end into a pan containing the powder which caused the main charge inside to ignite. In this way a 14–17 mm lead or iron pellet (later an armour-piercing bullet) or even, as at St Albans, 'arrows of an ell in length with feathers . . . and wild fire withal',[46] could be hurled towards the enemy. At short distances (approximately twenty yards) this impact could be very effective against armour plate; although the handgun had a range of about 200 yards, at this distance it was obviously far less accurate. The real drawbacks of the handgun during this period were that it was very slow to reload and clean out, it lacked the effect that greater numbers of handgunners had already achieved abroad and it was extremely temperamental, as

Field gun opening fire. (Paul Lewis Isemonger)

can be seen in the misfortunes of Warwick's Burgundian handgunners at St Albans when most of their guns exploded in their faces.[47]

The man-at-arms encased in his armour, the archer with his trusty longbow, the footman with his bill and the mercenary with his chosen continental weapon were now ready to fight. But what of the conditions that a soldier might face in medieval warfare? What were the sights, the sounds, the fears that accompanied this horrific one-to-one combat? This forms the theme of the next chapter.

CHAPTER 6

'In the footmen is all the trust'

PREPARATION FOR BATTLE

Wars of the Roses battles were not well recorded by contemporary chroniclers. What occurred in them is therefore generally regarded by historians to be at best conjectural, and always controversial. This does not mean, however, that we should disregard how battles were fought in the fifteenth century and focus more upon the political outcome of such encounters.

Two medieval 'battles' close with each other, archers to the fore. (Bibliothèque Nationale)

In this chapter a typical battle of the Wars of the Roses will be described. The evidence presented is firmly based on the few relevant documents we have of medieval warfare, taken from contemporary, or near contemporary, sources. An actual Wars of the Roses army cannot be analysed in terms of numbers and composition with any degree of accuracy, because of the huge amount of conflicting evidence in the chronicles – casualty figures, too, are unreliable – but a fictitious battleline can be described if we base it on the contingents of soldiers that were more accurately documented during the Wars of the Roses. The casualty rates, and the length of an engagement, can be assessed by analysing the practical mechanics of warfare and its effect upon the human body. From this factual and practical evidence we can begin to analyse the 'feel' of a typical Wars of the Roses army, apply this knowledge to battlefield conditions, and thereby arrive at a better understanding of the armies that fought in these unusual wars.

Terrain must also be taken into account in any battlefield scenario. This can be deduced from examples that were briefly described by contemporary chroniclers, some of whom may have been eye-witnesses of the events described. We may also consult early maps and local documents to interpret the fifteenth-century English landscape. Finally, when attempting to analyse the medieval soldier's experience of battle, we must make use of the extensive amount of modern research on medieval arms and armour, and then apply this to the 'mechanics' of war. But first, what of the mental state of the soldier?

Human feelings have not changed with the passage of time. A vivid kaleidoscope of emotions can be seen in the Paston, Stonor and Plumpton letters, for example: these fifteenth-century families' hopes, fears, sorrows and joys are no different from those expressed today. However, outside influences have changed, and it is only when an individual is faced with an uncertain future that all these human feelings come into much sharper focus. The reality of this danger for the men who fought the Wars of the Roses was the very real threat of being killed in battle, and this acceptance of death is manifest in the soldiers' preparation for it before battles took place.

Piety and warfare were inexorably linked in any battle fought in the medieval period, when it was deemed that all events were influenced in a very real way by the external forces of Heaven and Hell. Prayer was of great importance to knights and commoners alike, but especially to the the higher classes who had plenty of time to devote to it. Before troops moved into their final positions on the battlefield, masses were held in the open fields, just as they were at Agincourt in 1415 when the English army was heavily outnumbered and hence fearful of the consequences of defeat.[1] The more pious knights sought private absolution in the company of the various priests who always travelled with the army, sometimes under duress. This mass might be repeated many times before actual battle commenced (Henry V heard mass three times in succession before Agincourt), but because of the huge scale, in this case the whole of a medieval army, the ceremony would probably only last for a few minutes. Many soldiers may also have consulted with a priest some time before this in anticipation of action. Priests are usually mentioned by name in Wars of the Roses attainder documents, and consequently they were regarded as just as treasonable as soldiers in the eyes of a king, even though they had not actually been physically involved in the fighting.[2] The very fact that priests were so commonplace in armies of the period proves that the ceremony of mass was crucial to medieval soldiers. Absence of religious guidance may have resulted in low morale. The Croyland Chronicler carefully points out that priests were absent in Richard III's army at Bosworth – could this have been significant on the day?

Sudden death was also a more commonplace event in medieval times and an individual had to be purged of sin before facing it, or else enter Purgatory. Death was not a great unknown, because medieval man was told what to expect in the afterlife. Such piety sat uncomfortably beside the glorification of war. It is even documented that there were several pathological killers in the Wars of the Roses.[3] Some nobles were hell-bent on revenge, such as Lord Clifford; some inflicted torture on others, such as John Tiptoft, Earl of Worcester; and several individuals also committed 'war crimes' against non-combatants to satisfy their blood-lust or greed. Several writers revelled in the thought of body-strewn battlefields running with human blood and gore, and described very graphically in prose and verse the consequences of being sliced in two by swords and axes. Many contemporary illustrators graphically depicted such scenes, pandering to the higher classes' obsession with war. Even some church chroniclers were obsessed with the apocalyptic vision of English fields, streets and rivers running with Christian blood. It is therefore not surprising that the whole atmosphere surrounding the medieval battlefield experience is somewhat blurred, coloured as it was with this morbid fascination with death and propaganda.

The Wars of the Roses as a whole were not bloodbaths, but isolated battles in them undoubtedly were; therefore we cannot underestimate the ferocity of hand-to-hand combat. The effect of sharp and concussive weapons upon the human body, and the attitude of soldiers to this when experiencing the 'red mist' of total war, can be shown all too vividly in the injuries of some of the soldiers who did not survive the ordeal. Battlefield graves vividly bear witness to this kind of killing, and in some instances over-kill. When we discuss the men who suffered the very limits of human endurance, we should also bear in mind that many soldiers came to the battlefield cold, hungry and exhausted. Some were so surprised at the enemy's appearance that they were not able to

Stained glass window depicting Sir Thomas Montgomery, Long Melford Church, Suffolk. (Geoffrey Wheeler)

feed themselves, or indeed hear mass given by their priests before battle commenced. There is evidence that the Yorkist army before the battle of Towton was in bad shape because of its long march, for example, and both armies before Tewkesbury had suffered long, gruelling forced marches.[4]

During the most inactive periods before battles commenced, copious amounts of alcohol might be consumed by soldiers, in some instances to numb the senses, but in most cases to induce courage or create a diversion from the event which was about to take place. Philippe de Commines, an eye-witness of medieval warfare on the continent, described the scene and condition of some English archers who had been recruited into Burgundian ranks before the battle of Montl'héry in July 1465:

> and we found all the archers dismounted, and every man with a stake planted before him; several pipes of wine had been broached, and were set for them to drink; and from the little I saw, never men had more desire to fight, which I took for a good omen, and which comforted me extremely.[5]

Many of these English archers were outwardly prepared for battle, and Commines obviously found great comfort himself in their attitude to the imminent experience of combat. Some early battles of the Wars of the Roses were fought after long-drawn-out negotiations between the king and his rebellious nobles where heralds and members of the clergy tried in vain to avert imminent bloodshed. The condition of the soldiers and their attitude to combat was directly affected by these delays. It is documented that it had been raining heavily before the battle of Northampton in 1460 when various churchmen tried to stop the inevitable from occurring; snow and ice were central to many contemporary chroniclers' accounts of the 1461 campaigns; and damp mist and fog enveloped the battlefield of Barnet in April 1471. Such conditions not only had their part to play in the battles themselves, but also dictated how soldiers would eventually fight, and in what physical state they would have to endure the ultimate test of battle. Whether they were wet and weary from marching, cold and hungry from insuficient provisioning, tired of the prospect of warfare overall, or ruthless, well-fed and watered veteran soldiers, on top of this was a natural fear of what was about to take place. It is here that we find the true role of comradeship in arms.

Much has been said about the problem of marshalling medieval armies before they finally clashed, as well as the tactics that were employed in the confusion of combat. Medieval warfare *was* simply very confused, and contemporary chroniclers give us little in the way of clues as to how battles ebbed and flowed. What we can attempt to analyse, however, is how the soldier saw his role in a battle, and, to place this in context, the placement and composition of armies needs to be examined.

As discussed in Chapter 3, how armies were recruited rested on the structure of bastard feudalism and Commissions of Array; more precisely it rested on the local mustering of troop contingents. This dictated which soldiers would be sent where, with which noble, in which battle formation and where this would be finally placed on the battlefield to fight. This is true for all medieval armies, but particularly Wars of the Roses armies which were made up of regional, and essentially private, forces that were all brought together to fight for a particular reason. Because of fifteenth-century recruitment practices, a medieval 'battle' has been described as 'a great household, composed, in part at least, of smaller houscholds',[6] and armies were made up from 'confederations of private forces' that were each led by a leading figure.[7] In fact, if we look at the different methods of recruitment discussed in Chapter 3, we see that there was a far more complex mixture of common soldiers from villages, towns, cities and shires with a small nucleus of well-trained professionals who kept them under control. Contingents were composed under local leaders, and battle commanders – the 'great captains' of the army – needed to be appointed before any contact with the enemy took place.

The day before the battle of Tewkesbury, for example, King Edward, according to the *Arrivall*, 'advanced his banners and divided his whole host in three battles, and sent afore him his foreriders, and scourers, on every side of him'.[8] Later the Yorkist army arrived at Cheltenham, five miles from Tewkesbury, where it briefly rested and then moved on to encamp three miles from the Lancastrian position. The following morning (the day of the battle) Edward again set 'all his host in good array; ordained three wards; displayed his banners; did blow up the trumpets . . . and advanced directly upon his enemies'.[9] The process of forming such battles under leading nobles was nothing new to commanders in the Wars of the Roses, and most chronicles like this one, and indeed the military manuals of the period, indicate that this was standard practice both when armies were fully gathered and when they were on the march.

At the battle of Towton the vanguard of the Yorkist army was given to Lord Fauconberg, who, in fact, had commanded it ever since its departure from London. Unfortunately, however, like many other Wars of the Roses battles, it is unclear how the rest of the Yorkist army was divided to fight on Palm Sunday 1461, although we may suppose that the Earl of Warwick and King Edward were in command of the rest of the Yorkist force, with the Duke of Norfolk's contingents forming the rearward when they eventually arrived on the field. The vanguard of the army at Towton was well in advance of the other two wards the day before the battle; in some instances the vanguard might move faster because it contained mounted troops.[10] The vanguard was also usually comprised of greater numbers of men than the other two wards, in case it came into contact with the enemy first. This occurred at the battle of Stoke in 1487 when the Earl of Oxford was forced into giving battle, while Henry VII brought up the rear of the Tudor army some time later.[11] If this premature encounter did occur, then a competent leader was equipped with the necessary manpower and weapon types to offer battle while the mainward and rearward took their final positions, either to the left of the anchored vanguard abreast (protecting their line of advance and forming a screen in front of the enemy) or in battles astern, one ward behind the other. However, it must be stressed that the vanguard did not always take up position on the right flank of the army according to chronicled evidence, and we must also take into account the effects of chance, difficult terrain and the ongoing blood feud during the Wars of the Roses, all of which could dictate the opening battle positions.

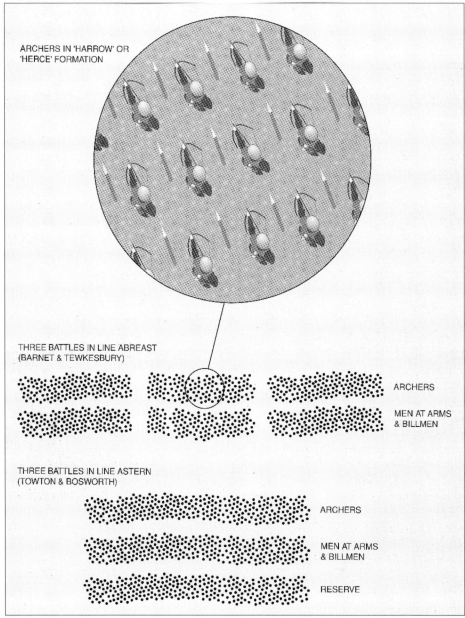

ARCHERS IN 'HARROW' OR 'HERCE' FORMATION

THREE BATTLES IN LINE ABREAST (BARNET & TEWKESBURY)

ARCHERS

MEN AT ARMS & BILLMEN

THREE BATTLES IN LINE ASTERN (TOWTON & BOSWORTH)

ARCHERS

MEN AT ARMS & BILLMEN

RESERVE

Types of 'battle' formation used by the armies in the Wars of the Roses, and a diagrammatic representation of the 'herce' or 'harrow' as adopted by longbowmen of the period. (Author)

Taking all the above factors into account it is doubtful that there was ever a model way to array an army 'by the book' during the Wars of the Roses, because any, or all, of the above circumstances might dictate the order of battle. It is highly likely that some armies were strung out, with groups of stragglers forming the flanks and rear of a battleline; archers may have formed an entire frontage for an effective missile attack, as occurred at Towton, for instance. When space was limited, as at Bosworth, the armies' traditional three battles might be astern of each other, well out of effective communication distance. In other situations, like the street fighting which occurred twice at St Albans, separate contingents of soldiers might be given specific individual tasks to perform. In short, there was no one set of rules that dictated how a Wars of the Roses army might fight. Although the 'ordaining' of battles, or wards, constituted a way of distributing and ordering lots of local and private contingents into manageable divisions which would march, as Edward's army did in 1471, and ultimately fight, around a specific banner as one. Once the opening archery duel was over, tactics and troop management were notoriously limited on the medieval battlefield – it was then that separate contingents of soldiers came into their own under the command of their nominated local captains.

As described earlier, comradeship played an important part in the medieval battle, and this even encompassed the 'great captain' himself who was commander-in-chief of the army. Before battle commenced it was up to the king or the leading noble to exhort his men to fight. As most commanders were literate, and had read military theory, they may have followed to the letter the precepts of Vegetius's *De Rei Militari*:

> Therefore that day that thy knights should fight, take them before thee and ask them frankly about their wishes, and without any doubts thou shalt soon perceive and espie, either by their cheer, or by their words, or their swift and hasty going, or their slow moving and tarrying, which be bold and which be afraid . . . Therefore in this case it needeth that the duke comfort his people with good cheer and bold words, rehearsing too the falsehood of his enemy's quarrel and right of his own cause.[12]

As the snow began to fall at the battle of Towton both armies 'gave a great shout' when they saw each other for the first time across the fields, and no doubt most battles started with much vocal abuse, swearing and instinctive gestures at the enemy. Rival banners would have pinpointed the position and composition of enemy forces, and the testing, teasing and ranging of single shots of arrows warned of the approach of combat, while in general a great noise must have been carried back and forth over the dense ranks of men. The running to and fro of messengers, the scurrying of pages, squires, grooms and servants with nobles' war horses, and the carrying and supplying of thousands of bundles of arrows to the front line would have taken up much of the waiting period – while the soldiers themselves, under the sweet smell of sweat and the plying of sour ale and wine to their mouths, waited for the inevitable to occur. Rosaries may have been fumbled with in quiet solitude, the ground was invariably kissed as a sign of final judgement and longbows would have been drawn and tested in the forward ranks in anticipation of repeated use. Then shouts and trumpets may have signalled, among the clattering and rattling of armour and weapons, the arrival of leading figures as they took centre stage. Catching a glimpse of the King of England, seated bolt upright astride his horse decked in gaudy colours with mace or sword in hand, must have been a heart-warming sight for the unified army, however miserable and mud-spattered the soldiers might have been.

Edward IV made speeches to his men in which he gave them a chance to depart if they regarded his cause and quarrel not to be good (echoes of Henry V at Agincourt).[13] He committed his cause and quarrel to Almighty God and all the saints before he entered into battle, he caused trumpets to split the air and shouts of obedience were, more often than not, given by his soldiers in unison with the appropriate propaganda issues that were rehearsed, and passed back and forth, from soldier to soldier along the line. Orders of no quarter were given by Edward on occasion, which sometimes would be emended by a cry to 'spare the commons, kill the nobles'[14] when an army was routed, and against this backcloth of frenzy and fright veteran soldiers and raw recruits alike would soon have felt the onrush of foreboding which hung like a leaden cloud over both contending armies. Now soldiers literally had no other option but to await their fate and obey the orders they were given, whether these were to shoot, to move in the direction of the enemy or to stand and face an all-arms assault.

At the battle of Bosworth Richard III wore a golden crown over his helmet to boost his troops' morale. Henry VI to a lesser degree encouraged patriotism with well-worded criticisms of the Yorkist captains at St Albans in 1455, saying that he would 'destroy them every mother's son'[15] for their treachery, and warned of what might befall the Yorkists before Ludford Bridge in 1459 with similar stern words prompted by others of his party. King Henry, as we have seen, did not personally command his armies in the field during the Wars of the Roses to any great extent. At some battles he was not even present on the field, preferring to let others take control of military matters, such as the Duke of Buckingham or the Duke of Somerset, mainly to avoid being witness to the inevitable bloodshed of which he had the utmost dread. The King's absence and unchivalrous detachment from martial affairs had a marked effect on the Lancastrian armies of the Wars of the Roses, and undermined Henry's authority. This directly affected the unity of his troops, and contributed to their higher than average proportion of defeats in battle during the wars. It was Henry's queen, Margaret of Anjou, who was forced into clawing back what she could of royal power and authority on the battlefield by using her son, the Prince of Wales, as a pawn to encourage her troops into unified action for the common good. Unceremoniously dragged from one camp to another during the most intense periods of the conflict, Henry VI was undoubtedly the saddest character in the Wars of the Roses. Unfortunately the horror of warfare had already carved its bloody mark on his unstable mind in 1455 when he himself was wounded, and saw his personal standard irreverently left abandoned in the face of Yorkist aggression. This event probably stayed with Henry for the rest of his life; his weak constitution was probably no match for battlefield conditions afterwards.

The anticipation in the air on the Wars of the Roses battlefield must have been extreme and many men may have thought twice about fighting. Priests, by this time, would have retired to the baggage area and, accompanied by the heralds, as non-combatants, they could only watch the unfolding horrors of war while the soldiers found their strength in comradeship, or in the fear of failing their local superiors now the ultimate test of loyalty was upon them.

A Wars of the Roses battleline would have contained various troop types, but only two of these counted when it came to organization on the field of battle – bows and bills. Archers would have been set forward of their local contingent, so that there would be, in effect, a continuous frontage of longbowmen, with a force of billmen and men-at-arms forming the ranks behind. As we have seen, in Sir Walter Strickland's case this would have amounted to an equal split, archers to the fore, while the rest of his soldiers fell in behind and around Strickland's personal banner (290 men). Strickland, along with others who were retainers of the Earl of Salisbury, may have formed a battle commanded by the Earl himself, these retainers obviously being beholden to Salisbury by contract of indenture. Much of Salisbury's battle would have comprised northerners from the West March of England, including men like Lord Ogle who commanded 600 'men of the marches' in the attack on St Albans in 1455.[16] The Earl of Salisbury himself had a riding retinue of some 500 men in 1458, which accompanied him to St Paul's for the celebration known as 'Love Day'.[17] The combined totals of these forces gives us some idea of the size of the battle which he could command (1390 men).

Salisbury's son, the Earl of Warwick, as captain of the Calais garrison, could command a similar size force to that of his father, that is to say the documented 1,000 men who were in his employment. These garrison troops could be used on the Wars of the Roses battlefield; in addition, as a great landowner in his own right, Warwick could call upon a substantial array of troops from his own lands. As hired men the garrison's loyalty was always questionable, even though mercenaries were habitually in use during the Wars of the Roses from about 1460, and the 500 Flemings that Edward IV brought to London in 1471 might be included in any particular battle out of necessity, as they were at both Barnet and Tewkesbury, for example.

In a later period, nobles like John, Duke of Norfolk, could command approximately 800 men, according to his household accounts in 1484, of which 500 were recruited from 44 manors. A further 180 were promised by 43 named individuals, who were probably Norfolk's household men, which takes his contingent's total up to about 1,000 men. These soldiers were probaby the men who fought for Norfolk at Bosworth in 1485, although on this occasion a small proportion of them, namely the 180 men promised by some of his more fickle retainers (Paston for one), may not have even turned up to fight.[18]

As we have seen, through his indentured retainers Lord Hastings could also command a substantial array of men – 904 soldiers according to the 1475 muster[19] – but here again there is reason to believe that Hastings could call upon many more of his retainers and tenants to serve him on English soil. Indeed, it is abundantly clear that in all the above named retinues the evidence points to much larger forces than have been calculated here, especially when we take into account that 'extraordinary retainers' and their troops, who generally owed allegiance to others, could also be called upon to serve when required for military duty.

If we take a look at the town and city militias who were commissioned to serve, we see that a town like Bridport, for example, could field 211 men,

The Towton Grave: healed blade wound and depression fracture to the head. In addition there are three puncture wounds to the top of the skull, possibly made by arrowheads. (Bradford University)

comprising archers and a motley crew of others who were armed with jacks, sallets, swords and daggers. However, cities like York and Coventry could field much larger contingents of men when called upon to do so, albeit by varying amounts, throughout the Wars of the Roses. The city of York may have sent as many as 400 men to our fictitious battle, and Coventry an average of 100 soldiers according to a contemporary document of 1455.[20] It is suggested that these militias would have complemented the above nobles' bastard feudal retinues. However, it is clear that some towns, such as Nottingham, were only able to field small contingents of soldiers (30 archers in 1453), and that even whole areas, such as the Ewelme half hundred, were struggling to muster 85 soldiers from 17 villages.[21] All these figures not only give us some idea of the numbers of men that served in the Wars of the Roses, but also speak volumes of the small percentage of the population that followed the drum during this period.

All the above figures are contemporary, but fall short of the totals that could actually be mustered for a Wars of the Roses battle according to other chronicled evidence. (Warwick's force, for instance, must have been massive according to contemporary accounts.) The abundance of livery badges that were made and distributed to soldiers, for instance, give us cause to wonder at the numbers of men who would eventually wear the 2,000 Stafford knot badges and the 8,000 white boar badges of the Duke of Gloucester. It is for this reason that the battle of Towton in 1461 was seen by contemporaries as the longest, biggest and bloodiest battle for a thousand years because the armies that fought at Towton were so proportionately larger than the norm.

THE LONGBOW

Extensive modern research carried out on the traditional English medieval weapon, the longbow, provides us with conclusive proof of how devastating this weapon was when used by large numbers of archers in advantageous battlefield positions.[22] In the fourteenth century, and chiefly in the Hundred Years War, the longbow was used to inflict very heavy casualties on advancing infantry or charging cavalry detatchments (and all the more so if this infantry or cavalry was outflanked or in disarray). Arrows could obviously cause more havoc when they found larger targets such as horses; in turn, their unfortunate riders could be catapulted out of their saddles when their horses floundered because of repeated wounding by arrows. This kind of arrow storm also caused an immense amount of confusion among dismounted infantry.

In all these situations the longbow reigned supreme as a missile weapon used from a defensive position. Largely unprotected horses, their riders and any advancing footman could be instantly turned into the ghastly vision of 'hedgehogs with quills' which is so often described by the chroniclers.[23] When hit, a knight's horse might career out of control into others, which in turn could cause major breaks in formation, and holes in supporting divisions, if horses ran into advancing infantry contingents, as they did at Agincourt in 1415. Vast confused masses of falling horses and wounded men could therefore tear huge gaps in a battleline; a flank attack by archers could funnel men closer and closer together, providing a still greater target for archers to exploit with their deadly weapon. Absolute mayhem could result from sustained 'showers' of literally thousands of arrows per minute onto a specific target area.

During the Wars of the Roses, however, both the use of the longbow and the archers' tactics developed somewhat. Primarily, both sides' knowledge of the longbow, learned and well rehearsed by commanders in the Hundred Years War, meant that now soldiers would advance and fight on foot against the terrible deluge of arrows. There were only minor exceptions to this rule. Consequently, archery did not win battles in the Wars of the Roses. More often than not it forced the side that was getting the worst of the barrage of arrows to manoeuvre, or to advance to the attack under a hail of still more missiles. The longbow also became less effective against advancing infantry at long distance, chiefly because of the improvements in knightly armour but also because of the acquisition of various other types of protection by common soldiers, such as the jack and brigandine.

If we compare fourteenth- and early fifteenth-century battles to battles that were fought in the Wars of the Roses we also see a marked difference in the longbow's effect. Against the Scots, such as at Dupplin Moor (1332), Halidon Hill (1333) and Homildon Hill (1402), the longbow did its job extremely well by permitting hardly any close-quarter fighting. However, all major engagements in the Wars of the Roses inevitably came to hand strokes, and indeed most battles were decided by this intensely brutal all-arms struggle in the end. Was this change as a result of better armoured protection, or were fewer bows being used on the battlefield at this time? It seems to have been a combination of both these factors and a few others.

A Wars of the Roses army employed its archers in the best possible place on the battlefield, which generally meant screening the front of the battleline, in other words fronting the traditional three medieval 'battles'. How were they organised? As we have seen, local contingents were mustered together, and they marched together: why should they not fight together as well, with 'a bow and a bill at his back'?[24] According to this theory, and following the chronicled evidence, longbowmen would, upon orders, take a few paces forward out of their own all-arms contingent and prepare to shoot. This movement forward would occur all along the battleline, by contingent, in order for the archers to be able to deliver the thousands of arrows that would be required to inflict the maximum amount of damage and disorganisation upon the enemy. It is unthinkable to my mind that any medieval commander would knowingly split his locally mustered contingents of soldiers to form a single body (vanguard) of strangers, without taking into account the backing of their own captains, men-at-arms and billmen. After they had loosed their arrows upon the enemy, they would step back in line again to fight hand-to-hand around their own banners, and with their comrades and captains, when the time came. This 'stepping forward' out of the main battleline was recorded at the battle of Crécy in 1346 when 'the English archers stepped forth one pace and let fly their arrows so wholly together and so thick it seemed [like] snow'.[25] There is also evidence this advance took place at the battle of Towton in 1461, and also in the actions of many other armies during this period.

At Stoke Field, the unfortunate Irish levies in the Earl of Lincoln's army were shot to pieces because of their lack of armoured protection, and according to the chronicler they soon took to their heels. However, more than one arrow wound to a soldier's body was a common occurrence in the Wars of the Roses. The Duke of Buckingham was wounded by three arrows in the face at the first battle of St Albans, and survived. At the same battle Henry Fenyingley, a nephew of Fastolf, 'fought manly, and was shot through the arms in three or four places'.[26] We may conclude, therefore, that at long distance many arrow wounds may have brought a man to his knees, and may have eventually killed him, but one or two superficial wounds would not. However, at close range the the 100–120 lb longbow was absolutely lethal, as it was capable of causing deep penetrating wounds up to the goose feathers at its end. Crossbow bolts, on the other hand, at 1000 lb draw weight, would probably be able to rip through several bodies at once, easily severing and cutting through any major organs in its path.

If deployed in open fields the archers in our fictitious Wars of the Roses army would have already hammered their six-foot sharpened wooden stakes into the ground for added protection against any pre-emptive cavalry attack. The Yorkists at Blore Heath (1459), under the command of the Earl of Salisbury, placed their stakes in anticipation that Lord Audley might foolishly launch a Lancastrian cavalry attack uphill, which he eventually did – several times, by all accounts. The nearby wood to the rear of the Yorkist line may have been useful in providing the raw materials for this type of spiked defence, and, standing within what fifteenth-century chroniclers metaphorically called the 'herce' or 'harrow' (that is, a chequerboard) formation, the Yorkist archers made short work of their adversaries from within what was, by then, a well tried and tested infantry formation.

The archer's task was to deliver as many arrows as possible, as fast as possible, to one specific target area. The 'right a sharp shower' that was delivered upon the Lancastrians at Tewkesbury might have been unleashed in unison along with artillery, or with mercenary crossbowmen, but primarily it was the longbowmen that caused an adversary who was unable to endure the ordeal to launch an attack. To inflict this damage and disorganisation longbowmen needed a good supply of arrows (possibly a hundred each), some of which were stuck into their belts from supplies provided by the baggage train. A large supply of arrows would also be stuck into the ground to enable the archer to shoot faster. We can therefore calculate that approximately 130,000 arrows were carried in our fictitious army, given that archers formed 50 per cent of the total force (48 arrows per man). If this formula is applied to the Yorkist archers who fought at the battle of Towton, we see that the number is even more staggering – one million arrows, weighing in transit approximately 40 tons.

When a battle commander was ready he gave his captains the order for their archers to 'notch', 'draw' and 'loose' their arrows upon the enemy, sending the first wave (for it must have looked like a wave breaking from one side of the battleline to the other) high into the air. Before the first arrows had reached their target another volley was following on behind it, given the time it took an archer to re-load his bow, and another shower of arrows were in flight at the same time – but this time coming from the direction of the enemy lines.

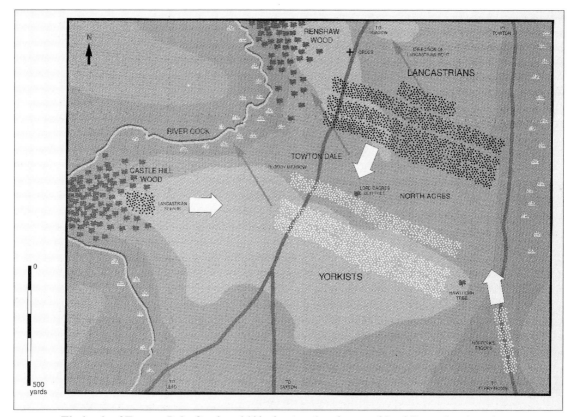

The battle of Towton, Palm Sunday, 1461, showing the advance of Lord Fauconberg's archers (Yorkist front line) and the main movements on the field which ended in the bloody Lancastrian rout. (Author)

Many references are made to arrow wounds during the Wars of the Roses, some taking many months to heal properly, some unmistakably fatal, still more being infected by dirty clothing, then later proving fatal. John Paston was wounded by an arrow in his right elbow at the battle of Barnet in 1471; the Earl of Warwick was injured in his leg by a stray arrow at Ferrybridge in March 1461; Henry VI and Buckingham were both wounded in the face and neck at St Albans in 1455; Lord Dacre and Lord Clifford were also shot in the head and neck at the battle of Towton when they removed their protective bevors, and so forth.[27] Many soldiers who did not have adequate protection would have come to grief in this way, and those men who had jacks would invariably suffer wounding to their arms and legs, if not to their upper body, depending on the padded or armoured quality of their jackets. The sound of thousands and thousands of clattering and ricocheting missiles would have been briefly interspersed by an instant of silence between volleys, and then the process would start all over again in a deadly rhythmic sequence. These brief silences must have been a clear indication for archers to respond, but returning fire under these dreadful circumstances must have been extremely difficult; greater numbers of longbowmen, placed in advantageous tactical positions, may have caused further action on the battlefield to take place, in this case by provoking the enemy to advance.

At the battle of Tewkesbury the *Arrivall* tells us that the Yorkist archers, after delivering a barrage of arrows to one flank of the Lancastrians, did 'again-ward to them, both with shot of arrows and guns, whereof never the less they had not so great plenty as had the King'.[28] At Towton it was the following wind that enabled Lord Fauconberg to take advantage of the Lancastrian archers who were blindly shooting short of Yorkist ranks in a snowstorm:

The Lord Fauconberg, which led the forward of King Edward's battle being a man of great policy and of much experience in martial feats caused every archer under his standard to shoot one flight and then made them stand still. The northern men, feeling the shoot, but by reason of the snow, not perfectly viewing the distance between them and their enemies like hardy men shot their sheaf arrows as fast as they might, but all their shot was lost and their labour in vain for they came not near the southern men by 40 tailor's yards. When their shot was almost spent the Lord Fauconberg marched forward with his archers, who not only shot their own sheaves, but also gathered the arrows of their enemies and let a great part of them fly against their own masters.[29]

As the Earl of Pembroke's forces at Edgecote, and the Irish contingent at Stoke, were deficient of archers, the former were forced to advance, and the latter to be annihilated where they stood; the Duke of Somerset advanced his battle at Tewkesbury because 'his fellowship were sore annoyed in the place where they were, as well with gun shot, as with shot of arrows, which they would nor durst abide'.[30] Wherever the advantage was exploited, the effect of the cloth–yard arrow was the same. It caused only about ten to fifteen minutes of disorganisation, but this was enough for only a few volleys to cause major disruption in the ranks. The arrow storm must have been difficult to bear even for a brief period of time; as the Monk of Malmesbury states, 'After the third or fourth, or at the very most the sixth, draw of the bows, men knew which side would win.'[31] In this situation the morale of soldiers was all-important.

Along with thousands of others with their helmeted heads bowed instinctly in defence, soldiers would have huddled desperately together to await the next volley. Splintering and bouncing off at deadly obtuse angles, arrow shafts that had hit their targets might not penetrate the well-protected areas of a soldier's body, but might find their mark elsewhere in the feet, hands, legs, arms and faces of all who were in range. If hit, archers and footsoldiers would have tried to pull arrowshafts out themselves in an effort to continue shooting back, and to survive the ordeal of battle when it came to hand-to-hand combat. However, those nobles and men-at-arms who were encased in complete harness would find consolation in the fact that their costly investment in armour plate was proving invaluable. Listening to the weird clanking sound coming from the outside of their body armour, while their visors were tightly closed to the falling wooden hail, the 'chivalrous' could only watch the bizarre spectacle unfold. At this point the cries of pain and confusion coming from the ranks would have drowned out any orders that they could give, so much so that returning fire would have become instinctive and decidedly erratic.

There is no doubt that archers were, as Philippe de Commines put it, 'the chiefest strength of an army in the day of battle'.[32] As long as they could shoot they needed not be great masters of their art, or indeed be veterans of other battles. Veteran archers, after all, knew that they would be receiving back across the 'no man's land' of the medieval battlefield as much as they delivered to the enemy. This explains Commines's interesting viewpoint on the usefulness, or otherwise, of experience during this testing duel of arrows:

> I would have them [the archers] indifferently mounted, that they may not be afraid of losing their horses, or rather that they had none at all; and for one day it is better to have raw soldiers that have never been in any action, than those that have been trained up in the wars; and in this I am of the same opinion with the English, who, without dispute, are the best archers in the world.[33]

HAND-TO-HAND COMBAT

Large numbers of dead or dying soldiers would not have been apparent at this stage of the battle. Men would no doubt be wounded, some horrendously so with arrows, but most soldiers would be hoping to move forward, or alternatively away from the incessant arrow storm, if only to present a continuously moving target to their opponents' longbowmen. Commanders would have been impatiently waiting to give the order to advance because of the worry, and fickle nature, of their troops who faced such a hellish situation. However, it was how this advance was instigated, and responded to, that presented great problems to Wars of the Roses armies, not only with regard to command, communication and cohesion, but also in the will of others to support the attack.

Archers might shoot as they ventured forward from the supplies of arrows that they had stuck through their belts, and also from the spent arrows that had fallen on the ground, and it is certain that they caused more casualties at this closer range, as the advance got nearer to the enemy line, chiefly because of the longbow's great penetrating power at this distance. An attack made in a confined area, such as that attempted at the second battle of St Albans in 1461 where archers were stationed at the top of an uphill street, failed miserably against the power of the longbow, and other ways to outflank the enemy had to be found. Prominent nobles who were leading a charge at the enemy line might be felled by arrows, as Lord Audley was at Blore Heath, adding to the overall confusion of an assault with regard to command. Some attacks were launched impetuously and were promptly dealt with by various forms of ambush, surprise attack and chance response: at Tewkesbury, for example, the Duke of Somerset's battle arrived at the junction of two Yorkist battles because they misread the terrain. Armies also had to march up steep slopes and scramble up redoubts, some of the soldiers in full armour, against a withering hail of missiles in snow, mud and, as at Barnet,

Bloody Meadow in the snow. The Lancastrian right wing advanced from right to left up this slope towards the Yorkist line during the battle of Towton in 1461, and made a fighting retreat back this way when their ranks broke in the afternoon. Five gravepits are said to have been dug near here due to the appalling mass slaughter which occurred in the rout. (Author)

through the animated uncertainty of a swirling mist. In such cases banners made of satin and worsted, set permanently on the fly with buckram, would have kept local contingents, and therefore the armies' battles, together in some sort of swarming and disjointed way while advancing, but inevitably there would have been some problems of cohesion as the drums beat the advance and the men slowly closed upon each other.

It has been chronicled that many halts were needed when troops advanced towards the enemy. Aside from the effect of difficult terrain, soldiers had to catch their breath, especially men encased in armour, and these pregnant pauses often resulted in more casualties and confusion. Many Wars of the Roses battlefields had hedges and ditches in the no man's land between the armies, not to mention ploughed ridge and furrow field systems and rivers, which had to be negotiated and crossed by armies. At St Albans, back gardens, houses and the narrow medieval streets prevented a more straightforward assault, and at Ferrybridge a bridgehead had to be established, with wooden planks placed over broken palings in order to get at the enemy. At sieges, especially at Bamburgh in 1464, soldiers had to scramble up mounds of rubble and get through breeches in curtain walls, and at Northampton an entrenched camp had to be infiltrated. When we consider all these factors, therefore, we can see that it was not by chance that a great many of the pitched battles fought during this period were lost by the side who advanced first.

Contemporary chronicles also provide instances where battle commanders were reluctant to support others in an advance. Jean de Waurin states that the Earl of Northumberland was slow to engage at the battle of Towton, which eventually caused a pivotal swing in the Lancastrian battleline.[34] Similarly, Lord Wenlock, a notorious turncoat, failed to support an attack launched by Edmund, Duke of Somerset, at Tewkesbury, which may have led later to Wenlock's death from a blow by his enraged superior's battle-axe.[35] The wily Earl of Northumberland decided not to support Richard III at the battle of Bosworth, which instilled distinct feelings of treachery in the Yorkist ranks, and in the end contributed to their defeat on a grand scale.[36] Thus the medieval battle group could become isolated even before it reached the point of contact with the enemy.

The disunity so often seen in a Wars of the Roses army comes more sharply into focus when we explore the rifts that existed between the nobles and gentry who decided that political and family issues should be worked out on the battlefield. The Gascoigne and Plumpton blood feud, which came to a head in the 1470s, was maintained by two retainers who fought on the same side in the Wars of the Roses, in this case for their benefactor the Earl of Northumberland. However, they held such grudges against each other that Northumberland found it difficult to control them.[37] Similar feuds forced contending lords and gentry onto opposing sides, where political and family issues were ultimately settled at the point of a sword, or with the headman's axe after battles were over. Major feuds, such as the York–Beaufort conflict and the Neville–Percy 'vendetta', were perpetuated for generations, and gave the Wars of the Roses a particularly sharp edge when it came to the final all-arms confrontation on the battlefield. The blood feuds between Molynes and Paston, Harrington and Stanley, Talbot and Berkeley and Bonville and Courteney were just as important, and potentially as dangerous, as the major quarrels that sparked off the Wars of the Roses. When nobles and their retainers faced each other across the small space that separated life from death, and gain from loss of goods or territory, anything was possible on the battlefield.

During the savage hand-to-hand fighting, when blows would be falling on an individual from all directions at once, the household men of a noble or retainer were invaluable for protection. The ability of the knight to exploit the support of his household to achieve great renown in battle is seen in King Edward IV's actions at the battle of Barnet in 1471:

For the king, trusting verily in God's help, our blessed Lady, and Saint George, took to him great hardiness and courage for to suppress the falsehood of all them that so traitorously had conspired against him, where through, with the faithful, well-beloved and mighty assistance of his fellowship, that in great number dissevered not from his person, and were well assured unto him as to them was possible, he manly, vigorously and valiantly assailed them, in the midst and strongest of their battle. Where with great violence, he beat and bare down afore him all that stood in his way and then turned to the range, first on one hand, and then on the other hand, in length, and so beat and bare them down, so that nothing might stand in the sight of him and the well assured fellowship that attended truly upon him.[38]

In this life and death struggle the attitude of individuals to combat was crucial. Written in about 1466, Jean de Bueil's *Le Jouvencel* sets out the attitude of a fifteenth-century nobleman to combat and tells of the glory and self-sacrifice that was expected in this bloody environment:

What a joyous thing is war, for many fine deeds are heard and seen in its course, and many good lessons learnt from it . . . You love your comrade so much in war. When you see that your quarrel is just and your blood is fighting well, tears rise in your eyes. A great sweet feeling of loyalty and pity fills your heart on seeing your friend so valiantly exposing his body to execute and accomplish the command of our Creator. And then you prepare to go and live or die with him, and for love not abandon him. And out of that there arises such a delectation, that he who has not tasted it is not fit to say what a delight is. Do you think that a man who does that fears death? Not at all; for he feels strengthened, he is so elated, that he does not know where he is. Truly he is afraid of nothing.[39]

Here the attitude of the nobility to war, comradeship and death, is set in the context of religion. In all medieval accounts these feelings are so closely linked together that in the mind of the 'chivalrous' they became one and the same on the battlefield. According to de Beuil, for the higher classes at least, fighting to the death in plate armour is seen as a highly spiritual, even ecstatic experience. This feeling must have been so powerful in medieval warfare that mutilation and over-kill were the most likely results of any sustained combat.

Descriptions of actual fighting in the Wars of the Rose are rare and vague; the few eye-witness reports that we do have describe only the immediate area of combat of the author. This, for example, from the Flemish chronicler Jean de Waurin, who fought at the battle of Verneuil in 1424, and went on to chronicle the whole of the Wars of the Roses:

The Duke of Bedford, as I heard say for I could not see or understand everything, because I was pretty well occupied defending myself, performed marvellous feats of arms and slew many a man. He laid about him with his axe which he held in both hands – there was nothing he did not strike down; he was a man of great physical strength, with very powerful limbs, and both prudent and fearless in arms.[40]

Amid the incessant noise and confusion of medieval warfare and above the forest of blades, poll-axes and other instruments of death, the heraldic banners of those who fought were the only rallying point on the battlefield for the men who fought the Wars of the Roses. Fighting close to the banner would have been the noble or captain commanding the contingent, and it is recorded in contemporary chronicles that soldiers were kept as close as possible to this rallying point when hand-to-hand fighting began. At the battle of Bosworth the Earl of Oxford, 'afraid that in the fighting his men would be surrounded by the multitude, gave out the order through the ranks that no soldier should go more than ten feet from the standards'.[41] This had the effect of contracting his battleline for a short while, thereby making a new assault, in a new formation, possible. Thus some order could be maintained amid the confusion, but only at a local level. Communication throughout the whole army, or the large battle group, was almost impossible when armies were finally pushed together into a writhing mass of bodies and weapon points. The metallic din of battle consumed all, and over the shouts and cries of the soldiers it is highly likely that nothing meaningful could productively pierce the confusion. Thus the importance of the small local contingent of soldiers. Soldiers who fought cohesively beneath their own town's or noble's banner were as important as the regiments of 'Pals' that were exploited to the full during the First World War. Comradeship is irreplaceable in the thick of battle, whatever the century, and on the Wars of the Roses battlefield this factor of fighting spirit, cohesion and communication was often the difference between victory or defeat.

The group fighting of the tourney was the training ground for the contingent captains. It allowed knights and men-at-arms to become conversant with simple battle tactics whereby the banner and the soldier's livery jacket, as uniform symbols of unity and control, helped to keep contingents together amid increasing battlefield confusion. Queen Margaret's troops were all given livery badges of the Prince of Wales to wear in 1461, beside their own livery colours and emblems, probably as an attempt to solve this confused aspect of warfare on a much larger scale, and perhaps also to promote unity in the ranks of an allied army. Whether this added to the overall confusion in Queen Margaret's Lancastrian army is not known, but the importance of recognition on the Wars of the Roses battlefield is not to be ignored. The mistaken identity of the Earl of Oxford's troops at the battle of Barnet reminds us of what could happen in confused circumstances – in this case defeat for the Earl of Warwick.

Cries of loyalty, or warning, like 'A Clarence', or 'A Warwick', were used by men to rally troops, as well as to create some sort of order out of the mayhem which surrounded the Wars of the Roses soldier on the battlefield. However, it is still difficult for us to imagine what sort of order existed when fighting was at its height, and when horrendous injuries were being inflicted all around. To add to this chaos, piles of dead would also be forming in mounds between the armies, hindering those that fought. Some of these human 'barriers' were recorded in medieval chronicles as being as high as a spear, although this is an exaggeration. Six bodies on top of each other is not an impossibility, and this unsteady platform must have been far from easy to fight on, or clamber over, in order to renew the conflict with the enemy. Soldiers in this case would try to find an uncluttered area of ground to fight upon, perhaps only a few feet away from them, providing they had the room or the time to do this. A continuously moving and see-sawing front line would have resulted, which contradicts the static picture of close-quarter combat that is often assumed. In fact, several battles during the Wars of the Roses were 'tidal', incessantly swaying backwards and forwards; some battlelines pivoted, some were overlapped and rotated and yet others were renewed after several short pauses, sometimes over the space of many hours of fighting. In this situation the feats of arms so cherished and sought after by knights were important for morale; the common soldiers obviously responded to their superiors' exposure to danger on a local level, as the well-protected knight laid waste to all before him with his poll-axe.

In the thick of the fighting several blows may have been needed to bring a man to the ground; only as more room opened up were weapons such as the bill and the halberd useful. At the battle of Flodden – some years after the Wars of the Roses, but nevertheless comparable for military purposes – it was recorded that it took four or five blows from a bill to fell a man, whereas it took only one from a halberd. Close-quarter weapons such as long thrusting swords, axes, maces,

The Towton Grave: multiple trauma to the back of the head. There are two criss-cross penetrating blows, a superficial blade injury, and two dagger wounds to the base of the skull. (Bradford University)

daggers and mauls would be used when space was limited or when the pushing and shoving of bodies prevented poll-arms from being used in such limited areas. Battlefield graves bear silent witness to the ghastly injuries inflicted, primarily on the human skull, from such heavy weapons. A sword thrust to the body might not produce any great pain initially because of the vast amounts of adrenaline pumping through the body at the height of combat, but as the adrenaline subsided, the agony would result in the soldier collapsing, causing a slow death from loss of blood and later hypothermia if he was left out on the field of battle to die. Filthy clothing or stuffing from padded jacks would have been pushed inside wounds, including arrow wounds, which would cause blood poisoning and death from infection, even if tended by a physician. A heavy blow from a mace, war hammer or axe would, given the right circumstances, be more lethal, as it could penetrate a helmet and shatter the skull, causing massive haemorrhaging.

Close-quarter combat must therefore have been short-lived. Chroniclers often increased the length of battles to enhance their stories, or for propaganda purposes. The ten hours recorded in the chronicles for the battle of Towton, for example, not only represent it as a battle of biblical proportions, but also indicate the chroniclers' confusion as they mistakenly linked it with the battle of Ferrybridge, fought the previous day.[41] The battle of Wakefield, on the other hand, is recorded as lasting only half an hour, which is probably a lot nearer the truth, although here too chroniclers may have distorted such information for their own ends. The main question to answer is how long a human being could have fought non-stop, especially in armour, under the stress and strain of what was clearly a terrific test of human endurance. For knights, at least, two to four hours' fighting at the tourney was not uncommon, providing that servants could lead them out of combat to refresh themselves at certain intervals. So did this occur on the battlefield?

Contemporary accounts record that men did come out of the line to take liquid because of the threat of heat exhaustion and dehydration, and that they were sometimes killed because of it. Lord Dacre, for example, was killed by an arrow in the head at the battle of Towton when he took off his helmet to drink a cup of wine in the heat of battle.[42] In this case, the noble's household men could continue to fight in their master's absence on a fairly broad front because even minor knights had a great many followers. However, for the common soldier there could be no respite. Breaking off from the enemy meant certain death from wounding and blows to the rear of his body; falling in the press with others meant suffocation under the piles of dead that covered medieval battlefields; and continued fighting led to fatigue and heavy sword arms. The stamina of soldiers in such a dire situation is incomprehensible, but this strength is backed up by the massively boned bodies of those soldiers who have been found in battlefield graves.

THE ROUT

Success or failure in Wars of the Roses battles hinged on many factors. A brief look at the period between 1455 and 1487 gives us some indication of the various causes of victory or defeat.

The steep slope leading down to the River Cock valley, where many Lancastrian soldiers perished at the battle of Towton. The terrain played a decisive part in what occurred here, as it did in many other battles of the period. (Author)

The first battle of St Albans ended with a surprise attack by the Yorkists and the death of leading nobles on the Lancastrian side. Blore Heath reminds us of the folly of cavalry attacks during this period, and also of the loss of a commander at the crucial stage of a battle. The 'non-battle' of Ludford and the battle of Northampton were won as a direct result of treachery in the ranks, and the battle of Wakefield was decided by the death of the Duke of York who ventured blindly into the jaws of a numerically superior force. At the battle of Mortimer's Cross Lancastrian mercenary troops were inferior to English Marchmen who were largely protecting their own lands on the Welsh border, and some days later at St Albans we see that Warwick's men were hard pressed to redress their disjointed battleline which had been deployed irresponsibly and in the wrong direction. At Towton, the Duke of Norfolk's arrival at a crucial moment of the battle unbalanced the delicate situation and led to a massive Lancastrian rout. At Hedgeley Moor a leading noble was killed, while at Hexham the Duke of Somerset's army was pushed unexpectedly into a treacherous river. The battles of Edgecote and Losecote Field were decided by superior forces. At Nibley Green a purely local issue was decided by the death of contending nobles, and at Barnet in 1471 mistaken identity, then treachery, caused the defeat and death of the Earl of

Warwick and his brother Montague. When the third Duke of Somerset's attack at Tewkesbury faltered and broke, others fled the field, and at Bosworth treachery and an ill-fated cavalry charge played a crucial part in the events that led to the crowning of Henry Tudor. Stoke Field, on the other hand, hinged on the demise of the 'naked' Irish contingents at the hands of the longbow. In short, a number of outside influences took their toll on the fighting stamina of hard-pressed contingents and caused them to break and run for their lives as military loyalty gave way to the panic and fear of being caught in a rout.

It was here that the English countryside played a major part in the survival or otherwise of the Wars of the Roses soldier. It was also in the rout from the field that the most casualties occurred, especially among men encased in armour who were attempting to flee on foot in an effort to reach their mounts, which were tethered some distance away from the front line. It was also here where mass execution could occur, mutilation could take place, looting could be carried out and old scores settled with the consent of a superior or, at the highest level, at the behest of the king of England himself.

The severity of the rout from a medieval battlefield was largely dictated by the terrain over which the escape attempt was made. Even now, areas of the greatest battlefield slaughter are marked quite precisely on modern maps to remind us that, even if for only a brief period of time, the terrain witnessed the ugliest side of warfare. These areas are now recorded as the 'bloody meadows' of Wars of the Roses legend. Some killing fields even have their own descriptive names, such as 'Red Gutter', 'The Bridge of Bodies', 'Fall Ings' and 'Dead Man's Bottom'. Here both nobles and common soldiers were mercilessly cut down and invariably stripped and looted in the final act of the Wars of the Roses battlefield ordeal.

Casualties at the infamous battle of Towton in 1461 were exceptionally high because of the disadvantageous terrain which the Lancastrian army encountered as it broke and ran in panic. Steep, snow-covered slopes to the west of the battlefield meant that soldiers hurtling away from their Yorkist pursuers slipped, slid and tumbled towards one obstacle after another, finally reaching the steep-sided River Cock, where Yorkist cavalry went to work cutting down refugees in their thousands. In attempting to wade across the river, great numbers of fleeing Lancastrians must have turned the panic into the worst kind of confusion, and ultimately large-scale drownings, as men scrambled to gain the opposite bank in their desperate attempt to escape. It is not surprising that dead bodies choked the river and created human bridging points over which many other Lancastrian soldiers tried to cross. Ultimately the little River Cock burst its banks and started flowing with blood. The grisly platforms of the human dead helped the escaping Lancastrians to disperse into the countryside where the lucky ones found temporary hiding places. However, most soldiers headed for York, their initial mustering point before the battle, where yet again more drownings and death met them at Tadcaster bridge. Here the River Wharfe had to be crossed, but the bridge had been broken down previously, and we may be sure that from this point on death and destruction continued to follow the Lancastrians right up to the gates of York.

The terrain presented similar problems to other armies in the Wars of the Roses. At the battle of Northampton, for example, 'many men were drowned beside the field in the river at a mill';[43] at Wakefield the River Calder caused many men to be slaughtered in the rout, and at Hexham the river called Devil's Water hampered the Lancastrian army's escape; at Tewkesbury a similar scene of drowning and death awaited the Duke of Somerset's army as it fled in panic towards the town and the River Avon:

> Upon this his men, seeing that the king gave them enough to do before them, were greatly dismayed and abashed, and so took flight in the park, and into the meadow that was near, and into the lanes and dykes where they best hoped to escape the danger. Never the less, many were distressed, taken, and slain . . . And so it befell in the chase of them that many of them were slain, and at a mill, in the meadow by the town, many of them were drowned. Many ran towards the town, many to the church, to the abbey, and elsewhere, as best they might.[44]

Dominic Mancini observed that the 'English manner' of fighting was chiefly responsible for this type of large-scale slaughter, especially among the nobility. He states that because horses were abandoned behind the lines so that their riders could pursue the fight on foot, it was accepted that 'no one should hold any hope of flight'.[45] As a result of this, many men in armour were cut down and robbed in the rout from the battlefield, and it is here we find the reason behind the high casualty rate among the higher classes during the Wars of the Roses. Several footsoldiers could easily track down and pounce on a noble, break open his armour and kill him when he was isolated without the support of his household men. His valuables, including rings, purses, weapons and armour, could be then distributed as the spoils of war. To add to this terrifying situation, the rout would herald the arrival of soldiers on horseback who were given the task to ride down their opponents. Cavalry detachments with their long thrusting spears would have found their prey sapped by the ordeal of battle. At the second battle of St Albans the Lancastrians spurred their horses into action when the middle ward of the Earl of Warwick's army was routed on Barnards Heath. Abbot Whethamstede probably saw what occurred near his abbey:

> The southern men, who were fiercer at the beginning, were broken quickly afterwards, and the more quickly because looking back, they saw no one coming up from the main body of the king's army, or preparing to bring them help, whereupon they turned their backs on the northern men and fled. And the northern men seeing this pursued them very swiftly on horseback; and catching a good many of them, ran them through with their lances.[46]

Death tolls in the rout, therefore, in some cases exceeded the number of dead and dying already lying on the main battlefield. The terrain, however, was not the only culprit for causing the more disastrous routs of the Wars of the Roses: there was also the fact that everyone fought on foot, and therefore had also to try to escape on foot. Turning to run was obviously the worst possible scenario for a knight faced with defeat. Some who decided early that the battle was lost may have reached their horses, but death through repeated stabbing and crushing by heavy weapons was the usual result of a knight turning to run.

For the common soldier the prospect of running was very different. Lightly armoured men were nimble enough to avoid pursuers, and ultimately the common soldier's life did not hold out the prospect of great rewards for the victorious army. It is therefore not surprising that Edward IV 'plentifully used his mercy in saving the lives of his poor wretched commons'[47] on more than one occasion. Common soldiers at least would be able to live, and in some cases fight, another day if they managed to escape into the surrounding countryside.

CHAPTER 7

'Now are our brows bound with victorious wreaths'

The fate of the men who fought and died in the Wars of the Roses is graphically portrayed in the skeletal remains which were recovered from the grave that was found purely by accident in Towton village while this book was being written. The battle of Towton was fought on 29 March 1461 during severe wintry weather conditions by two massive medieval armies, both of which had everything to gain from the battle, as well as everything to lose, because of a blood feud which had reached fever pitch. The skeletal remains from the Towton grave are still the subject of major research and debate, but archaeologists have already indicated that the find is of great importance, not only with regard to our understanding of fifteenth-century warfare and medieval man, but also because the methods and processes used in the excavation may be invaluable when examining any other mass graves that may be found in the future.

The grave at Towton is comparable to the types of war graves that are mentioned in all the topographic histories, maps and chronicles that deal with this particular period in history: it is basically of rectangular shape, that is to say a trench grave. Preliminary excavation work soon revealed that the bodies had been tossed into the grave in a random fashion, and that most of the skeletons were orientated in an east–west compass direction next to the main medieval road from London to York. The grave also contained a slope at one end, presumably so that the grave diggers could fill it with bodies more easily, and further evidence suggests that backfill was carried out from the opposite end of the grave, towards this slight incline, when the bodies were first buried there in 1461.

As it is sited in very hard ground, and as shale, rocks and rubble as well as earth were used to cover the bodies over in 1461, it must have taken some time and effort to dig the grave out initially. The cold weather conditions during and after the battle of Towton must have helped the grave diggers' work considerably in that the bodies would have been preserved a little longer than normal. In short, the Towton casualties (some 20,000–28,000 according to the heralds' reports) need not have been buried immediately. Indeed, George Neville, who reported the battle only a few days later, confirms in his letter to Francesco Coppini that immediate burial may not have been possible, because the dead were spread over a vast area – six miles long by three miles four furlongs wide.[1]

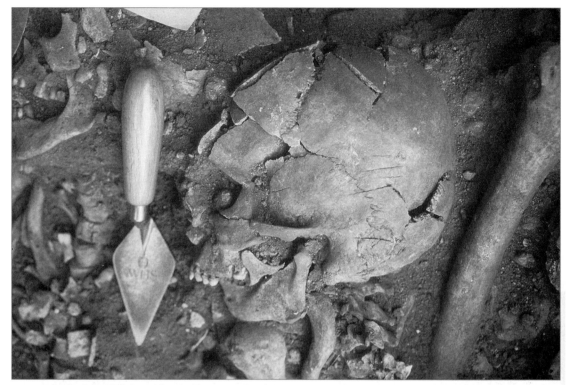

The face of medieval battle. Five superficial chopping wounds to the left side of the head indicate probably only a few of the many horrific injuries sustained by some of the soldiers found in the Towton Grave. (Bradford University)

In all, a maximum of thirty-seven male skeletons were found in the grave. Twenty-six more had immediately been re-buried before the current team of archaeologists were called in: this previous excavation of bones, therefore, was not examined or researched by archaeologists. No artefacts were found in the grave except for a very simple copper ring, a small piece from some kind of studded garment, possibly a fragment from a brigandine, and what might have been a bodkin arrowhead lodged in the spine of one of the skeletons. This absence of artefacts indicates that the bodies were stripped of all clothes and valuables before burial, which seems to have been common practice during this period after battles had taken place, and also fits in with the fact that looting was rife on medieval battlefields immediately after the fighting had ended. Twenty-nine of the bodies found in the grave were complete skeletons; they were laid head to toe in what became after decomposition only about half a metre of earth. The average ages of the bodies varied from late teens to men of forty-five years old, which is what we would expect from Commissions of Array, from the stipulations of the Statute of Winchester, and also from our knowledge of the average life expectancy of individuals in the later medieval period.

Almost all of the men from the Towton grave suffered multiple cranial injuries which undoubtedly caused their deaths in most cases. No doubt most also suffered other wounds in the more fleshy parts of the body, evidence of which cannot of course be discerned by examining the skeletal remains alone. The abundance of head trauma ranges from small sword and dagger cuts to massive depression fractures and punctures to the skull, sometimes in the shape of the weapon that made them. Arrow wounds are also apparent. Much heavier concussive weapons obviously caused the more serious major fractures, but some smaller holes were apparent, especially at the back of the skull of one individual, which were at first thought to be arrow wounds. However, upon further research, these holes suggest premeditated, deep penetrating dagger wounds, that were purposely grouped closely together for maximum effect. Indeed, several thrusts were aimed at the same area, and twisted into the skull in a calculated and deadly fashion. It seems that helmets were either ripped off by attackers or were not in place when most of these injuries occurred.

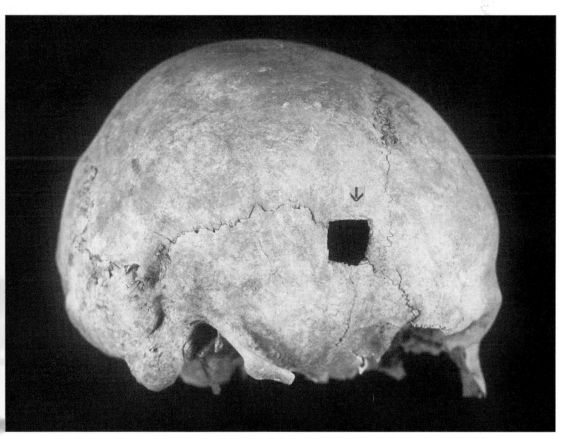

The Towton Grave: injury to the right side of the head, possibly made by the 'crow's beak' of a poll-axe or the spike from a bill. (Bradford University)

Injuries to the torso, including blows and cuts to the chest cavity, the rib cage and the back of the body, are generally not apparent, which confirms that these areas had armoured protection at the time of death. As has been described in previous chapters, brigandines and jacks were commonly worn by footsoldiers, not to mention plate armour which was worn by the more affluent men-at-arms. The evidence of the Towton grave pit seems to suggest that all of these body armours were in place when the soldiers were killed. However, given the fact that there seems to have been time to break open or rip through these garments, unbuckle armour and then kill individuals with several repeated blows, it is surprising that only head injuries were inflicted. The presence of other cuts to the shoulders, arms and neck of certain individuals indicates the haphazard nature of these frenzied attacks with heavy weapons, swords and daggers; it also provides some evidence to suggest that decapitation took place and throats were cut in the process.

The battlefield graves that were found at Wisby in Sweden in 1901–1929 show skeletal remains with an abundance of deep wounds (cuts to the bone) to the arms and legs of the medieval soldiers unearthed there.[2] This, at first sight, might have been expected of the Towton skeletons, bearing in mind the documented absence of armoured protection to all these more vital areas of movement. Generally, however, the Towton soldiers do not show any sign of these types of injury, except wounding to the backs of the arms. It has therefore been suggested that some of the victims of what appears to have been a 'massacre' at Towton village crossed their arms in front of their faces and heads in an attempt to prevent the blows from raining down on their skulls. Cuts to the forearms of some of the soldiers are therefore suggestive of a feeble, and instinctive, attempt at self-defence. The soldiers may also have been disarmed, or more than likely unarmed at the time of death.

The Towton grave is thus highly unusual. In fact, taking all the available evidence into account, it appears that this grave is not a battlefield grave at all, but contains the remains of many of the soldiers who were caught up with and killed in the rout. This claim can be supported by various facts. First, the grave is over half a mile away from the actual battlefield, in the direction of the Lancastrian rout (although one could argue that the rout *was* the battlefield); secondly, there is topographical evidence to suggest that there are other actual battlefield graves in existence; thirdly, the injuries to the soldiers in the Towton grave constitute repeated blows to one area of the body – the skull – which took time to effect – in fact, the extensive wounding to one individual (ten head wounds in all) suggest overkill; and fourthly, there is some mutilation on the bodies, which again took time to complete. Several small cuts to the skull, as well as repeated slashing and cutting to the side of the head, all indicate that speed was not an issue here.

Could all these horrific repeated injuries to the head have been carried out under battlefield conditions? I suggest not. In the confusion of battle a soldier would not have had the time to deliver several repeated blows to one individual, or one main area of the body, while other soldiers around him presented such an immediate danger. Therefore it must be concluded that the Towton grave contained soldiers who were killed in the Lancastrian rout from the battlefield, or

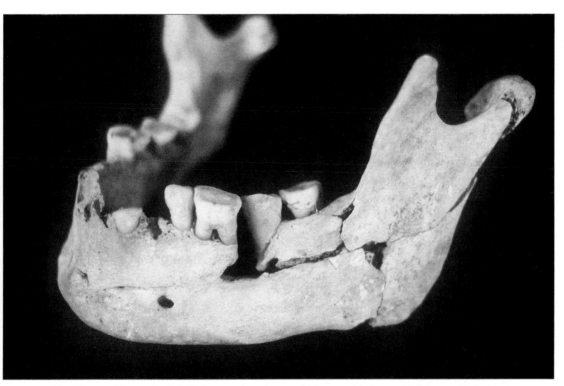

The Towton Grave: healed blade wound to the mandible, most likely resulting in permanent facial deformity. Incredibly this wound did not contribute to this soldier's death at Towton, as it had been sustained some time before the battle took place. (Bradford University)

soldiers who were captured and then killed after the battle was over. This hypothesis cannot be proved, of course, until the Towton grave can be compared to an actual battlefield grave pit.

Aside from the many major injuries that caused death to the individuals found in the Towton grave, many of the soldiers who were unearthed were veterans. Some cuts to the head and body were received well before the battle of Towton began, and the healing processes of bone indicate that many soldiers had survived previous fights with a surprising degree of resilience. One individual had previously suffered a terrible cut to his face, almost splitting his features in two at the jaw bone and through the mouth. The jaw had been very badly damaged and dislocated, resulting in what must have been a major stitching and cauterising process for the surgeon, not to mention immense deformity of the face for the soldier.

How resilient and tough some of these Wars of the Roses soldiers were can be seen from the massively boned skeletal remains that have been unearthed from the Towton grave. At the time of death most of the soldiers' teeth were also in good condition, indicating an adequate diet, and no major illnesses were detected

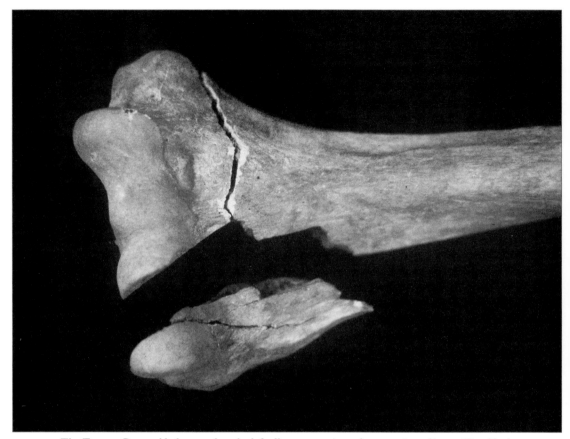

The Towton Grave: blade wound to the left elbow, removing a large section of bone. (Bradford University)

on the bodies. However, the amount of damage caused to the back and spines of some of the individuals suggests a life of hard manual labour. A skeleton recovered from Henry VIII's warship, the *Mary Rose*, shows repeated use of the shoulder blade and left forearm, the tell-tale sign of a longbowman; the same disjointed bone fragments found on the Towton skeletons must point to the same conclusion.[3]

As we have seen, arrow wounds from the longbow were very common. In April 1471, after the battle of Barnet, the Pastons received news that one of their family had been wounded in the left forearm by an arrow, just below the elbow. Even though John Paston had fought for the Earl of Warwick, and was therefore on the run from the Yorkists after the battle, he managed to survive, with the help of a paid surgeon. However, many other soldiers died both on and off the battlefield as a result of infected wounds caused by soiled arrowheads or from fragments of clothing entering deep within the body. Such a wound could result in tetanus, sepsis or eventually peritonitis, even though the initial wound might not have seemed to be dangerous at the time. Of course medieval surgeons were present in most Wars of the Roses armies (Humphrey Stafford's physician, for instance, was retained by military indenture), but treatment for wounds was still only rudimentary, especially under battlefield conditions.[4] John Paston was so concerned about his wound that he had to obtain money from his family to pay his surgeon for constantly attending his arrow wound with 'leechcraft' and 'physic', when all his goods had been lost in his escape from the battlefield in 1471.[5]

What of the fate of the soldiers who actually died in the fighting? Were they all buried on the field of battle, or were some taken from the field to be buried elsewhere? Were Wars of the Roses soldiers remembered at all? Were their widows provided for? All these questions need to be answered, in order to shed some light on the medieval attitude to warfare.

The abundance of dead and wounded on the medieval battlefield and their effect on the living, who sometimes even had to camp for the night where they had fought, is vividly recounted in the memoirs of Philippe de Commines. After the confusing battle of Montl'héry in 1465 part of the Burgundian army drew their wagons together in a laager to camp amid the carnage of the day's battle:

> In the meantime, the Count of Charolois ate and drank a little, and all the rest of the army did the same; after which the wound in his neck was carefully dressed. To make room for him, before he could sit down to eat, four or five dead bodies had to be removed, and two trusses of straw were brought for him to sit on. As we were removing the dead men, one of the poor stark naked creatures called out for some drink, and on putting a little ptisan (of which the Count had drank) into his mouth, he came to himself.[6]

No matter whether the Wars of the Roses soldier had experienced victory or defeat, he invariably had to return home – often a great distance from the battlefield. Victory would mean being discharged of his obligation to serve, and usually payment in loot and coins for his passage back to his own town or village would be provided. Defeated troops were not so fortunate. Some were wounded, others were deprived of goods, armour, horses and most of their money, and yet others were hunted down in the aftermath. Gerhard von Wesel commented on the state of soldiers returning home from the battle of Barnet in 1471:

> and with them many of their followers wounded, mostly in the face and lower half of the body, a very pitiable sight. May God preserve them . . . Those who set out with good horses and sound bodies returned home with sorry nags and bandaged faces, some without noses etc. and preferred to stay indoors. May God have pity at this wretched spectacle, for it is said that there had been no fiercer battle in England for the last 100 years than happened last Easter as I have described.[7]

After battles were over, men of noble birth were taken from the field after first being sought out by the heralds who traditionally had the laborious task of

Bloody Meadow, Tewkesbury. This thin tract of land, which eventually leads to the banks of the River Avon, was the scene of mass Lancastrian slaughter in 1471. (Author)

identifying, recording and numbering the dead. The Earl of Exeter after Barnet was 'greatly despoiled and wounded, and left for dead in the field, and so lay there from seven of the clock till four afternoon' with the rest of the corpses and dying men.[8] Some soldiers would gradually bleed to death on the battlefield, or suffer agony as the temperature began to drop towards night. Others who had been recognised by their heraldic devices, such as livery collars in the case of the aristocracy, were collected by their families and borne away to be buried elsewhere. Noted members of the ruling class were either buried nearby in consecrated ground, normally in local churchyards, as Lord Dacre was at Saxton after the battle of Towton, or they were transported back to their places of origin, their manors or local churches to be buried alongside their ancestors.

If they were rebellious nobles this final burial was carried out after their bodies had been given an appropriate viewing to the public. For example, the Earl of Warwick after his death in battle at Barnet was taken to London so that proof of his death could be established in an appropriately graphic and grisly manner. His scarred body was then taken to Bisham Abbey to be interred there alongside others of the Neville family. Some nobles after being executed had their heads spiked on London Bridge, or on other gateways leading into towns and cities. However, the common soldier was not so important, nor lucky enough to even be given burial in hallowed ground. Indeed, the vast majority of battlefield graves may not have been consecrated at all, and those shallow graves which were may have been eroded soon after when life returned to normal over the scarred battlefield landscape. The area known as 'The Graves' on Towton battlefield, for example, was soon ploughed up in the Tudor period, according to John Leland, when several village fields were extended. This prompted the Hungates, who were the lords of the manor at Saxton, to re-inter the bones which had come to the surface in the nearby parish church.[9]

Aside from graves on and off the field, various chantry chapels were set up on battlefields, although most have now disapeared. Towton's chantry chapel was built by Richard III 'to pray for the souls of those slain at Palmsunday Field',[10] and similar chantries were ordered to be set up by the Yorkists after the first battle of St Albans in 1455 in order that prayers could be said for the Lancastrians killed there. At Barnet, according to *The Great Chronicle of London*, there were killed 'three-thousand men or thereabouts which were buried in the said plain, well upon half a mile from the town, were after was built a little chapel to remember the souls of them that were slain at that field'.[11]

Such religious acts of remembrance signify that there was a reluctance to forget the Wars of the Roses dead. Richard Duke of Gloucester, who was probably the most pious King of England when he came to the throne – aside from Henry VI, of course – made an endowment at Queen's College Cambridge in July 1477 for priests to pray for a number of his humble servants who died fighting for him at Barnet and Tewkesbury. Six years later Richard could recall each one by name. Other nobles similarly made provision for their retinues, including William, Lord Herbert, who drew up his will in 1469 making provision for those who had fought and died in his service. Henry Earl of Northumberland before the battle of Bosworth also commanded the executors of his will to maintain all those who might be badly wounded while carrying out their duty. Thus there was not only a general respect for the wounded and the dead, but also sometimes provision for dependants on the death of a loved one, or some form of maintainence as compensation if they were wounded.[12]

Out of the estimated adult peerage who fought in the Wars of the Roses some thirty nobles were killed by one means or another and countless other knights were butchered in battle or through 'legitimate' execution. Other 'rebels' faced attainder and the penalties that were associated with it. Although some soldiers were reprieved, this was not done in the name of chivalry or mercy, but out of political necessity and family favour, such as in the case of the Lancastrian Lord Rivers who escaped his attainder in July 1461 for his action against Edward IV at the battle of Towton. Because the King had married Lord Rivers' sister (Elizabeth Woodville) fortuitous family connection forced a compromise to be arranged. Alternatively potential enemies could be received as friends in an effort to secure vital territorial areas of control traditionally under the influence of an opponent, such as in the case of the Percies of Northumberland and the Nevilles of Middleham, whose fortunes fluctuated under various Yorkist and Lancastrian kings. Necessity dictated that the Percies and Nevilles still generally retained power and control on the northern border, even after brief reprimands or changes in office. With the king's consent, both families could still retain their power or influence, and also recruit troops as long as the inherent threat of Scottish raiding existed. In the north of England the Percies and the Nevilles were regarded as petty kings in their own right, with their own ancestral line of power and influence, which in some ways outshone the king himself. As such, at least one member of both families was present in most battles of the period and consequently generally suffered because of it.[13]

Although the careers of most knights were short lived, to say the least, two knights in particular stand out from the rest as being rather fortunate, despite their active involvement in the Wars of the Roses. By looking at their lives, even if only very briefly, we can see just how precarious a soldier's existence was, especially when subjected to the political wheel of fortune of the time.

Sir Walter Devereux of Weobley, Herefordshire, who later became Lord Ferrers of Chartley, was Sheriff of Gloucestershire in 1455. In 1459 he became a staunch Yorkist who was forced after Ludford Bridge to submit to Henry VI after being attained in the Coventry Parliament of that year. Although he was deprived of some of his possessions because of his association with the Yorkist lords in 1459 he was back in their ranks in 1460 when he was given the responsibility of keeping order in Wales. After fighting for the Yorkists at the battle of Mortimer's Cross in 1461 he was among those who acclaimed Edward Duke of York as King Edward IV at Baynards Castle in London on 3 March 1461, after which he found himself fighting at the battle of Towton where he was created a Knight Batchelor by Edward IV for his services. He was later created Lord Ferrers (Devereux was summoned to court as Lord Ferrers in February 1462) and thereafter he became one of Edward's most trusted lieutenants in Wales and also during the border war of the same year. Later in the Wars of the Roses he was among those empowered to raise troops to pursue and arrest Warwick and Clarence and was also present, fighting for Edward, at the battles of Barnet and Tewkesbury in 1471. In 1475 he supplied men-at-arms and archers for Edward's abortive invasion of France where he was a signatory to the truce made with the French king, but when Richard III usurped the throne in 1483 his loyalty to the Yorkist cause seems to have wavered slightly, probably because he had sworn allegiance to Edward V and he resented Richard's usurpation of his throne. However, in 1485 he had a change of heart and he made the fatal miscalculation of being among those who fought for Richard at Bosworth. He was killed either on the field of battle, or more probably in the pursuit, after which his attainder was assured when Henry VII took the throne soon after.[14]

On the Lancastrian side Sir Richard Tunstall of Thurland (Lancashire) was luckier than most and outlived the Wars of the Roses despite his eventful military career. He was appointed by Henry VI as one of four Esquires of the King's Body on 3 September 1452 and he received his knighthood soon after this. Until about the middle of 1468 Tunstall was a prominent Lancastrian, being present at both the battle of Wakefield in 1460 and at the second battle of St Albans in 1461. After the Lancastrian retreat back to York in February of that same year Tunstall was ordered by Henry to recruit troops in the Knaresborough district which would eventually fight with him and Sir William Plumpton at the battle of Towton on 29 March. Towton was a dreadful blow to the Lancastrian cause, and Tunstall and his son were attained by Edward IV in July 1461 and were assumed dead, but it was later reported that both had escaped into the north with King Henry, where they immediately set about further resistance by capturing the northern border strongholds. The next we hear of Sir Richard is when he was captured along with the garrison of Bamburgh, and was likely to be beheaded by his own brother, but not for the last time in his eventful career he managed to escape death, as he was found again in the thick of military operations in Northumberland at Dunstanburgh Castle which was under siege from Lord Scrope. When Dunstanburgh surrendered Tunstall sought refuge with the Lancastrian defenders at Alnwick Castle until this too fell in January

Garter stall plate of Sir Richard Tunstall KG in St George's Chapel, Windsor. (Geoffrey Wheeler)

1463. Escaping from the clutches of the Yorkists yet again he slipped over the border into Scotland and later in the year he surfaced in Wales where he held Harlech Castle for the King against his enemies. Tunstall returned to the north of England in 1463/4 to fight for the Lancastrian cause at the battles of Hedgeley Moor and Hexham, after which, defeated and on the run, he managed to escort his King – the broken Henry VI – to Thurland Castle for safety, only to find his estates had been confiscated by Edward IV. He was later captured in Wales when he made a fateful decision to return to Harlech Castle. The castle surrendered to the Yorkists in 1468, and Tunstall was promptly sent to the Tower for his crimes against the Yorkist regime.

All now seemed lost for Sir Richard, but fortune once more smiled on him when somehow he managed to earn his reversal of attainder in 1473, and he was taken firmly into King Edward's favour despite his previous associations with the Lancastrian party. Consequently he was with Edward in France in 1475, proving that bending with the wind was to be ranked very highly among a knight's political qualities during the Wars of the Roses. Indeed, his new found favour secured him lofty diplomatic positions in France and Calais in the coming years, and in Richard III's reign he was made a Knight of the Garter for his agreeable service to the crown. His post in Calais was to save his skin during the dramatic events of August 1485 after which he was appointed the Steward of the Lordship of Kendal, and later he received the Stewardship of the Honour of Pontefract from Henry VII. As the new King's Councillor, Sir Richard served his Tudor king well for the last few years of his eventful life and was well rewarded for his services to the crown until his death in 1491 or 1492.[15]

Reversal of attainder was a common occurrence in the Wars of the Roses and attainder for treason was never usually inherited by an offspring when the father was killed or executed because of it, although lands were often forfeited back to the ruling monarch for such crimes in the interim period. In this way a good proportion of the English nobility survived the Wars of the Roses in some form or other, and there were even non-combatants among the nobility which ensured family survival. The Yorkist kings, especially, had an extremely narrow powerbase of loyal peers throughout the Wars of the Roses, and it was for this reason that King Edward IV tried to secure the support of die-hard Lancastrians after the battle of Towton in 1461. In the end, however, political necessity forced Edward to try to eliminate all the active Lancastrian support, which entailed extinguishing the male line of Beaufort, the Prince of Wales, King Henry VI and even his own brother in the process.

King Edward left his younger brother, Richard Duke of Gloucester, with even worse problems to solve because of his untimely death in 1483. Richard's ambition to usurp the throne also set him on a course of political alienation which meant that he too was to lack the support and loyalty of his nobility and their troops when it mattered most on the battlefield. His successor, Henry Tudor, soon discovered that in order to counter the insecure and unstable foundations then inherent in the English monarchy he had to try to curb bastard feudalism, in the end resorting to propaganda by effectively blackening the years of civil war and the Yorkist achievement with lies and distortion, the effects of which are still felt today. Such writers as Edward Hall, Sir Thomas More and later William Shakespeare produced propagandist tales of ambition, greed, child murder, fratricide, unlawful execution, carnage and battlefields soaked in English blood as effective weapons against Yorkist sympathies. Modern historiographical research has shown up the flaws in this picture of the period with increasing validity.

This study of the medieval soldier has shown us that any man who fought in the Wars of the Roses did not expect to serve for long in the army. He might fight in a battle, he might possibly be killed in combat, but his service and loyalty were governed by the way he was recruited in the first place: it was not governed by his violent nature. Military service was not sought out by the common man nor was it in any way heroic. However, for the higher classes it was the total opposite. The bloodstained battlefields of the Wars of the Roses tell the true story of a period of insecurity and blind obedience that had moments of extreme violence on the battlefield. Retainers and their masters would fight for territorial, political or family reasons, but the common soldier fought chiefly for wages, or because he was bound as a tenant to an estate. Men-at-arms were well-trained soldiers, and they tended to form the nucleus of the various ad hoc and extremely parochial contingents of levied soldiers who generally had had very little experience of large-scale pitched battles. Despite this, such common soldiers were tough, resilient individuals who were used to hard manual labour as a part of their everyday life and were therefore generally in good fighting condition if they happened to be led properly into battle by their superiors. Veteran soldiers might know the consequences of medieval warfare all too well, but raw recruits, as in all wars, were untrustworthy individuals, especially when they fought their own kind

Saxton parish church and the tomb of Lord Dacre of Gilsland. Killed at the battle of Towton in the afternoon of Palm Sunday 1461, Lord Dacre was buried here together with his horse. (Author)

in a civil war. Divisions in recruitment catchment areas made villages, towns, cities and even families take opposing sides. The blood feud, so common in the Wars of the Roses, fed off this method of recruitment and political polarisation.

Above all the life of the Wars of the Roses soldier shows us that fifteenth-century man was little different from the man of today. Just as he must have bowed his head in quiet contemplation when he surveyed the futile results of war, so do we when we gaze down upon the human remains laid irreverently in the Towton grave, and wonder at the far-off age of uncertainty and confusion in which the soldiers lived.

Notes

PREFACE

1. The first and the second battle of St Albans in H.T. Riley, ed., *Registrum Abbatis Johannis Whethamstede*, 1872.
2. See A. Gransden, *Historical Writing in England*, vol. 2, *C.1307 to the Early Sixteenth Century*, 1982, pp. 249–307.
3. On the theories behind this see J. Keegan, *The Face of Battle*, 1976, pp. 87–8.
4. See M.A. Hicks, *Bastard Feudalism*, 1995.

CHAPTER 1

1. See A.J. Pollard, *The Wars of the Roses*, 1994, p. 20. For Henry VI's character and John Blacman's view of the King see B. Wolffe, *Henry VI*, 1983, pp. 3–21.
2. For a simplified breakdown of the causes of the Wars of the Roses see J. Warren, *The Wars of the Roses and the Yorkist Kings*, 1995, p. 68. For a more in-depth study see R.L. Storey, *The End of the House of Lancaster*, 1966.
3. For Henry's madness see Wolffe, *Henry VI*, pp. 267–86.
4. Ibid., pp. 16–17.
5. See A. Johnson, *Richard Duke of York, 1411–1460*, 1988.
6. The fullest contemporary account is given in J. Gairdner, ed., *Gregory's Chronicle*, 1876, pp. 190–4.
7. A full explanation of these problems is given in A.J. Pollard, *North-Eastern England in the Wars of the Roses*, 1990.
8. See Pollard, *The Wars of the Roses*, p. 24.
9. See P. Haigh, *The Military Campaigns of the Wars of the Roses*, 1995, p. 182.
10. J. Gairdner, ed., *The Paston Letters*, vol. 3, pp. 25–30. C.A.J. Armstrong, *The Dijon Relation*, in *BIHR* 33, 1960, pp. 63–5. H.T. Riley, ed., *Registrum Abbatis Johannis Whethamstede*, vol 1, 1872, p. 171.
11. Gairdner, ed., *Gregory's Chronicle*, p. 198.
12. Ibid., p. 204. W. and E. Hardy, eds, *Jean de Waurin: Recueil des Chroniques d'Engleterre*, vol. 5, 1891, p. 269. J.S. Davies, ed., *An English Chronicle*, 1856, pp. 79–80.
13. J. Strachey, ed., *Rotuli Parliamentorum*, 1767–83, vol. 5, p. 348.
14. For the official account of Ludford Bridge see Strachey, ed., *Rotuli Parliamentorum*, vol. 5, p. 348. W. and E. Hardy, eds, *Jean de Waurin*, vol. 5, pp. 276–7.
15. Strachey, ed., *Rotuli Parliamentorum*, vol. 5, p. 348.
16. J.S. Davies, ed., *An English Chronicle*, 1856, pp. 85–90. *Foedera*, XI, 1704–13, p. 449.
17. Davies, ed., *An English Chronicle*, 1856, pp. 85–90. Also, W. and E. Hardy, eds, *Jean de Waurin*, vol. 5, pp. 282–4.
18. Also present were the Prior of St John, the Papal Legate Francesco Coppini and the Bishops of Exeter, Ely, Salisbury and Rochester.
19. An account of the battle is given in Davies, ed., *An English Chronicle*, 1856, pp. 94–8.
20. Riley, ed., *Registrum Abbatis Johannis Whethamstede*, vol. 1, pp. 376–8.
21. W. Shakespeare, *Richard III*, Act 1, scene 1.
22. Gairdner, ed., *Gregory's Chronicle*, pp. 209–10.
23. Davies, ed., *An English Chronicle*, 1856, pp. 106–7.
24. Accounts of the battle of Wakefield tend to differ, but see J. Stevenson, ed., *William Worcester: Annales Rerum Angelicarum*, 1884, p. 775. Davies, ed., *An English Chronicle*, 1856, pp. 106–7. W. and E. Hardy, eds, *Jean de Waurin*, vol. 5, pp. 325–6. H. Ellis, ed., *Hall's Chronicle*, 1809, pp. 249–51.
25. See H.T. Riley, ed., *Croyland Abbey Chronicle*, 1854, p. 423.
26. There is no reason to doubt Edward's presence at St Albans in 1455, even though

he was only thirteen years old. In Edward IV's 1475 campaign William (2nd) Herbert was fourteen years old, and brought 40 men-at-arms and 200 archers with him to France for his military education.

27. For the battle of Mortimers Cross see Gairdner, ed., *Gregory's Chronicle*, p. 211. Ellis, ed., *Hall's Chronicle*, p. 251.

28. Details of the second battle of St Albans can be found in Gairdner, ed., *Gregory's Chronicle*, pp. 213–14. Riley, ed., *Registrum Abbatis Johannis Whethamstede*, vol. 1, pp. 388–92.

29. The contemporary ballad 'The Rose of Rouen', in *Archaeologica* XXIX, pp. 343–7, gives details of the fear of the 'northerners'.

30. J. Stevenson, ed., *William Worcester: Annales Rerum Angelicarum*, pp. 775–7.

31. H. Ellis, ed., *Three Books of Polydore Vergil's English History*, 1844, p. 111.

32. Details of the Towton campaign can be found in A.B. Hinds, ed., *Calendar of State Papers of Milan*, vol. 1: *1385–1618*, 1912, pp. 99–105. Ellis, ed., *Polydore Vergil's English History*, pp. 110–11. Ellis, ed., *Hall's Chronicle*, pp. 255–6. W. and E. Hardy, eds, *Jean de Waurin*, vol. 5, pp. 337–42. 'Hearne's Fragment' in J.A. Giles, ed., *Chronicles of the White Rose of York*, 1834, pp. 8–9.

33. It has been proved that titles were passed on from father to son, or to brothers, or were ultimately perpetuated through the female line.

34. Strachey, ed., *Rotuli Parliamentorum*, vol. 5, pp. 477–8.

35. The war in Wales is detailed in H.T. Evans, *Wales and the Wars of the Roses*, 1915.

36. See J.O. Halliwell, ed., *John Warkworth: Chronicle*, 1839, pp. 2–3.

37. Ibid.

38. See Gairdner, ed., *The Paston Letters*, Letter 533, vol. 4, pp. 59–60. Gairdner, ed., *Gregory's Chronicle*, p. 219.

39. See Halliwell, ed., *John Warkworth: Chronicle*, p. 2.

40. The battle of Hedgely Moor is not well recorded by contemporary chroniclers, however; see Gairdner, ed., *Gregory's Chronicle*, pp. 223–24. W. and E. Hardy, eds, *Jean de Waurin*, vol. 5, pp. 440–41.

41. See Halliwell, ed., *John Warkworth: Chronicle*, p. 4. for the desertion of Somerset's levies in the face of the enemy.

42. For details of this see 'The Siege of Bamburgh Castle' in Giles, ed., *Chronicles of the White Rose of York*, pp. lxxxvi–lxxxix.

43. See Halliwell, ed., *John Warkworth: Chronicle*, p. 5.

44. Warwick had no male heir. Sir William Herbert, created Earl of Pembroke in 1468, and Humphrey Stafford, created Earl of Devon in 1469, also threatened Warwick's territorial ambitions.

45. 'False, Fleeting, perjur'd Clarence' in Shakespeare's *Richard III*, Act 1, scene 4.

46. See Haigh, *Military Campaigns*, pp. 189–93, for the identities of the two 'Robins'.

47. Redesdale's manifesto is given in Halliwell, ed., *John Warkworth: Chronicle*, pp. 72–3.

48. See 'Hearne's Fragment' in Giles, ed., *Chronicles of the White Rose of York*, p. 24.

49. For the battle of Edgecote see Halliwell, ed., *John Warkworth: Chronicle*, p. 6., and, more specifically, Hearne's Fragment in Giles, ed., *Chronicles of the White Rose of York*, p. 24. W. and E. Hardy, eds, *Jean de Waurin*, vol. 5, pp. 581–3.

50. Edward IV transferred Warwick's Welsh offices to his brother Richard of Gloucester, and Henry Percy was restored to the Earldom of Northumberland.

51. Thomas Burgh of Gainsborough.

52. For the best account of the Lincolnshire rebellion of 1470 see J.G. Nichols, ed., *Chronicle of the Rebellion in Lincolnshire 1470*, 1847.

53. All the events of 1471 are graphically retold by an anonymous servant of Edward IV in J. Bruce, ed., *The Historie of the Arrivall of King Edward IV, 1471*, 1838.

54. Ibid., pp. 18–21.

55. Ibid., p. 28.

56. Ibid., p. 29.

57. Ibid., pp. 30–1.

58. Ibid., pp. 33–8. See also A.H. Thomas and I.D. Thornley, eds, *The Great Chronicle of London*, pp. 218–21.

59. On King Henry's 'murder' see Halliwell, ed., *John Warkworth: Chronicle*, p. 21. Bruce, ed., *The Historie of the Arrivall*, p. 38. T. Hearne, ed., *Leland: Collectanea*, vol. 2, 1715, p. 507.

60. For more detail regarding Edward's army see F.P. Barnard, *Edward IV's French Expedition of 1475*, 1975. For Edward's invasion see A.R. Scoble, ed., *The Memoirs of Philippe de Commines*, 1911, vol. 1, pp. 251–87.

61. The events of 1483 are described in Ellis, ed., *Polydore Vergil's English History*. C.A.J. Armstrong, ed., *Dominic Mancini: The Usurpation of Richard III*, 1969. W.E. Campbell, ed., *Thomas More: The History of King Richard III*, 1931. Riley, ed. *Croyland Abbey Chronicle*.
62. On the deaths of the Princes see all the above, plus Thomas and Thornley, eds, *The Great Chronicle of London* pp. 236–7.
63. See Riley, ed. *Croyland Abbey Chronicle*, pp. 490–5.
64. The battle of Bosworth can be followed in Ellis, ed., *Polydore Vergil's English History*, pp. 221–4. The Ballad of Bosworth Field is from J.W. Hales and F.J. Furnivall, eds, *Bishop Percy's Folio Manuscript*, 1868, vol. 3, pp. 256–7. G. Doutrepont and O. Jodogne, eds, *Jean Molinet: Chronique*, 1935, vol. 1, pp. 434–6.
65. See D. Hay, ed., *The Anglica Historia: Polydore Vergil's English History*, 1950, pp. 10–13.
66. For the battle of Stoke Field see ibid., pp. 24–5. Doutrepont and Jodogne, eds, *Jean Molinet: Chronique*, p. 564. The Herald's Report, in Hearne, ed., *Leland: Collectanea*, vol. 4, pp. 212–15.

CHAPTER 2

1. The phenomenon of 'parhelion' is mentioned in J. Gairdner, ed., *Gregory's Chronicle*, 1876, p. 211, and H. Ellis, ed., *Hall's Chronicle*, 1809, p. 251.
2. *Foedera*, II, pp. 709–11.
3. For the dates of these two battles see J. Strachey, ed., *Rotuli Parliamentorum*, vol. 5, *1767–83*, pp. 477–8 (Towton), and J. Bruce, ed., *The Historie of the Arrivall of King Edward IV, 1471*, 1838, pp. 18–19 (Barnet).
4. See the Bishop of Exeter's words in A.B. Hinds, ed., *The Calendar of State Papers of Milan*, vol. 1, *1385–1618*, 1912, p. 62.
5. J.S. Davies, ed., *An English Chronicle*, 1856, pp. 81–2.
6. See N.P. Milner, ed., *Vegetius: Epitome of Military Science*, 1993.
7. For more information see D. Bornstein, *Military Manuals of the 15th Century* (Medieval Studies 38), 1975.
8. R. Dyboski and Z.M. Arend, eds, *Knyghthode and Bataile*, 1935, pp. 58–9.
9. J.G. Nichols, ed., *The Book of Noblesse*, 1860, p. 77.

10. Gairdner, ed., *Gregory's Chronicle*, p. 212.
11. W. and E. Hardy, eds, *Jean de Waurin: Recueil des Chroniques d'Engleterre*, 1891, vol. 5, pp. 325–34.
12. For examples of this see Bruce, ed., *Arrivall*, pp. 19–20. W. and E. Hardy, eds, *Jean de Waurin*, vol. 5, pp. 340–1.
13. With regard to the date when civil war broke out see A.J. Pollard, *The Wars of the Roses*, 1988, p. 24.
14. F. Devon, ed., *Issues of the Exchequer*, 1837, p. 501.
15. See A.H. Burne, *Battlefields of England*, 1950.
16. Ellis, ed., *Hall's Chronicle*, p. 268.
17. M. Vale, *War and Chivalry*, 1981, p. 26.
18. These views can be followed in more depth in Vale, *War and Chivalry*, and in M. Keen, *Chivalry*, 1984.
19. F. Saccheti, *Nouvelle*, III, 1804–5, p. 91.
20. 'Les grandes compagnies au XIVme siècle, *BEC*, V, 1833–4, p. 246.
21. L.T. Smith, ed., *Leland Itinerary*, IV, 1906–10, p. 162.
22. For Gascoigne see P. Routh and R. Knowles, *The Medieval Monuments of Harewood*, 1983, p. 40. For Trollope see Gairdner, ed., *Gregory's Chronicle*, p. 214.
23. G. Bernard, *The Tudor Nobility*, 1992, pp. 9–10.
24. See A.W. Boardman, *The Battle of Towton*, 1994.
25. E.M. Thompson, ed., *Chronicron Galfridi le Baker de Swynebroke*, 1889, p. 51. In fact it was Dupplin Moor: see R. Nicholson, *Edward III and the Scots*, 1965, pp. 87, 133.
26. See F.R.Twemlow, *The Battle of Blore Heath*, 1912.
27. A. Scoble, ed., *Memoirs of Philippe de Commines*, 1911, vol 1, p. 279.
28. Ibid., p. 192.
29. J.A. Giles, *Chronicles of the White Rose of York*, 1834, p. lxxxix.
30. G.C. Macaulay, ed., *The Chronicles of Froissart*, 1904, p. 104.
31. Scoble, ed., *Memoirs of Philippe de Commines*, vol. 1, pp. 24–5.
32. Keen, *Chivalry*, p. 237.

CHAPTER 3

1. C. Plummer, ed., *The Governance of England*, 1885, pp. 127–30.
2. Ibid., p. 14.

3. Namely Charles Plummer. Also K.B. McFarlane in *The Nobility of Later Medieval England*, 1973.
4. See M. Hicks, *Bastard Feudalism*, 1995, p. 19.
5. J. Maclean, ed., *The Lives of the Berkeleys*, 1884, vol. II, p. 109.
6. G.R. Owst, *Literature and the Pulpit in Medieval England*, 1961, p. 311.
7. J. Gairdner, ed., *The Paston Letters*, 1904, vol. 6, pp. 71–2.
8. A.R. Myers, *The Household of Edward IV*, 1959, pp. 96–110.
9. J.E. Gairdner, ed., *Gregory's Chronicle*, 1876, p. 212.
10. Gairdner, ed., *The Paston Letters*, vol. 6, p. 85.
11. H. Nicolas, *The Wardrobe Accounts of Edward IV*, 1830, p. 162.
12. J.O. Halliwell, ed., *The Song of Lady Bessy*, 1847, Version I, p. 33.
13. J.S. Davies, ed., *An English Chronicle*, 1856, p. 75.
14. The 50,000 figure alludes to the approximate strength of both armies at the battle of Towton in 1461. See A.W. Boardman, *The Battle of Towton*, 1994.
15. W.H. Dunham, *Lord Hastings' Indentured Retainers 1461–1483*, 1955, p. 25.
16. Ibid.
17. A. Goodman, *The Wars of the Roses*, 1981, pp. 227–8.
18. Gairdner, ed., *The Paston Letters*, vol. 4, p. 60.
19. See Dunham, ed., *Lord Hastings' Indentured Retainers*.
20. Ibid., p. 125.
21. A. Scoble, ed., *Memoirs of Philippe de Commines*, 1911, vol. 1, p. 251.
22. Compare Dunham, ed., *Lord Hastings' Indentured Retainers* with F.P. Barnard, *Edward IV's French Expedition*, 1975.
23. T. Stapleton, ed., *The Plumpton Letters*, 1839, p. 77.
24. Dunham, ed., *Lord Hastings' Indentured Retainers*, p. 133.
25. Historical Manuscripts Commission, Sixth Report, 1877–8, pp. 223–4.
26. C.L. Kingsford, ed., *The Stonor Letters and Papers*, vol. II, p. 161.
27. J. Strachey, ed., *Rotuli Parliamentorum, 1767–83*, vol. 4, p. 517.
28. Dunham, ed., *Lord Hastings' Indentured Retainers*, pp. 126–7.
29. Davies, ed., *An English Chronicle*, pp. 106–7.
30. Ibid.
31. Davies, ed., *Rotuli Parliamentorum*, vol. 5, pp. 447–8.
32. M.D. Harris, ed., *Coventry Leet Book*, 1907–13, pp. 342–3.
33. For more information on the workings of the array system see P.L. Hughes and F.J. Larkin, eds, *Tudor Royal Proclamations*, 1964, vol. I, no. 61, pp. 83–4.
34. C.L. Kingsford, ed., *The Stoner Letters and Papers*, vol. II, no. 258.
35. See J.O. Halliwell, ed., *John Warkworth: Chronicle*, 1839, and J.G. Nichols, ed., *Chronicle of the Rebellion in Lincolnshire, 1470*, 1847.
36. J. Bruce, ed., *The Historie of the Arrivall of King Edward IV, 1471*, 1838. p. 33.
37. Gairdner, ed., *The Paston Letters*, vol. 3, pp. 265–6. The exact date of this letter of 1461 is unknown, but it is more probable that the Norfolk troops mentioned in the letter were mustered in January or February 1461 to protect London (see later in the letter) when the advancing Lancastrian army was robbing and pillaging its way southward.
38. See Boardman, *The Battle of Towton*.
39. See *The Bridport Muster Roll, 1457*, Dorset County Record Office, DL/BTB:FG3 (Ph 694).
40. *Calendar of Patent Rolls 1452–61*, vol. 6, 1910–16, pp. 406–10.
41. A. Raine, ed., *York Civic Records*, vol. I, 1939, p. 135.
42. J.E. Oxley, *The Fletchers and Longbowstring Makers of London*, 1968.
43. J. Nicolson and R. Burn, *A History of Westmorland*, 1777, p. 96.
44. Gairdner, ed., *Gregory's Chronicle*, p. 212.
45. See Harris, ed., *Coventry Leet Book*.
46. 'The Rose of Rouen', *Archaeologia*, XXIX, pp. 343–7.
47. W.H. Stevenson, ed., *Records of the Borough of Nottingham*, 1883–5, vol. II, p. 377.
48. Harris, ed., *Coventry Leet Book*, pp. 282–3.
49. See A.J. Pollard, *North-Eastern England during the Wars of the Roses*, 1990, pp. 150–3. R.L. Storey, *The Wardens of the Marches of England Towards Scotland, 1377–1489*, 1957.
50. '1468 Statute of Livery', *Historical Research*, LXIV, 1991, p. 21.
51. See Pollard, *North-Eastern England*, p. 151.
52. A. Hanham, ed., *The Cely Letters, 1472–1488*, 1975, pp. 147–8.

53. For further information on the Calais garrison see G.L. Harriss, 'The Struggle for Calais: An Aspect on the Rivalry Between Lancaster and York', *English Historical Review*, 75, 1960, p. 30.
54. Gairdner, ed., *Gregory's Chronicle*, p. 213.
55. Ibid., pp. 213–14.
56. See J. Gillingham, *The Wars of the Roses*, 1981, p. 29.
57. Ibid., p. 64.
58. W. Campbell, ed., *Materials [for a History of the Reign of Henry VII]*, 1873, vol. I, pp. 188, 251.
59. H.T. Riley, ed., *Registrum Abbatis Johannis Whethamstede*, 1872, vol. 1. pp. 168, 390.
60. A.H. Thomas and I.D. Thornley, eds, *The Great Chronicle of London*, 1938, p. 216.
61. Bruce, ed., *The Historie of the Arrivall*, p. 7.
62. Gairdner, ed., *Gregory's Chronicle*, p. 213.

CHAPTER 4

1. J.O. Halliwell, ed., *John Warkworth: Chronicle*, 1839, p. 12.
2. See F.P. Barnard, *Edward IV's French Expedition*, 1975, pp. 141–5.
3. Ibid., pp. 140–1.
4. Ibid., pp. 134–5.
5. See MS.2. M.16. College of Arms, in Barnard, *Edward IV's French Expedition*.
6. For overwhelming evidence of this fact see numerous examples in W.H. Dunham, *Lord Hastings' Indentured Retainers, 1461–1483*, 1955.
7. T.B. Pugh, 'The Magnates, Knights and Gentry', in S.B. Chrimes, C.D. Ross and R.A. Griffiths, eds, *Fifteenth-century England, 1399–1509*, 1972, pp. 101–9.
8. N.B. Lewis, 'The Organisation of Indentured Retainers in 14th-century England', *Transactions of the Royal Historical Society*, 4th series, XXVII, 1945, p. 30.
9. J.P. Collier, ed., *Howard Household Books*, vol. 2, 1844, pp. 480–92.
10. A.R. Myers, ed., *English Historical Documents 1327–1485*, 1969, p. 272.
11. For payments made to Edward in defence of the realm see *Calendar of Fine Rolls*, PRO, 1461–1471, pp. 84f.
12. F. Devon, ed., *Issues of the Exchequer*, 1837, pp. 501–4.
13. See M.D. Harris, ed., *The Coventry Leet Book*, 1907–13, p. 309. For details of other payments made to soldiers during this

period see *Records of the Borough of Nottingham*, vols 2–3, 1883–5, and W.H. Hudson and J.C.Tingey, eds, *The Records of the City of Norwich*, vol. 1, 1906.
14. *York House Books*, Books 2/4, f.169, trans. L. Attreed in P.W. Hammond and A.F. Sutton, *The Road to Bosworth Field*, 1985, p. 213.
15. For Towton see A. Raine, ed., *York Civic Records*, vol. 1, 1939, p. 135.
16. R. Dyboski and Z.M. Arend, eds, *Knyghthode and Bataile*, 1935, pp. 41–2.
17. Jean de Waurin, *Recueil des Chroniques d'Engleterre*, ed. W. and E. Hardy, 1891, vol. 5, p. 333.
18. Rye and Lydd, *Royal Commission on Historical Manuscripts: Fifth Report*, vol. 1, 1876, p. 523.
19. De Waurin, *Recueil des Chroniques*, vol. 5, p. 338.
20. See A.W. Boardman, *The Battle of Towton*, 1994.
21. J. Gairdner, *The Paston Letters*, 1904, vol. 3, pp. 265–6.
22. H. Ellis, ed., *Hall's Chronicle*, 1809, p. 255.
23. J.G. Nichols, ed., *Chronicle of the Rebellion in Lincolnshire, 1470*, 1847, pp. 16–17.
24. Accounts of the battle of Wakefield vary (see above notes), but the rescuing of the Yorkist foragers is significant, and is featured in most contemporary accounts.
25. J. Bruce, ed., *The Historie of the Arrivall of King Edward IV, 1471*, 1838, p. 28.
26. Ibid., p. 27.
27. J.E. Gairdner, ed., *Gregory's Chronicle*, 1876, p. 214.
28. De Waurin, *Recueil des Chroniques*, vol. 3, p. 319.
29. H.T. Riley, ed., *Croyland Abbey Chronicle*, 1854, p. 423.
30. Gairdner, ed., *Gregory's Chronicle*, p. 214.
31. Ibid., p. 207.
32. G. Poulson, *Beverlac*, 1829, pp. 227–8; Harris, ed., *Coventry Leet Book*, p. 356.
33. See J. Keegan, *The Face of Battle*, 1976, pp. 113, 326.
34. British Library, Cotton MS. Julius B.XII, ff. 27d–29d.
35. Halliwell, ed., *John Warkworth: Chronicle*, p. 2.
36. Ibid., p. 6.
37. 'Hearne's Fragment', in J.A. Giles, ed., *Chronicles of the White Rose of York*, 1834, p. 24.
38. Bruce, ed., *The Historie of the Arrivall*, p. 18.

39. A.H. Thomas and I.D. Thornley, eds, *The Great Chronicle of London*, 1938, pp. 189–90.
40. Gairdner, ed., *Gregory's Chronicle*, p. 211.

CHAPTER 5

1. All these points are detailed in C. Ffoulkes, *The Armourer and his Craft from the XIth to the XVIth Century*, 1912; C. Blair, *European Armour: Circa 1066 to Circa 1700*, 1958; D. Edge and J.M. Paddock, *Arms and Armour of the Medieval Knight*, 1988.
2. See R. Hardy, *Longbow*, 1992, pp. 222–36.
3. See *The Bridport Muster Roll 1457*, Dorset County Record Office, DL/BTB:FG3 (Ph 694).
4. Milanese armours are discussed in L. Boccia, F. Rossi and M. Morin, *Armi et Armature Lombarde*, 1979; Gothic armours in T. Bruno, *Deutsche Platternkunst*, 1944.
5. See 'War Wounds of the Cranium in the Middle Ages: As Disclosed in the Skeletal Material from the Battle of Wisby', *Bulletin of the Los Angeles Neurological Society*, vol. 30, 1965, pp. 27–33.
6. See *The Bridport Muster Roll 1457*.
7. For a detailed discription of the defence measures at the battle of St Albans in 1461 see J.E. Gairdner, ed., *Gregory's Chronicle*, 1876, p. 213.
8. See notes 5, 14 and 19 on Chapter 1 for all these battles.
9. 'Brief Latin Chronicle' in J. Gairdner, ed., *Three Fifteenth-century Chronicles*, 1880, p. 169.
10. The most recent study of the armourer's craft is M. Pfaffenbichler, *Armourers*, 1992.
11. Pierpont Morgan Library, MS 775 f.122, circa 1480.
12. H. Ellis, *Edward Hall: Hall's Chronicle*, 1809, p. 255.
13. R. Whittaker, *Loidis and Elmete*, 1816, p. 156.
14. A. Scoble, ed., *Memoirs of Philippe de Commines*, 1911, vol. 1, p. 27.
15. J. Gairdner, ed., *The Paston Letters*, 1904, vol. 3, pp. 193–4.
16. Edge and Paddock, *Arms and Armour*, p. 110.
17. Ibid., p. 135.
18. See R.E. Oakeshott, *The Sword in the Age of Chivalry*, 1964, and R.E. Oakeshott, *Records of the Medieval Sword*, 1964.
19. J.W. Hales and F.J. Furnivall, eds, *Bishop Percy's Folio Manuscript*, 1868, vol. 3, pp. 256–7.

20. For English knights dismounting to fight see Dominic Mancini, *The Usurpation of Richard III*, ed. C.A.J. Armstrong, 1969, pp. 98–101.
21. See Chapter 4 for Gregory's views on spearmen.
22. Mancini, *Usurpation*, pp. 98–9.
23. The absence of levies, etc., in Henry's army at the first battle of St Albans is based on the fact that the Lancastrian force was only comprised of the riding retinues of the nobles present, and not their fully mustered tenantry.
24. See *The Bridport Muster Roll 1457*; C.L. Kingsford, *The Stoner Letters and Papers*, vol. 2, no. 258; and Gairdner, ed., *Gregory's Chronicle*, p. 205.
25. M. Burgess, *The Mail-makers Technique*, 1953.
26. J.P. Collier, ed., *Household Books of John Duke of Norfolk and Thomas Earl of Surrey, 1481–1490*, 1844.
27. See also 'Remains of a Jack of Plate Excavated from Beeston Castle in Cheshire', *Journal of the Arms and Armour Society*, 13.2, 1989, pp. 81–154.
28. Edge and Paddock, *Arms and Armour*, p. 135.
29. In 1381 some of Wat Tyler's rebels attacked the Duke of Lancaster. They were unable to penetrate the Duke's brigandine with arrows and in the end they literally had to hack it to pieces.
30. C.L. Kingsford, 'Hardyng's Chronicle', *English Historical Review*, 27, 1912, p. 749.
31. See C. Plummer, ed., *The Governance of England*, 1885, chapter 12.
32. See Hardy, *Longbow*.
33. A. Calmette and F. Perinelle, *Pièces Justificatives*, no. 63, Royal Armouries. See also F.P. Barnard, *Edward IV's French Expedition*, 1975.
34. See Hardy, *Longbow*, pp. 222–36.
35. Scoble, ed., *Memoirs of Philippe de Commines*, vol. 1, p. 71.
36. See J.E. Oxley, *The Fletchers and Longbowstring Makers of London*, 1968.
37. Extract from part of George Ashby's poem, 'The Active Policy of a Prince', circa 1470, in *George Ashby's Poems*, Early English Text Society.
38. See G.M. Wilson, ed., *European Crossbows: A Survey by Josef Alm*, trans. H.B. Wells, 1994.
39. Bills were used in large numbers at the battle of Formingy (1450). See, M. Troso,

Le Armi in Asta: Delle Fanterie Europee, 1000–1500, 1988, for the evolution of staff weapons.
40. Gairdner, ed., *Gregory's Chronicle*, p. 214.
41. See A.L. Thompson, 'Medieval Daggers', *Military History*, 102, 1996, p. 52.
42. See P. McGill and J. Jones, *Standards, Badges and Livery Colours of the Wars of the Roses*, 1992. Also 'Hobilar 11', *Journal of the Lance and Longbow Society*.
43. 'Wardrobe Accounts of 1483', *Archaeologia*, 1, p. 394.
44. See Gairdner, ed., *The Paston Letters*, no. 734, MS Phillipps, 9735, no. 201.
45. J. Bruce, ed., *The Historie of the Arrivall of King Edward IV, 1471*, 1838, p. 18.
46. Gairdner, ed., *Gregory's Chronicle*, p. 213.
47. For early artillery and firearms see H. Brackenbury, *Ancient Cannon in Europe*, vols 1 and 2, 1865–67. Also T.F. Tout, 'Firearms in England in the Fourteenth Century', *English Historical Review*, 26, 1911, p. 43. A full account of fifteenth-century firearms has yet to be written, but see R.D. Smith and R.R. Brown, *Bombards: Mons Meg and her Sisters*, 1989.

CHAPTER 6

1. F. Taylor and J.S. Roskell, eds, *Gesta Henrici Quinti*, 1975, p. 84.
2. For example see the Yorkist attainder after the battle of Towton: J. Strachey, ed., *Rotuli Parliamentorum*, vol. 5, *1767–83*, pp. 477–8.
3. Lord Clifford, Sir Thomas Courtenay and Lord Egremont, to name only three.
4. See A.W. Boardman, *The Battle of Towton*, 1994. P.W. Hammond, *The Battles of Barnet and Tewkesbury*, 1990. M. Bennett, *The Battle of Bosworth*, 1987.
5. A.R. Scoble, ed., *Memoirs of Philippe de Commines*, 1911, vol. 1, p. 21.
6. J.M.W. Bean, *From Lord to Patron*, 1989, p. 48.
7. See R.L. Storey, *The End of the House of Lancaster*, 1986, p. 7.
8. J. Bruce, ed., *The Historie of the Arrivall of King Edward IV, 1471*, 1838, p. 28.
9. Ibid., pp. 28–9.
10. See Boardman, *The Battle of Towton*, p. 49.
11. 'The Herald's Report', in T. Hearne, ed., *Leland's Collectanea*, 1774, vol. 4, pp. 210–15.
12. Milner, ed., *Vegetius, De Rei Militari*.

13. For Edward's speech before Towton see W. and E. Hardy, eds, *Jean de Waurin: Recueil des Chroniques d'Engleterre*, 1891, vol. 5, p. 340.
14. Scoble, ed., *Memoirs of Philippe de Commines*, vol. 1, p. 192.
15. J. Gairdner, ed., *The Paston Letters*, 1904, vol. 3, p. 26.
16. Ibid., p. 30.
17. A.H. Thomas and I.D. Thornley, eds, *The Great Chronicle of London*, 1938, pp. 189–90.
18. J.P. Collier, ed., *Household Books of John Duke of Norfolk and Thomas Earl of Surrey, 1481–1490*, 1844, pp. 480–93.
19. See, W.H. Dunham, *Lord Hasting's Indentured Retainers, 1461–1483*, 1955, and F.P. Barnard, *Edward IV's French Expedition of 1475*, 1975.
20. A. Raine, ed., *York Civic Records*, 1941, p. 135. M.D. Harris, ed., *Coventry Leet Book*, 1907–13, pp. 282–3.
21. Strachey, ed., *Rotuli Parliamentorum, 1767–83*, p. 232. C.L. Kingsford, *The Stoner Letters and Papers*, 1919, vol. 2, no. 258.
22. R. Hardy, *Longbow*, 1992.
23. For example at Stoke Field (1487): G. Doutrepont and O. Jodogne, eds, *Jean Molinet: Chronique*, 1935, vol 1, pp. 562–5.
24. 'The Herald's Report', pp. 212–15.
25. G.C. MacCaulay, ed., *The Chronicles of Froissart*, 1904, p. 104.
26. Gairdner, ed., *The Paston Letters*, vol. 3, p. 30.
27. See Gairdner, ed., *The Paston Letters*, vol. 5, p. 99. G.L. Harriss and M.A. Harriss, eds, 'John Benet's Chronicle', *Camden Miscellany*, 24, 1972, p. 230. For Towton see Boardman, *The Battle of Towton*.
28. Bruce, ed., *The Historie of the Arrivall*, p. 29.
29. H. Ellis, ed., *Hall's Chronicle*, 1809, pp. 255–6.
30. Bruce, ed., *The Historie of the Arrivall*, p. 29.
31. William of Malmesbury, *De Gestis Regum Anglorum*, W. Stubbs, ed., vol. 2, p. 291.
32. Scoble, ed., *Memoirs of Philippe de Commines*, vol. 1, p. 24.
33. Ibid.
34. W. and E. Hardy, eds, *Jean de Waurin: Recueil des Chroniques*, vol. 5, p. 340.
35. Bruce, ed., *The Historie of the Arrivall*, pp. 29–30.
36. See Bennett, *The Battle of Bosworth*, p. 114.

37. See T. Stapleton, ed., *The Plumpton Letters*, 1839.
38. Bruce, ed., *The Historie of the Arrivall*, pp. 19–20.
39. Jean de Bueil, *Le Jouvencel*, ed. C. Favre and L. Lecestre, 1887–9, vol. 2, pp. 20–1.
40. W. and E. Hardy, eds, *Jean de Waurin: Recueil des Chroniques*, vol. 5, p. 76.
41. H. Ellis, *Polydore Virgil's English History*, Camden Society, 1844, pp. 221–6.
42. Boardman, *Battle of Towton*, p. 132.
43. J. Gairdner, ed., *Gregory's Chronicle*, 1876, p. 207.
44. Bruce, ed., *The Historie of the Arrivall*, p. 30.
45. Mancini, *Usurpation*, pp. 132–3.
46. H.T. Riley, ed., *Registrum Abbatis Johannis Whethamstede*, 1872, vol. 1, pp. 388–92.
47. J.G. Nichols, ed., *Chronicle of the Rebellion in Lincolnshire, 1470*, 1847.

CHAPTER 7

1. A.B. Hinds, ed., *Calendar of State Papers of Milan*, vol. 1, *1385–1618*, 1912, p. 100.
2. See B. Thordeman, *Armour from the Battle of Wisby, 1361*, 1939.
3. See M. Rule, *The Mary Rose*, 1982, pp. 184–6, and R. Hardy, *Longbow*, 1992, p. 217.
4. For Paston's injury see J. Gairdner, ed., *The Paston Letters*, 1904, vol. 5, pp. 99 and 102–3. A.C. Reeves, *Humphrey Stafford's Military Indentures*, 1972, p. 91.
5. J. Gairdner, *Paston Letters*, vol. 5, p. 99.
6. A.R. Scoble, ed., *Memoirs of Philippe de Commines*, 1911, vol. 1, p. 31.
7. J. Adair, 'The Newsletter of Gerhard Von Wesel, 17 April 1471', *Journal of the Society for Army Historical Research*, 1968.
8. J.O. Halliwell, ed., *John Warkworth: Chronicle*, 1839, pp. 16–17.
9. See A.W. Boardman, *The Battle of Towton*, 1994, p. 89.
10. 'John Leland's Itinerary, 1558', in *Yorkshire Archaeological and Topographical Journal*, 10, 1889, p. 234.
11. A.H. Thomas and I.D. Thornley, eds, *The Great Chronicle of London*, 1938, p. 217.
12. See M.K. Jones, 'Richard III as a Soldier', in J. Gillingham, ed., *Richard III: A Medieval Kingship*, 1993.
13. See A.J. Pollard, 'Percies, Nevilles, and the Wars of the Roses', *History Today*, September 1993, p. 42.
14. See F.P. Barnard, *Edward IV's French Expedition of 1475*, 1975, pp. 25–8.
15. Ibid., pp. 86–95. A. Goodman, *The Wars of the Roses*, 1981, p. 132.

Bibliography

PRIMARY SOURCES

Benet's Chronicle 1400–62 (ed.) G.L. Harriss and M.A. Harriss, Camden Miscellany, vol. 24, 1972
Beverlac, G. Poulson, 1829
Bishop Percy's Folio Manuscript (ed.) J.W. Hales and F.J. Furnivall, vol. 3, 1868
The Book of Fayttes of Arms and of Chivalry (ed.) A.T.P. Byles, 1937
The Book of Noblesse (ed.) J.G. Nichols, 1860
Bridport Muster Roll 1457, Dorset County Record Office B3/FC3
The Brut Chronicle (ed.) F.W.D. Brie, 2 vols, 1906
Calendar of Fine Rolls 1461–71, PRO, 1935–62
Calendar of Patent Rolls 1452–61, vol. 6, 1910–16
Calendar of State Papers of Milan, vol. 1 (ed.) A.B. Hinds, 1912
The Cely Letters 1472–88, (ed.) A. Hanham, 1975
Chronicle of the Rebellion in Lincolnshire 1470 (ed.) J.G. Nichols, 1847
Chronicron Galfridi le Baker de Swynebroke (ed.) E.M. Thompson, 1889
Commines, Philippe de, Memoirs of, 2 vols (ed.) A.R. Scoble, 1911
The Coventry Leet Book (ed.) M.D. Harris, 1907–13
Croyland Abbey Chronicle (ed.) H.T. Riley, 1854
'The Dijon Relation' in *British Institute of Historical Research*, 33, C.A.J. Armstrong, 1960
Drake, F. *Eboracum*, 1736
An English Chronicle of the Reigns of Richard II, Henry IV, Henry V and Henry VI, (ed.) J.S. Davies, 1856
English Historical Documents, vol. 4, 1327–1485 (ed.) A.R. Myers, 1969
Foedera (ed.) T. Rymer, XI, 1704–13
Froissart Chronicles (ed.) G.C. Macaulay, 1904
Gesta Henrici Quinti (ed.) F. Taylor and J.S. Roskell, 1975
The Governance of England (ed.) C. Plummer, 1885
Les Grandes Compagnies au XIVme Siècle, Bibliothèque de L'École des Chartes, V, 1833–4
The Great Chronicle of London (ed.) A.H. Thomas and I.D. Thornley, 1939
Gregory's Chronicle in *The Historical Collections of a Citizen of London* (ed.) J. Gairdner, 1876

Hall, Edward, Chronicle of (ed.) H. Ellis, 1809
Hardyng, John, Chronicle of (ed.) H. Ellis, 1812
'Hardyng's Chronicle' in *English Historical Review*, 27, C.L. Kingsford, 1912
'Hearne's Fragment' in *Chronicles of the White Rose of York* (ed.) J.A. Giles, 1843
Historical Manuscripts Commission, Sixth Report, 1877–87
Historie of the Arrivall of King Edward IV, 1471 (ed.) J. Bruce 1838
The Household Books of John Duke of Norfolk and Thomas Earl of Surrey 1481–1490 (ed.) J.P. Collier, 1844.
Issues of the Exchequer (ed.) F. Devon, 1837
Le Jouvencel (ed.) C. Favre and L. Lecestre, 1887–89
Knighthode and Bataile (ed.) R. Dyboski and Z.M. Arend, 1935
Leland's Collectanea (ed.) T. Hearne, 1774
Loidis and Elmete, R. Whittaker, 1816
'John Leland's Itinerary of 1558' in *Yorkshire Archaeological and Topographical Journal*, vol. 10, 1889
Mancini, Dominic, *The Usurpation of Richard III* (ed.) C.A.J. Armstrong, 1969
Materials [for a History of the Reign of Henry VII] (ed.) W. Campbell, 1873
Molinet, Jean, *Chronique* (ed.) G. Doutrepont and O. Jodogne, 1935
More, Thomas, *The History of King Richard III* (ed.) W.E. Campbell, 1931
Nouvelle, Clio Series, III, F. Saccheti, (Milan), 1804–5
The Paston Letters, 6 vols (ed.) J. Gairdner, 1904
The Plumpton Letters (ed.) T. Stapleton, Camden Society, 1839
Polydore Vergil's English History (ed.) H. Ellis, 1844
The Records of the Borough of Nottingham, vol. 2, London, 1883–5
The Records of the City of Norwich, I (ed.) W.H. Hudson and J.C. Tingey, 1906
'The Rose of Rouen' in *Archaeologia XXIX*
Rotuli Parliamentorum, 6 vols, 1767
Royal Commission on Historical Manuscripts: Fifth Report, 1876
The Song of Lady Bessy (ed.) Halliwell, 1847
The Stonor Letters and Papers, 1290–1483 (ed.) C.L. Kingsford, 1919
Warkworth, John, *Chronicle* (ed.) J.O. Halliwell, 1839
Waurin, Jean de, *Recueil des Chroniques D'Engleterre* (ed.) W. and E. Hardy, 1891
Registrum Abbatis Johannis Whethamstede, (ed.) H.T. Riley, 1872
Worcester, William, *Annales Rerum Anglicarum* (ed.) J. Stevenson, 1884
York Civic Records (ed.) A. Raine (Yorkshire Archaeological Society Record Series), 1939

SECONDARY SOURCES

Alm, J. *European Crossbows* (trans.) H.B. Wells. (ed.) G.M. Wilson (Royal Armouries), 1994
Barnard, P.F. *Edward IV's Expedition of 1475*, 1975
Bean, J.M.W. *From Lord to Patron*, 1989
Bellamy, J.G. *Bastard Feudalism and the Law*, 1989
Bennett, M. *Lambert Simnel and the Battle of Stoke*, 1993
——. *The Battle of Bosworth*, 1987

Bernard, G. *The Tudor Nobility*, 1992

Blair, C. *European Armour*: c. *1066 to* c. *1700*, 1958

Boardman, A.W. *The Battle of Towton*, 1994

Boccia, L., Rossi, F. and Morin, M. *Armi e Armature Lombarde*, 1979

Bornstein, D. 'Military Manuals of the 15th Century' in *Medieval Studies*, 38, 1975

Brackenbury, H. *Ancient Cannon in Europe*, vols 1 and 2, 1865–67

Bradbury, J. *The Medieval Archer*, 1992

Brooke-Little, J.P. *Boutell's Heraldry*, rev. 1973

Brooke, R. *Visits to Fields of Battle in England*, 1857

Bruno, T. *Deutsche Platternkunst*, 1944

Burgess, M. *The Mail-Maker's Technique*, Society of Antiquaries, 1953

Burne, A.H. *Battlefields of England*, 1950

Chrimes, S.B. *Lancastrians, Yorkists and Henry VI*, 1966

——, Griffiths, R.A and Ross, C.D. (eds) *Fifteenth-Century England 1399–1509*, 1995

Dockray, K. and Knowles, R. *The Battle of Wakefield*, 1992

Dunham, W.H. *Lord Hastings' Indentured Retainers 1461–1483*, 1954

Edge, D. and Paddock, J.M. *Arms and Armour of the Medieval Knight*, 1988

Evans, H.T. *Wales and the Wars of the Roses*, 1915

Ffoulkes, C. *The Armourer and his Craft from the XIth to the XVIth Century*, 1912

Foss, P.J. *The Field of Redemore: the Battle of Bosworth 1485*, 1990

Gillingham, J. *The Wars of the Roses*, 1981

——. (ed.) *Richard III: A Medieval Kingship*, 1993

Goodman, A. *The Wars of the Roses*, 1981

Gransden, A. *Historical Writing in England, vol. 2*, c. *1307 to the early sixteenth century*, 1982

Haigh, P.A. *The Battle of Wakefield 1460*, 1996

——. *The Military Campaigns of the Wars of the Roses*, 1995

Hardy, R. *Longbow*, 1992

Hammond, P.W. *The Battles of Barnet and Tewkesbury*, 1990

Hammond, P.W. and Sutton, A.F. *Richard III: the Road to Bosworth Field*, 1985

Hicks, M. *Bastard Feudalism*, 1995

Hughes, P.L. and Larkin, F.J. *Tudor Royal Proclamations*, 1964

Jacob, E.F. *The 15th Century*, Oxford History of England, 1992

Johnson, P.A. *Richard Duke of York, 1411–1460*, 1988

Journal of the Arms and Armour Society, 13.2, 1989

Journal of the Society for Army Historical Research, 1968

Keegan, J. *The Face of Battle*, 1991

Keen, M. *Chivalry*, 1994

Kendall, P.M. *The Yorkist Age*, 1967

Kingsford, C.L. *English Historical Literature in the 15th Century*

Koch, H.W. *Medieval Warfare*, 1978

Lander, J.R. *The Wars of the Roses*, 1965

Maclean, J. *The Lives of the Berkeleys*, 1884

McFarlane, K.B. *The Nobility of Later Medieval England*, 1973

McGill, P. *Heraldic Banners of the Wars of the Roses*, 1990

—— and Jones J. *Standards, Badges and Livery Colours of the Wars of the Roses*, 1992

Milner, N.P. *Vegetius: Epitome of Military Science*, 1993

Myers, R.A. *Household of Edward IV*, 1959

Nicolas, H. *Wardrobe Accounts of Edward IV*, 1830

Nicholson, R. *Edward III and the Scots*, 1965

Nicolson J. and Burn R. *A History of Westmorland*, 1777

'The Northern Retainers of Richard Neville Earl of Salisbury' in *Northern History*, 11, 1976

Oakeshott, R.E. *European Weapons and Armour*, vol. 2, 1980

——. *Records of the Medieval Sword*, 1964

——. *The Sword in the Age of Chivalry*, 1964

Oman, C. *The Art of War in the Middle Ages*, vol. 2, 1991

Owst, G.R. *Literature and the Pulpit in Medieval England*, 1961

Oxley, J.E. *The Fletchers and Longbowstring Makers of London*, 1968

Perges, G. 'Army Provisioning, Logistics and Strategy in the Second Half of the 17th Century', *Acta Historica*, 16, 1857

Pfaffenbichler, M. *Armourers*, 1992

Pollard, A.J. *North-Eastern England During the Wars of the Roses*, 1988

——. 'Percies and Nevilles', *History Today*, Sept. 1993

——. *The Wars of the Roses*, 1994

Prestwich, M. *Armies and Warfare in the Middle Ages*, 1996

Pugh, T.B., Chrimes, S.B., Ross, C.D. and Griffiths, R.A. *Fifteenth-Century England 1399–1509*, 1972

Rawcliffe, C. *The Staffords, Earls of Stafford and the Dukes of Buckingham 1394–1521*, 1978

Ross, C. *Edward IV*, 1983

——. *The Wars of the Roses*, 1967

Routh, P. and Knowles, R. *The Medieval Monuments of Harewood*, 1983

Seymour, W. *Battles in Britain 1066–1547*, 1975

Smith, R.D. and Brown, R.R. *Bombards: Mons Meg and Her Sisters* (Royal Armouries), 1989

Smurthwaite, D. *The O.S. Complete Guide to the Battlefields of Britain*, 1984

Storey, R.L. *The End of the House of Lancaster*, 1986

Tarassuk, L. and Blair, C. *The Complete Encyclopedia of Arms and Weapons*, 1982

Thompson, J.A.F. 'Gregory's Chronicle – A Possible Author', *British Museum Quarterly*, 36, 1971–2

Thordeman, B. *Armour from the Battle of Wisby 1361*, 1939

Troso, M. *Le Armi in Asta: Delle Fanterie Europée, 1000–1500*, 1988

Twemlow, F.R. *The Battle of Blore Heath*, 1912

Vale, M. *Piety, Charity and Literacy among the Yorkshire Gentry 1370–1480*, Borthwick Papers, 1976

——. *War and Chivalry*, 1981

Warren, J. *The Wars of the Roses and the Yorkist Kings*, 1995

Whittaker, R. *Loidis and Elmete*, 1816

Wolffe, B. *Henry VI*, 1983

Young, P. and Adair, J. *Hastings to Culloden*, 1964

Index

Numbers in italics indicate illustrations